# The Citizens at Risk

# The Citizens at Risk

## From Urban Sanitation to Sustainable Cities

Gordon McGranahan
Pedro Jacobi
Jacob Songsore
Charles Surjadi
Marianne Kjellén

STOCKHOLM ENVIRONMENT INSTITUTE

Earthscan Publications Limited, London and Sterling, VA

First published in the UK and USA in 2001 by
Earthscan Publications Ltd

Copyright © Stockholm Environment Institute, 2001

ISBN: 1 85383 561 7 paperback
       1 85383 562 5 hardback

Typesetting by JS Typesetting, Wellingborough, Northants
Printed and bound by Creative Print and Design (Wales), Ebbw Vale
Cover design by Declan Buckley
Cover photo © Dermot Tatlow/Panos Pictures

For a full list of publications please contact:

Earthscan Publications Ltd
120 Pentonville Road
London, N1 9JN, UK
Tel:  +44 (0)20 7278 0433
Fax: +44 (0)20 7278 1142
Email:  earthinfo@earthscan.co.uk
http://www.earthscan.co.uk

22883 Quicksilver Drive, Sterling, VA 20166–2012, USA

Earthscan is an editorially independent subsidiary of Kogan Page Ltd and publishes in
association with WWF-UK and the International Institute for Environment and
Development

A catalogue record for this book is available from the British Library

Library of Congress Cataloging-in-Publication Data

The citizens at risk : from urban sanitation to sustainable cities / Gordon McGranahan ...
[et al].
        p. cm.
    Includes bibliographical references and index.
    ISBN 1-85383-562-5 (cloth : alk. paper) – ISBN 1-85383-561-7 (pbk. : alk. paper)
        1. Human ecology–Developing countries. 2. Urban ecology–Developing countries.
3. Urban pollution–Developing countries. 4. Sustainable development–Developing
countries. 5. Environmental policy–Developing countries. 6. Environmental justice–
Developing countries. 7. Developing countries–Environmental conditions. I.
McGranahan, Gordon. II. Title.

GF900 .C57 2001
307.72–dc21                                                        2001003254

# Contents

# List of Tables, Figures and Boxes

## TABLES

# FIGURES

# BOXES

# List of Acronyms and Abbreviations

| | |
|---|---|
| AMA | Accra Metropolitan Area |
| CBO | community-based organization |
| CEDEC | Centro de Estudos de Cultura Contemporânea |
| CO | carbon monoxide |
| CVM | contingent valuation method |
| GAMA | Greater Accra Metropolitan Area |
| GEMS | Global Environmental Monitoring System |
| GDP | gross domestic product |
| GRO | grass-roots organization |
| HDIS | high-density indigenous sector |
| Jakarta-DKI | special capital district of Jakarta |
| KIP | Kampung Improvement Programme |
| LPG | liquified petroleum gas |
| MARC | Monitoring and Assessment Research Centre |
| MDIS | medium-density indigenous sector |
| NGO | non-governmental organization |
| POP | persistent organic pollution |
| PPP | purchasing power parity |
| PRA | participatory rapid appraisal |
| RF | rural fringe |
| RSP | respirable particulates |
| SAP | structural adjustment programme |
| SEI | Stockholm Environment Institute |
| Sida | Swedish International Development Cooperation Agency |
| TSP | total suspended particulates |
| UNCED | United Nations Conference on Environment and Development |
| UNDP | United Nations Development Programme |
| UNEP | United Nations Environment Programme |
| UNICEF | United Nations Children's Fund |
| WHO | World Health Organization |

# About the Authors

**Pedro Jacobi** is Associate Professor in the Economics of Education Department of the School of Education of the University of São Paulo, and has been President of the Graduate Programme of Environmental Sciences (1998–2000). He has a Masters Degree in Urban and Regional Planning from Harvard University, and a PhD in Sociology from the University of São Paulo. Two recent publications related to the topic of this book are: Jacobi, P (1999) *Cidade e meio ambiente* (*The City and the Environment*), Annablume, São Paulo, and Jacobi, P, Baena Segura, D and Kjellén, M (1999) 'Governmental responses to air pollution: summary of a study of the implementation of *rodízio* in São Paulo', *Environment and Urbanization,* vol 11, no 1, pp79–88. He can be contacted at the Programa de Pós-Graduação em Ciência Ambiental da Universidade de São Paulo (PROCAM-USP), Rua do Anfiteatro, 181, Colmeia/Favo 15, 05508-900 Cidade Universitária, São Paulo, Brazil; email: prjacobi@uol.com.br

**Marianne Kjellén** is a researcher at the Stockholm Environment Institute, and a doctoral student at the Department of Human Geography, Stockholm University. She has a Masters of Social Science and Bachelor of Science in Business Administration and Economics. Two recent publications related to the topic of this book are: Kjellén, M and McGranahan, G (1997) *Urban Water – Towards Health and Sustainability,* Stockholm Environment Institute, Stockholm (which provides the basis for Chapter 3); and Kjellén, M (2000) 'Complementary water systems in Dar es Salaam, Tanzania: the case of water vending', *International Journal of Water Resources Development,* vol 16, no 1, pp143–154. She can be contacted at the Stockholm Environment Institute, Box 2142, 10314 Stockholm, Sweden; email: marianne.kjellen@sei.se

**Gordon McGranahan** is a researcher at the International Institute for Environment and Development and, until recently, headed the Urban Environment Programme at the Stockholm Environment Institute. He received his PhD in Development-Economics from the University of Wisconsin-Madison, in 1986. Two recent publications of relevance are: McGranahan, G, Songsore, J and Kjellén, M (1996) 'Sustainability, poverty and urban environmental transitions' in Pugh, C (ed) *Sustainability, the Environment and Urbanization,* Earthscan, London, pp103–133;

and McGranahan, G, Leitmann, J and Surjadi, C (1998) 'Green grass and brown roots: understanding environmental problems in disadvantaged neighbourhoods', *Journal of Environmental Planning and Management*, vol 41, no 4, pp505–518 (which provided the basis for Chapter 6). He can be contacted at IIED, 3 Endsleigh Street, London WC1H 0DD, UK; email: gordon.mcgranahan@iied.org

**Jacob Songsore** is Professor and former Head of the Department of Geography and Natural Resource Development at the University of Ghana-Legon. He received his PhD in Geography from the University of Ghana. Two publications of relevance are: Songsore, J and Goldstein, G (1995) 'Health and environment analysis for decision-making (HEADLAMP): field study in Accra, Ghana', *World Health Statistics Quarterly*, vol 48, no 2, pp108–117; and Songsore, J and McGranahan, G (1998) 'The political economy of household environmental management: gender, environment and epidemiology in the Greater Accra Metropolitan Area', *World Development*, vol 26, no 3, pp395–412 (which provided the basis for Chapter 7). He can be contacted at the Department of Geography and Natural Resource Development, University of Ghana, Box 59, Legon-Accra, Ghana; email: j_song sore@hotmail.com

**Charles Surjadi** is Professor of Public Health at the Faculty of Medicine of Atma Jaya University (Jakarta, Indonesia) and Senior Researcher at the Center for Health Research also at Atma Jaya University. He is a medical doctor with a PhD in Public Health from the Faculty of Medicine, University of Amsterdam. Two relevant publications are: Surjadi, C (1993) 'Respiratory diseases of mothers and children and environmental factors among households in Jakarta', *Environment and Urbanization*, vol 5, no 2, pp78–86; and Surjadi, C and Handayani, Y S (1999) *The Problem and Management of Solid Waste in Jakarta*, Center for Health Research, Atma Jaya Catholic University, Jakarta. He can be contacted at the Center for Health Research, Atma Jaya Catholic University, Atma Jaya Hospital Complex, Jalan Pluit Raya 2, Jakarta 14440, Indonesia; email: surjadi@fk.atmajaya.ac.id

# Acknowledgements

We would like to thank the Swedish International Development Cooperation Agency for financial support, and the Stockholm Environment Institute for the institutional support that made this book possible.

This book grew out of a comparative study of Accra, Jakarta and São Paulo. We would like to thank those who co-authored the reports and articles that resulted from the study, as well as the many other study team members and residents who contributed their time and ideas to the study. Thanks are also due to the Port Elizabeth team, and especially Liz Thomas and John Seager, for demonstrating that the approach we applied could be adapted and improved upon for other cities.

Some of the initial findings were published in the journal *Environment and Urbanization*, and the journal and its editor David Satterthwaite have been a constant source of inspiration. We would also like to thank the *Journal of Environmental Planning and Management* and *World Development* for permission to base chapters on papers first published in these journals (see first notes to Chapters 6 and 7).

Over the years, numerous colleagues have reviewed the materials presented here, contributing their own ideas and examples. After compiling a list of some 50 individuals, we decided that a collective acknowledgement would be more appropriate. Thanks to you all.

# Preface

This book is one outcome of research collaboration dating back to 1991, when the Stockholm Environment Institute initiated a study of environmental burdens in Accra, Jakarta and São Paulo. Sustainability had already become the watchword in environmental circles. Our initial focus, however, was on the environmental health threats that residents face in their homes and neighbourhoods, threats that tend to be more severe in conditions of poverty. It soon became clear that these local environmental health issues did not sit well on the sustainability agenda – if anything, the standard measures to address sustainability seemed to threaten environmental health and vice versa. Since many of the organizing themes of this book concern the relationship between urban environmental health and sustainability, our use of these terms requires some clarification.

We define 'environment', 'sustainability' and 'health' narrowly and in largely physical terms. The 'environment' is defined as physical surroundings, and when we discuss 'environmental problems' it is usually in relation to deficiencies brought about inadvertently by human activity: pollution, resource depletion, ecosystem destruction and the like. 'Sustainability' is defined as the capacity of being maintained indefinitely, and 'threats to sustainability' are generally taken to be activities that create appreciable environmental burdens for future generations. 'Health' is defined as the state of being free of disease or disability.

This goes against the tendency in international development circles to apply very broad definitions to goal-demarcating words, allowing them to encompass a wide range of socio-economic as well as physical concerns. Thus, for example, the environment is often taken to include social conditions, sustainability is often taken to include social stability, and health is often defined as an overall state of well-being. We share the concern that:

- Environmental problems, defined narrowly, cannot be understood or addressed in isolation.
- Sustainability, defined narrowly, is not in itself a goal.
- Health, defined narrowly, is only one aspect of human well-being.

We do not, however, believe that broader definitions can help to address these concerns.

While broad definitions can be a useful means of drawing attention to otherwise neglected issues, and at least superficially would seem to support a more holistic analysis, they quickly become counterproductive. There are, for example, close links between social and environmental problems, but defining social conditions as part of the environment neither helps to articulate these links, nor provides a useful conceptual framework for understanding social problems. It is very distorting, for example, to treat violence as an 'environmental' problem. Similarly, defining sustainability to include social stability, and pronouncing poverty unsustainable on these grounds provides a very dubious basis for representing the interests of the poor – it virtually implies that the problem with poverty is that poor people are disruptive. And defining health as overall well-being implies, incorrectly, that health specialists are in a good position to understand and address the full panoply of human aspirations.

There are also dangers in using broad definitions of health and sustainability to construct goals for urban development. Broadly defined, a sustainable city embodies all the good qualities a city can have, and perhaps a few more besides. A healthy city is much the same. Yet the goals of sustainability and health, more narrowly defined, are by no means identical. And however valiantly one tries to extend the concept of the sustainable city to cover contemporary deprivations, it implies a special concern not to compromise the future. Likewise, however valiantly one tries to extend the concept of a healthy city, it implies an emphasis on traditional environmental health concerns.

Environmentalists and health specialists need to be aware that their concerns are not all-important, and cannot be addressed in isolation. Defining 'environment', 'sustainability' and 'health' to encompass more issues does not serve this purpose, however. There are no well-bounded definitions of environment, health and sustainability, however widely one casts the net. Indeed, broad definitions can easily create the illusion that important issues and interconnections have been taken into account, when they have merely been named. Thus, at least for the purposes of this book, we have chosen to stick with narrow definitions, but to be as explicit as possible about the limitations of these key concepts and of the book itself. While we believe the topics covered in this book to be of critical importance, many equally important urban issues are barely touched upon.

# 1

# Introduction

At one level, this is a book about the challenge of improving environmental health conditions in deprived urban settlements. At another level, it is about the challenge of sustainable urban development in a globalizing world. But perhaps most accurately, it is about environmental justice and urban development in a rapidly changing world.

Urban living has always been accompanied by environmental risks. These risks have varied significantly, of course, over time and space. So have the ways that people have interpreted and responded to them. The shifts over the last hundred years are particularly relevant to the concerns of this book.

A century ago, sanitary reform was in full swing, and the urban environmental agenda of the industrializing world had relatively well-defined priorities. Economic growth had brought wealth to some, but also new forms of urban poverty, ill health and social discontent. For much of the 19th century, average urban life expectancy was lower even in affluent cities than in the surrounding countryside (Bairoch, 1988). Sanitary reform, which at the time referred to a wide range of local environmental improvements, promised to reduce ill health and thereby combat poverty and discontent. By the end of the century, it seemed to be delivering on at least the first of these promises.

In the intervening century, urban populations have mushroomed throughout the world, and disparities have grown. A number of cities have undergone a sanitary revolution, and their residents are virtually assured adequate water, sanitation and waste collection. More recently, some cities have undergone what could be termed a pollution revolution, and cleaned up their ambient air and water. A few even aspire to a sustainability revolution, and are taking steps to reduce their overall ecological burden. But urban environmental challenges have never loomed larger: there are more people without adequate sanitation, more cities with serious pollution, and a greater global ecological burden from cities than ever before.

A concern for equity has always held a prominent place in urban environmental debates. Sanitary improvements have long been promoted in the name of the poor. Controlling ambient pollution has often been portrayed as a means of protecting unsuspecting residents from suffering at the hands of immoral polluters. And sustainability is typically pursued in the name of the as yet unborn.

The international urban environmental agenda, however, has tended to track the concerns of the affluent cities. When the most affluent cities in the world were rife with infectious diseases, the sanitary movement came to the fore. When the most affluent cities had addressed their most serious sanitary problems, but citywide pollution continued to grow, reducing ambient air and water pollution became the order of the day. Now that the quality of the ambient environment in many affluent cities has improved, but affluent urban lifestyles increasingly threaten the global environment, sustainability has become the watchword.

A number of superficially sensible reasons might seem to justify these shifts in international environmental priorities (other than the 'sensible' desire to cater to the concerns of the politically powerful). From a research perspective, is it not sensible to focus on the new and poorly understood challenges, rather than on the old problems for which solutions have already been demonstrated? From a policy perspective, is it not sensible to focus international attention on global burdens and let local problems be addressed locally? And from a 'green' perspective, is it not sensible to treat problems like poor sanitation as symptoms of poverty, and restrict the label 'environmental' to problems that clearly constitute a threat to nature.

The evidence and arguments presented in this book suggest that such reasoning is misguided. There is still a lot to learn about the local environmental health problems that spurred the sanitary revolution, and many of the orthodox technical and organizational solutions are no longer appropriate. International efforts can provide critical support for local environmental improvement (as they did during the 19th century sanitary movement), even if the form of support needed is unlikely to emerge from the sorts of international agreements that are being developed to address the new global environmental burdens. And at least from an anthropocentric point of view, the complex of problems that arise when sanitation is inadequate, waste goes uncollected, water supplies are intermittent, and smoky fuels are used for cooking, are just as 'environmental' as any of the burdens of industrial pollution and excessive material consumption.

Before summarizing the structure and arguments of the book, the remainder of this introduction will describe the 'greening' of the concept of development; introduce the 'brown' and the 'green' urban environmental agendas that reappear in various contexts throughout the book; summarize some of the features of globalization that have a bearing on both the 'brown' and the 'green' agendas; and bring together some of these concerns in a discussion of the city, sustainable development and globalization.

## THE GREENING OF THE CONCEPT OF DEVELOPMENT

Most international research and policy analysis on urban issues in 'developing countries' is heavily influenced by the prevailing development paradigms. Not surprisingly then, the 'greening' of development debates, and the emergence of sustainability as a major concern, has had an appreciable impact on how urban issues, and urban environmental issues in particular, are framed and filtered. This section provides a brief summary of some of the relevant changes in the concept of development. A more systematic critique of the ascendance of sustainability as an overarching goal is provided in the concluding chapter.

The concept of development, around which a significant post-Second World War consensus was forged, contained an implicit compromise – the 'less developed' would follow the lead of the 'more developed', and in return the 'more developed' would help them to do so. Conventional theories of development had cities and nations proceeding through a series of stages, the affluent showing the poor the image of their own future. East–West conflict complicated the politics, but was essentially a dispute between geopolitical groupings with opposing visions of unilinear development. For Western powers, demonstrating the viability of the market road to development was all the more important, given that the principal alternative – the socialist or communist road – was geopolitically undesirable.

Until recently, most criticism of this development agenda came from 'below'. In the 1960s, dependency theorists argued that poverty and affluence were different facets of the same global economic system, rather than different points on a common economic trajectory (Frank, 1969). The concept and pursuit of development is still often blamed for helping to create the power relations that oppress those implicitly, if no longer explicitly, defined as underdeveloped (Escobar, 1995). Such criticisms typically claim that pursuing conventional development is not in the interests of those it is ostensibly meant to serve, but rather serves the interests of the affluent Northern, and Southern elites.

The global environment critique of development takes a very different tack, and is intrinsically more disruptive of Northern support for the development agenda. First popularized by the *Limits to Growth* study (Meadows et al, 1972), the notion that conventional economic development is damaging the global environment has been receiving increasing attention. It does not require sophisticated mathematical models to infer that if the affluent lifestyle of some 1 billion Northerners is taxing the environmental limits of the earth, then adding several billion Southerners to the ranks of the affluent would be devastating. If profligacy is the force behind the world's environmental problems, then, for the currently affluent, one of the worst scenarios of the future is for the rest of the world to replicate their consumption patterns.

In promoting 'sustainable development', the Brundtland Commission attempted to redirect the development agenda and create consensus around a more unifying goal (World Commission on Environment and Development, 1987). Rather than attempting to replicate Western affluence globally, the common goal should be to meet the needs of the present, without compromising the ability of future generations to meet their own needs. From the perspective of sustainable development, all nations are underdeveloped. For some the development priority may be to meet better the needs of the present. For others it may be to provide better for the needs of future generations. But the sustainable development challenge is common to all nations, and indeed to all people.

Despite the popularity of the concept, the pursuit of 'sustainable development' has not much influenced economic policy, either internationally or locally. Indeed, the concept has remained at the margins of economic policy debates. In the last decades of the 20th century, structural adjustment was the most influential economic policy package in large parts of the world, and structural adjustment programmes are environmentally ambiguous at best (Munasinghe, 1999; Reed, 1996). In the Washington Consensus of the early 1990s, which John Williamson identified as a body of economic advice that deserves to be endorsed across the political spectrum, environmental issues were notable for their absence (Williamson, 1993). The Post-Washington Consensus, presented only somewhat tongue-in-cheek by Joseph Stiglitz (then Senior Vice President and Chief Economist at the World Bank), refers to the goal of sustainable development and takes environmental issues more seriously, but only just (Stiglitz, 1998).

Even as the environmental dimension to sustainable development has proved difficult to put into economic practice, the concept of sustainability applied to sustainable development has been extended to include, more explicitly, non-environmental dimensions. The initial attraction of sustainable development was that it brought environmental concerns to the centre of the development agenda. But sustainability is now often taken to include a social dimension that many feel is also lost in the narrow pursuit of economic growth (see, for example, the annual *Human Development Reports* published by Oxford University Press for the United Nations Development Programme). At times this has involved intellectual contortions, including, for example, convoluted arguments to the effect that poverty is unsustainable (see Chapter 8). But the critical point is surely correct: if sustainable development is to provide an overarching goal for humankind, it must encompass more than the fulfilment of economic needs in an environmentally sustainable way. And, as indicated in the following section, this means recognizing the environmental dimensions of poverty as well as the social dimensions of sustainability.

# THE EMERGENCE OF TWO URBAN ENVIRONMENTAL AGENDAS

Historically, the citizens most at risk from urban environmental threats have been those in poverty. People lacking economic assets, political power and social resources are invariably the most exposed to a city's bad water and sanitation, polluted air, poorly managed waste and other localized environmental insults. Malnourishment and poor healthcare compound the attendant health risks. This still holds true today, and in many parts of the world accounts for a large share of the burden of disease (Murray and Lopez, 1996). With a large and growing share of the world's poverty now urban, ensuring that the urban poor have the opportunity to secure healthy living environments is one of the major challenges of the new millennium.

Increasingly, future generations, natural systems and distant people are also put at risk from urban environmental insults. There are physical reasons for this: many environmental burdens are more diffuse and delayed than those of the past. But there are socio-economic dimensions here too. Future generations, like the poor though for different reasons, cannot deploy their (future) economic resources and political power to influence contemporary decisions. The welfare of distant people and ecosystems are also easily overlooked. From this perspective, cities are also of critical importance: they concentrate damaging activities and the people who must change their ways if improvements are to be achieved. For many contemporary environmentalists, this is the essence of the urban challenge, not the environmental health burdens that persist in poor cities and neighbourhoods.

In short, it is now possible to distinguish between two urban environmental agendas. Of particular relevance to poor urban dwellers is the 'brown' agenda, prioritizing environmental health, and addressing local issues relating to, for example, inadequate water and sanitation, urban air quality and solid waste disposal. Of particular relevance to future generations and natural systems is the 'green' agenda, prioritizing ecological sustainability, and addressing issues relating to resource degradation, contributions to global environmental burdens, and other largely extraurban problems. Cutting across both agendas is the need for better governance to ensure that complex environmental issues are actively addressed, taking into account both intra- and intergenerational equity.

Much of this book concentrates on environmental and health problems in poor cities and neighbourhoods. Many of the central topics are, in a sense, old fashioned. The ultimate concern is the physical dimension of the urban environment, and issues such as safe water, sanitation and air pollution. The social environment, ecological concerns and global impacts receive less attention. But it is important not to confuse 'old' with resolved, simple or uncontentious. Improving environmental health in cities is not just a matter of mustering the political will to secure finance, and then installing the requisite pipes, drains, sewers and electricity lines. The notion that local environmental problems can be engineered away was a convenient fiction, itself designed in part to secure public funds. Once this fiction is stripped away, one is left with a complex of environmental problems as challenging, interesting and demanding of innovation as any. (There is always the danger, of course, that one is also left with fewer public funds.)

The local environmental health hazards that still threaten a large share of the world's population are also bound up with new economic, social and ecological processes, many of which are global in scale. It is one of the many paradoxes of urban development that to cope with the 'old' we first need to understand the 'new'. Globalization is as pertinent to the brown agenda as it is to the green.

## THE RELEVANCE OF GLOBALIZATION

If sustainable development has gained vocal support to comparatively little effect, globalization has had major effects with comparatively little support. This is not surprising: the term globalization was coined to describe what is happening in the world, not what ought to happen. Like sustainable development, globalization means different things to different people. At times it is treated as virtually synonymous with international economic liberalization and the fall of communism (which of course did have considerable support from many quarters). At other times it is treated as an environmental or cultural phenomenon. But the popularity of the concept derives from the fact that somewhat analogous processes can be perceived in a range of different dimensions. At least to some degree, the significance of spatial distance has changed, environmentally, economically and even socially.

In its environmental dimension, globalization can be taken to refer to the increasingly interconnected nature of environmental problems. With global warming, to take the most obvious example, greenhouse gas emissions from around the world combine to alter the global climate (Jepma and Munasinghe, 1998). The oil crisis of the 1970s provided more immediate evidence of global interdependence: supply restrictions in a small number of countries created a global shortage. Behind these highly publicized examples, a wide range of global environmental threats are emerging: stratospheric ozone depletion (United Nations Environment Programme, 1996), the dispersion of persistent organic pollutants (POPs) (Vallack et al, 1998), loss of biodiversity (Wilson, 1992), emerging and re-emerging diseases (Fidler, 1996; Morse, 1993), and so on. All of these problems involve the interplay of global processes, leaving even nations powerless to take preventive action alone, and creating enormous obstacles to effective negotiation between those creating the environmental burdens and those likely to suffer.

Economic globalization can be taken to refer to the increasingly interconnected nature of the world economy (Dicken, 1992). An increasing share of production is traded internationally. International financial exchanges, with the help of new information technology, are growing even more rapidly. Corporations are increasingly transnational in character (Sklair, 1991). Economic activities are becoming functionally more integrated: a single product is increasingly likely to contain both labour and material inputs from many countries. With capital and products flowing ever more easily, labour too faces more international competition (and unlike corporations, unions have not been able to adapt successfully to globalization), and nation states have less scope for economic management. While in some senses a world economy has existed for centuries (Hirst and Thompson, 1996; Wallerstein, 1979), it is at the very least taking on a new form. The disintegration of the Soviet Union and recent measures to promote 'free trade' have reinforced this process.

Social globalization can be taken to refer, very roughly, to the increasingly transnational character of social processes and networks. With the help of new information technologies, ideas can be communicated rapidly around the world. Some researchers argue that this has changed the whole dynamic of development around the world, and that it is increasingly important to understand the world in terms of communications and culture (Castells, 1996). At the very least, it must be recognized that corporations and the international media have been particularly quick to take advantage of the new information technologies, and expanding consumerism remains an obvious cultural aspect of globalization. But political processes, social movements and even personal networks are also adapting. From a sociological perspective, globalization can also be taken to refer to people's increasing *consciousness* of the world as a whole (Yearley, 1996). Some sociologists see this as part of a shift towards a more 'reflexive modernization' that is calling into question traditional (Enlightenment) views of science, progress and development, and undermining political categories such as 'left' and 'right' (Beck, 1997; Beck et al, 1994; Giddens, 1994).

These different dimensions of globalization are themselves closely interrelated. Together, they not only bring new challenges, but also transform old ones. Thus, for example, globalization helped to place intergenerational equity on the development agenda, but it is also changing the nature of intragenerational inequities and social exclusion. Environmental, economic and social differences are not declining, but are being spatially restructured. Globalization has reduced the scope of the action of national governments, but places new demands on governance at every level. The implications for cities are far from clear, but are undoubtedly substantial and go well beyond the confines of spatial planning (Marcuse and van Kempen, 2000).

## The City, Sustainable Development and Globalization

Superficially, it might also seem that the process of globalization and the pursuit of sustainable development must reduce the relevance of cities. Cities are, after all, local agglomerations of doubtful sustainability. But this is to confuse globalization with homogenization and sustainable development with anti-development.

One of the most renowned aspects of globalization is that national boundaries and governments are becoming less pivotal. In the words of one of the best known scholars of globalization:

> *Globalization 'pulls away' from the nation state in the sense that some powers nations used to possess, including those that underlay Keynesian economic management, have been weakened. However, globalization also 'pushes down' – it creates new demands and also new possibilities for regenerating local identities* (Giddens, 1998).

Most national governments are purposefully decentralizing, and others are having fiscal withdrawal forced upon them. Globalization is creating new opportunities for cities, even as it is closing off others (Cohen et al, 1996). It is far from clear how cities will rise to their new challenges, and some are far better positioned than others (Savitch, 1996). But the notion that globalization is making cities less significant is unfounded. Indeed, at least for the new 'global' cities, and London, Tokyo and New York in particular, the reverse would seem to be true (Sassen, 2000).

Alternatively, the fact that cities have large ecological 'footprints' makes them more, not less, important to the pursuit of sustainable development (Rees and Wackernagel, 1996). Cities concentrate, and in many ways symbolize, environmentally destructive practices, but only a few urban activities would become less environmentally harmful if they were transplanted to rural areas. Our urban present may be more destructive of nature than our rural past, but a rural future could be even more destructive. Indeed, it is noteworthy that one of the most commonly prescribed measures to reduce the ecological burden of cities is to make them more compact (Haughton, 1999) – a strange notion indeed if dispersing human settlement and economic activity to rural areas were the key to sustainability.

In any case, as indicated in Table 1.1, the share of the world's population living in urban areas is growing and is expected to continue growing for the foreseeable future. Increasingly, they are home to the world's poor, as well as its affluent (Satterthwaite, 1995). Efforts to intervene directly to reverse urbanization have been notoriously unsuccessful, whether pursued in the name of the poor (eg Pol Pot's Cambodia) or the affluent (apartheid, South Africa). On the other hand, efforts to better manage urban environments have had some notable successes. For all its problems, the sanitary movement of the 19th century is perhaps the most striking example of successful environmental reform.

From a 'green' perspective, the importance of urban initiatives is implicit in the environmentalist call of the 1970s to 'think globally, act locally'. Many environmentalists still have a firm conviction that global environmental improvement must be grounded locally, and hence that cities have a key role to play in achieving sustainability (Brugmann, 1994; Brugmann, 1996). Indeed, this is no

**Table 1.1** *Estimated percentage of population living in urban areas by major region – 1960, 1980, 2000, 2020*

| Region | 1960 | 1980 | 2000 | 2020 |
|---|---|---|---|---|
| Africa | 18 | 27 | 38 | 49 |
| Asia | 21 | 27 | 38 | 50 |
| Europe | 58 | 71 | 75 | 80 |
| Latin America[a] | 49 | 65 | 75 | 81 |
| North America | 70 | 74 | 77 | 82 |
| Oceania | 66 | 71 | 70 | 72 |
| *More developed*[b] | 61 | 71 | 76 | 81 |
| *Less developed*[c] | 22 | 29 | 41 | 52 |
| *World* | 34 | 39 | 47 | 57 |

*Notes:* a Includes Caribbean
b All regions of Europe and North America, Australia, New Zealand and Japan
c All regions of Africa, Asia (excluding Japan), Latin America and the Caribbean, and Melanesia, Micronesia and Polynesia
*Source:* United Nations (1998) *World Urbanization Prospects: The 1996 Revision: Estimates and Projections of Urban and Rural Populations and of Urban Agglomerations,* United Nations, New York

longer just a radical vision – it has become an establishment vision. The first major United Nations conference was held in Stockholm in 1972. When the Earth Summit was held in Rio 20 years later, the resulting action plan (Agenda 21) explicitly called on local authorities to create the foundations for sustainability. The Secretary General of the conference went so far as to say that: 'If sustainable development does not start in the cities, it will not go – cities have got to lead the way' (Brugmann, 1996). A few years later the Global Plan of Action of the Habitat II Conference underlined the need to link local governance with global sustainability.

This is not to say that the groundwork for a world of sustainable cities, in harmony with the global environment, has already been laid. Even in very affluent cities, global issues like climate change are still peripheral concerns for local authorities. Some initiatives are being taken (Collier and Löfstedt, 1997; Lafferty and Eckerberg, 1998; Lambright and Changnon, 1996), and numerous networks of city authorities are being developed. By and large, however, while it is clear that global improvement must be based on local initiatives, it is not at all clear that local authorities can or will take a leading role. The notion that local participatory processes are going to reduce global environmental burdens remains little more than wishful thinking. Transforming this wishful thinking into reality is one of the key challenges for the next millennium. Improving urban environmental management, especially in affluent cities, is central to this challenge.

From a 'brown' perspective, cities are of even more obvious importance. The brown agenda addresses environmental problems whose physical causes and effects are largely intraurban. It is the city's residents that suffer if their air is polluted, their water and sanitation is inadequate, their waste is not disposed of, and the urban environment is generally unhealthy. The problem here is not ensuring that cities are in harmony with their surrounding environment, but improving the quality of urban environment for local residents. There is no need to bring global interests to bear, since the people whose interests are threatened live within the cities concerned. The core of the brown agenda lies in addressing better the concerns of disadvantaged local residents, not in adding the concerns of the global community or of future generations. Superficially, at least, cities would seem to be in the position to solve such problems themselves.

However, just as action on global issues needs to be grounded locally, so action on local issues needs to be situated and even supported globally. The physical aspects of the 'brown' issues may be primarily local, but their socio-economic aspects are not. Globalization has made it all the more critical that the 'brown' agenda be recognized as an international issue. It would be truly unfortunate if the 'brown' agenda were marginalized in the international arena on account of its local character, and doubly unfortunate if it were inappropriately subsumed within such 'green' concerns as sustainability. We return to this point in the concluding chapter.

Even if one goes back to the sanitary reform of the 19th century, urban environmental improvement has always depended on extraurban support. When sanitary reform started, urban initiatives were critical. It was innovative efforts at the local level that eventually provided the basis for the more standardized sanitary reforms that spread across a large part of the world. However, the movement itself was not at all a local affair. Scientists, public figures and local activists succeeded because of national and international connections and support. Chadwick's highly influential *Report on the Sanitary Condition of the Labouring Population of Gt Britain*, first published in 1842, was based on the work of a national commission. Despite the British government's renowned preoccupation with free trade, it increasingly accepted responsibility for improving local environmental conditions so as to protect public health. Many other national governments did likewise (Rosen, 1993).

As we move into the 21st century, the antiquated science and paternalist approach of the sanitary movement may seem quaint and outdated, perhaps even pernicious. The importance of the 'brown' agenda is undiminished, however. Contemporary globalization poses different challenges from 19th century industrialization and free trade, but as in the 19th century, economic change is outpacing urban environmental management and the achievement of social justice. Moreover, there is a serious danger that as new 'green' concerns are added to the environmental agenda, the 'brown' concerns will be neglected or misrepresented.

# THE STRUCTURE AND ARGUMENTS OF THIS BOOK

This book is the outcome of nearly ten years of collaborative research on the part of the authors. The principal focus of this research has been on the environmental problems faced by households and neighbourhoods in Accra, Jakarta and São Paulo. Much of the analysis has been very practical and down-to-earth. Many of the conclusions and recommendations have been specific to these cities or areas within them. This book is reflective. It attempts to situate the local analysis within the broader context of international environmental debates. In its own way, this more reflective work is also intended to be very practical. After all, international debates influence local practice. Moreover, despite all their diversity, we believe that local environmental problems deserve a central place in the international arena, and not just because the 'green' agenda needs to be locally grounded. The 'brown' agenda is itself in desperate need of revitalization, and deserves the best that science, governance and international cooperation have to offer.

Chapters 2 and 3 present what we term the 'urban environmental transition'. This transition captures, in stylized terms, some of the most evident differences in the environmental burdens of poor, middle-income and affluent cities. In short, with increasing affluence, environmental problems become spatially more dispersed and temporally more delayed. This is evident in the contrasts among existing cities and in the history of currently affluent cities. These patterns do not have to be accepted. They do not reflect inevitable stages of urban development. Indeed, they reflect unsustainable as well as inequitable tendencies. But it is only by understanding how and why such patterns have emerged that more desirable and sustainable development paths can be identified.

Chapter 2 examines the environmental transition in some detail, outlining its structure, reviewing some of the empirical evidence and examining some of the complexities. What emerges is a picture of urban environmental change that is very complex, but also reflects some relatively straightforward tendencies.

For all cities, environmental problems tend to be:

- the unintended outcomes of human activity;
- closely interconnected;
- only resolvable through collective action; and
- most damaging to economically and politically disadvantaged groups.

On the other hand, the most pressing environmental burdens change as cities become more affluent:

- In poor cities, the most pressing environmental problems are usually local, immediate and threaten health directly.

- In middle-income cities (especially those that are large and industrialized), the most pressing environmental problems are typically city-regional, often including both ecological and health damages.
- In affluent cities the living environment is usually comparatively healthy, but urban activities and lifestyles account for a large environmental burden, and contributions to long-term and global problems are appreciable.

Chapter 3 focuses on one critical environmental medium: water. This allows for a more detailed analysis of environmental displacement, and the shift from 'brown' issues of health to 'green' issues of sustainability. Few would dispute that urban water systems should be both healthy and sustainable. Ideally, along with efficiency and equity, these are the central pillars of a sound water strategy. Unfortunately, the narrow pursuit of health can undermine the sustainability of water systems, and vice versa. Such trade-offs are examined in this chapter.

Chapter 4 looks in more detail at three specific cities: Accra (the poorest and smallest), Jakarta and São Paulo (the largest and most affluent). When we started to work on these cities, many of their problems seemed remarkably similar. Each of the cities has their low-income neighbourhoods, with the familiar litany of water, waste, pest and air-pollution problems. Judging from the first situation analysis, size seemed to be the most important difference; with Jakarta and especially São Paulo, a host of new environmental burdens appeared to overlay the longstanding environmental problems of urban poverty. As the research proceeded, however, it became clear that the differences were more radical than we had supposed, and both within and between the cities, affluence emerged as the critical parameter. This chapter starts by reviewing the character of some of the most serious local environmental health threats, and then goes on to compare the results across the three cities.

Chapter 5 summarizes three idealized models of how local environmental improvements ought to be organized, their relative strengths, and whether and how these strengths can be combined. The three models are labelled the planning model, the market model and the local collective action model. These models represent three forms of social interaction: bureaucratic organization (which attempts to apply rationality of a higher order to people's behaviour); market processes (which rely on the 'invisible hand' of the market to transform individual preferences into aggregate outcomes); and voluntary association (whereby group decisions are collectively negotiated outcomes). To some degree, the public sector has a vested interest in the planning model, the private sector in the market model, and the voluntary sector in the voluntary association model. But low-income urban dwellers have an interest in how markets, public sector activities and voluntary associations function and combine to help them achieve healthier living environments. This generally supports the claim that partnerships and the coproduction of environmental services are desirable, but it is also important not to idealize hybrid models.

Understanding neighbourhood conditions can play an important role in urban environmental management, especially when environmental services are lacking. Chapter 6 turns to three different approaches to local environmental assessment, following roughly the same tripartite division introduced in Chapter 6. The three approaches are broad-spectrum surveys, participatory appraisal and contingent valuation. To a first approximation, the broad spectrum survey is a tool of government, participatory appraisal a tool of the voluntary sector, and contingent valuation a tool of market economics. But the case studies summarized in this chapter illustrate how each technique can provide important and often complementary insights, and should not be viewed as inherently tied to particular interest groups.

Chapter 7 examines gender aspects of local environmental management in Accra. Affluence, and implicitly class, is the central social distinction employed in this book. There are, however, many other social distinctions that are relevant to urban development and the environment, of which gender is perhaps the most obvious, particularly with reference to household environmental problems. In many cities, women are the *de facto* managers of the home environment, and as cooks, child-carers and cleaners are exposed to a disproportionate share of the hazards. This chapter examines the micropolitics of power that surround household environmental management in Accra. It also provides a quantitative analysis of some of the environmental risks that women and children are exposed to, and their possible health effects.

Chapter 8 concludes with a reassessment of both the 'brown' and the 'green' agendas from the perspective of environmental justice. It is argued that the tendency to use sustainability as an overarching goal either marginalizes the 'brown' agenda or frames it incorrectly. Similarly, in the attempt to wed poverty and environmental concerns within the rubric of sustainable development, poverty is often portrayed as a major threat to sustainability, again marginalizing or misconstruing the 'brown' agenda. Environmental justice, on the other hand, is shown to provide a sound basis for reconciling the 'brown' and 'green' agendas. The conclusions end with a brief look at urban environmental management and equity in a globalizing world.

# 2

# Urban Affluence and Shifting Environmental Burdens

Most of this chapter is devoted to a few simple claims about the relationship between affluence and urban environmental burdens. The claims centre on the tendency for urban environmental burdens to be more dispersed and delayed in more affluent settings (Bartone et al, 1994; Lee, 1994; McGranahan, 1993; McGranahan et al, 1996; Pugh, 1996; Satterthwaite, 1997). This relationship is then used to develop a somewhat stereotypical account of the environmental priorities of poor, intermediate and affluent cities. In summary, the most significant environmental burdens tend to have the following character:

- Poor cities – localized, immediate and health threatening.
- Middle-income cities – citywide or regional, somewhat more delayed, and a threat to both health and (ecological) sustainability.
- Affluent cities – global, intergenerational and primarily a threat to sustainability.

This shifting locus of environmental burdens reflects predispositions rather than predetermined outcomes, and affluence is only one factor among many. Particularly important, some cities are far more successful than others are at taking action to reduce their environmental burdens. A poor city that is well managed is likely to have far fewer environmental problems than a poor city that is badly managed. Much the same holds for intermediate and affluent cities, even if their most critical environmental challenges are usually quite different.

This relates to an important common feature of environmental burdens of poor, intermediate and affluent cities alike: typically they involve the unintended consequences of human activity, and the complex interplay of physical and socio-economic systems. They do not simply reflect human preferences at different levels of economic development. They also reflect social inequities and the failure to accommodate human preferences that are not easily represented or negotiated within the prevailing political and economic systems. The needs of both low-income groups and future generations typically fall into this category. But most environmental problems, in both poor and affluent cities, also have physical features that make them prone to both market and public sector failures.

Affluence clearly influences the environmental quality of a city, but the grounds for singling it out as the central axis in this analysis is as much its political relevance as its empirical significance. As indicated in Chapter 1, the issues of environmental rights and responsibilities have become closely intertwined with those of economic growth and distribution. For this reason alone, environmental differences that relate to a city's economic status are particularly relevant. Moreover, the economically powerful are more politically powerful and articulate. This adds a second reason. Where class conflict is rife, these reasons are compounded but they are also relevant to the politics of geography and identity.

There is a strong tendency for policies, whether local, national or international, to represent the interests of the affluent disproportionately. Measures taken in the name of the poor are often inefficient or ineffective (Kundu, 1993). In many settings, there is far more pressure on politicians to make ambitious claims about their plans to help the poor than there is to design and implement effective measures. Thus political compromises tend to retain the rhetoric of poverty alleviation, but to give in on substantive detail. The stages between setting policy goals, designing responses and implementing them are critical to policy-making, and it is here that groups whose interests are expressed primarily through crude political instruments, such as electoral politics or mass mobilization, lose out the most. Similarly, issues of particular concern to the affluent tend to receive more attention from researchers who must follow the funding opportunities. And while, for example, business studies that try but fail to serve the interests of business are likely to be rejected, with consequence, by the business establishment, the same cannot be said of poverty studies.

This tendency warrants careful scrutiny, especially when the goal is to provide a framework for policy analysis. Making wealth a more explicit part of the analysis can help to draw out the equity dimensions of environmental management. Even the stereotyped account of the environmental burdens of poor, intermediate and affluent cities presented above can help to serve this purpose. It indicates, for example, that while the environmental burdens of urban poverty primarily affect the poor living in the immediate locality, the environmental burdens of affluence can affect both rich and poor people around the globe. Thus, environmental burdens reinforce existing inequalities. Equally important, decisions about which scale of environmental burdens to prioritize are simultaneously decisions about whose environmental problems are to be addressed. Moreover, if only 'stakeholders', narrowly defined, are to take responsibility for addressing environmental problems, then everyone must take responsibility for the problems of affluence, while the poor are left to deal with the problems of poverty. (Alternatively, if stakeholders are given a voice in proportion to their 'stake', then inequities are inevitably perpetuated.)

Needless to say, however, simplifications can also be actively misleading. A great deal is left out, and from some perspectives what is left out is as important as what is included. Following the stylized presentation, a few of the more significant qualifications are discussed, including:

- **Intraurban variation** There are important socio-economic and environmental differentials within cities. These differentials clearly qualify some of the conclusions one might be tempted to draw from an assessment of interurban differentials alone.
- **The role of governance** Unqualified accounts of interurban differences can create a false sense of inevitability. They fail to explain why most cities do not address adequately the environmental burdens that are characteristic of their level of affluence, and why some cities come far closer to succeeding than others. At least part of the explanation lies in qualities of governance, and the manner in which the challenge of addressing environmental problems in a cooperative and equitable manner is met.
- **Interscale effects** A sharp distinction between different scales of environmental burden is inevitably somewhat artificial. Problems at different scales often interact. In explaining the urban environmental transition, emphasis is placed on environmental displacement, but there are also interscale effects that provide opportunities for reducing burdens at several scales simultaneously.
- **Urban–rural interactions** Urban development changes rural environments in ways that go well beyond the environmental impacts of urban production and consumption patterns. For some purposes it is best to treat urban and rural development as different components of a single system. Again, this highlights the need for caution in interpreting the urban environmental transition presented here.

## STYLIZED OUTLINES OF AN URBAN ENVIRONMENTAL TRANSITION

### *From Sanitation to Global Climate Change*

Urban affluence is often blamed for creating environmental problems (Rees and Wackernagel, 1996). So is urban poverty (McGranahan, 1998) and the rapid industrialization and uncontrolled growth often characteristic of middle-income cities (Kasarda and Rondinelli, 1990). The apparent contradiction between these three views is at least partially explained by the fact that those who are concerned with the environmental burdens of poverty focus on a very different set of environmental problems from those concerned with industrializing or wealthy cities. Even to begin to generalize about the relationship between urban affluence and the environment, it is clearly necessary to distinguish between the different types of environmental burdens.

Figure 2.1 portrays, in very stylized terms, the relationship between affluence and three comparatively well-documented urban environmental indicators: the share of the population without adequate access to sanitary facilities; ambient concentrations of sulphur dioxide; and per capita emissions of carbon dioxide. Statistically grounded versions of these curves, including scales, were presented in the 1992 *World Development Report* to make the point that: 'rising economic activity can cause environmental problems but can also, with the right policies and institutions, help address them' (World Bank, 1992). However, indicators such as these also reveal the outlines of an urban environmental transition.

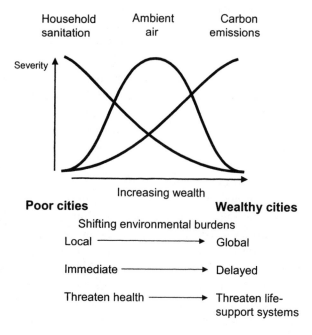

**Figure 2.1** *An urban environment transition: from sanitation to sustainability*

It is not surprising that the share of the urban population without access to adequate sanitary facilities tends to decline with affluence.[1] The dangers of poor sanitation are widely acknowledged, and the effects are immediate and local. Many of the urban sanitary facilities still considered adequate were already developed more than a century ago. There are a variety of relatively standardized institutional mechanisms for providing and servicing these facilities, as well as for punishing sanitary offenders. Wealthier people can better afford these 'adequate' facilities, and wealthier governments can better afford to provide and service them, and enforce sanitary regulations.

---

1 While statistics on urban sanitation levels are imperfect and not necessarily comparable across countries, it is unlikely that anyone would seriously dispute with this general finding

Nor is it surprising that the per capita emissions of carbon dioxide from fossil fuel combustion tend to increase with affluence.[2] Most economic activities require energy conversions, and fossil fuels are still the world's principal energy source. The danger that carbon dioxide emissions will adversely affect climate change has only recently gained widespread recognition. The effects are delayed and highly uncertain. Moreover, the costs of reducing carbon emissions are borne by those who take preventive action, while the costs of failing to reduce emissions are distributed globally and on to future generations. International mechanisms of the sort needed to ensure that there are suitable incentives for preventive action remain rudimentary and heavily disputed. Wealthier people can afford to consume more fossil fuels, both directly and indirectly, and wealthy governments still have relatively little incentive to prevent their own citizens from doing so. While some commitments towards limiting carbon emissions have been made, the question of how the responsibilities should be shared remains largely unresolved.

The rise and fall of ambient concentrations of sulphur dioxide is superficially surprising, but actually conforms more closely to what is sometimes portrayed as the normal relationship between pollution and affluence (Grossman and Krueger, 1995). Sulphur dioxide emissions, like carbon dioxide, are closely associated with fossil fuel combustion, but can be reduced by measures such as lowering the sulphur content of the fuels burned, and are hence less central to energy conversion processes. The dangers of sulphur dioxide concentrations are less widely acknowledged, immediate and localized than poor sanitation, but more so than global climate change: most of the burden falls on the city and the surrounding region, and many of the effects are incurred within a normal planning time-horizon.

Generally, the poorest cities do not consume sufficient fuel to create high concentrations of sulphur dioxide. On the other hand, many cities in affluent countries have implemented control measures that, together with a shift away from industry and into services, have led to appreciable improvements in recent decades. To the extent that these measures can overcome the effects of higher energy use, this leaves middle-income cities, and particularly large industrialized middle-income cities, with the highest concentrations of sulphur dioxide in their ambient air.[3]

---

2 The statistics normally employed to analyse the relationship between carbon emissions and affluence are national rather than urban, but the form of the relation is unlikely to be affected by such considerations. Of more relevance, fuel combustion is almost invariably ascribed to the nation where the fuel is consumed, even when that fuel is used to produce goods that are themselves consumed elsewhere. Generally, however, accounting for indirect effects would simply make the positive association between affluence and carbon emissions somewhat stronger

3 It should be noted that there are some indications that sulphur dioxide concentrations begin to rise again at very high income levels. Moreover, total sulphur dioxide emissions do not show the same tendency to decline in more affluent cities

In summary, while these curves are not the straightforward result of simple laws of development, they are related to the underlying features of these three environmental problems. Some of the key features referred to in the preceding paragraphs are summarized in Table 2.1. Even from these three examples, it should be clear that it is not a coincidence that the local, immediate, health-threatening problem is most evident in the low-income cities; that the global, very delayed, life-support system threatening problem arises from affluent urban lifestyles; and that the spatially and temporally intermediate problem is most evident in middle-income cities.

**Table 2.1** *Comparing selected features of three environmental indicators: access to sanitation, ambient concentrations of sulphur dioxide and carbon emissions*

|  | Inadequate sanitation | Ambient concentrations of sulphur dioxide | Carbon emissions |
| --- | --- | --- | --- |
| *Highest Incidence* | Poor urban centres | Middle-income urban centres | Affluent urban centres |
| *Impact* | Strong on human health | Moderate on health but also on ecology | Potentially strong on life-support systems |
| *Scale of impact* | Household–neighbourhood | City-region | Globe |
| *Timing of impact* | Immediate | Immediate–cumulative | Cumulative–intergenerational |
| *Achieved prominence* | Late 19th century | Mid-20th century | Late 20th century |

Within the context of these examples, more affluent urban centres tend to have environmental burdens that are more:

- spatially dispersed;
- temporally delayed; and
- damaging to life-support systems rather than to human health directly.

Alternatively, with increasing affluence, the local, immediate, easily discerned environmental burden tends to diminish.

The environmental shifts that come with affluence can be explained superficially in very simple terms. On the one hand, human activities have environmentally disruptive side-effects. As the activity levels increase, these effects are compounded and extend over time and space. On the other hand, affluence brings increased capacity and political willingness to take measures to avoid environmental threats. Localized, immediate and detectable impacts tend to receive the most attention, and are politically and institutionally the easiest to address. These impacts are, simultaneously, those that are most likely to affect human health directly. In this simple account, as affluence increases, the physical consequences of higher activity levels explain the increasingly dispersed and delayed character of environmental burdens, and purposeful measures that the wealthy are in a better position to implement explain the declining local burdens. That some burdens of intermediate scale rise and then fall can then be explained as the combined outcome of these two tendencies.

That some citywide and regional problems grow rapidly, even as local environments improve, can also be explained in terms of physical displacement. Local burdens are often shifted on to the broader environment, rather than being reduced at source, as indicated in the previous section. One means of solving the local sanitation problem is to use water to carry faeces and other wastes out of the city. One means of solving the local solid-waste problem is to dump it beyond the city boundaries. One means of solving the local air-pollution problems is to build higher smokestacks, or to shift the combustion site outside the city and bring in electricity.

To warrant describing these tendencies as an urban environmental transition, they should be evident for other contemporary urban environmental problems, and in the historical development of currently affluent cities. Thus, the next subsection focuses on contemporary cities, and the shifting environmental burdens evidenced in a selection of problem areas, such as water, air, waste and resource depletion). This is followed by a more detailed attempt to stereotype the environmental problems of poor, intermediate and affluent cities, and a simplified environmental history of affluent cities, applying the same framework. This then provides the basis for re-examining some of the complexities that can make an overly narrow interpretation of this transition very misleading.

## Shifting Urban Air, Water and Waste Burdens

In this section, we attempt to re-examine the tendencies described in the previous section in the context of a range of environmental problems encountered in different cities around the world. Table 2.2 is a checklist of city-related environmental problems taken from a recent United Nations Development Programme (UNDP) document. The classification is closely linked to the scale of the problems, and the tendencies noted above would imply that the more affluent the city, the lower down the list its principal environmental burdens are likely to be. While it is not possible to examine all these problem areas, there is a clear shift from

**Table 2.2** *Checklist for city-related environmental problems by context and nature of the hazard or problem*

| Context | Nature of hazard or problem | Some specific examples |
|---|---|---|
| Within house and its plot | Biological pathogens | Water-borne, water-washed (or water-scarce), airborne, food-borne, vector-borne including some water-related vectors (such as *Aedes* mosquitoes breeding in water containers where households lack reliable piped supplied). Note that insufficient quantity of water may be as serious in terms of health impact as poor water quality. Quality of provision for sanitation also very important. Overcrowding/poor ventilation aiding transmission of infectious diseases. |
| | Chemical pollutants | Indoor air pollution from fires, stoves or heaters. Accidental poisoning from household chemicals. Occupational exposure for home workers. |
| | Physical hazards | Household accidents – burns and scalds, cuts, falls. Physical hazards from home-based economic activities. Inadequate protection from rain, extreme temperatures and so on. |
| Neighbourhood | Biological pathogens | Pathogens in wastewater, solid waste (if not removed from the site), local water bodies. Disease vectors such as malaria-spreading *Anopheles* mosquitoes breeding in standing water or filariasis spreading *Culex* mosquitoes breeding in blocked drains, latrines or septic tanks. If sanitation is inadequate, many people will defecate on open sites – so lots of faecal contamination, including the sites where children play. If drainage is inadequate, flooding will also spread faecal contamination. If a settlement is served by communal standpipes, latrines and/or solid-waste collection points, these need intensive maintenance to keep them clean and functioning well. |
| | Chemical pollutants | Ambient air pollution from fires, stoves, from burning garbage if there is no regular garbage collection service. Air pollution and wastes from 'cottage' industries and from road vehicles. |
| | Physical hazards | Site-related hazards, such as housing on slopes with risks of landslides, sites regularly flooded, sites at risk from earthquakes. Traffic hazards. Noise. Health hazards to children if open sites have wastes dumped there because of no regular service to collect household wastes. |
| Workplace | Biological pathogens | Overcrowding/poor ventilation aiding transmission of infectious diseases. |

| Context | Nature of hazard or problem | Some specific examples |
|---|---|---|
| | Chemical pollutants | Toxic chemicals, dust. |
| | Physical hazards | Dangerous machinery, noise. |
| City (or municipality within larger city) | Biological pathogens | Quality and extent of provision for piped water, sanitation, drainage, solid-waste collection, disease control and healthcare at city or municipal level a critical influence on extent of the problems. |
| | Chemical pollutants | Ambient air pollution (mostly from industry and motor vehicles, motor vehicles' role generally growing), water pollution, hazardous wastes. |
| | Physical hazards | Traffic hazards, violence, 'natural' disasters and their 'unnaturally large' impact because of inadequate attention to prevention and mitigation. |
| | Citizens' access to land for housing | Important influence on housing quality directly and indirectly (such as through insecure tenure discouraging households investing in improved housing and discouraging water, electricity and other utilities from serving them). |
| | Heat island effect and thermal inversions | Raised temperatures a health risk, especially for vulnerable groups (such as the elderly and very young). Pollutants may become trapped, increasing their concentration and the length of exposure. |
| City-region (or city periphery) | Resource degradation | Soil erosion from poor watershed management or land development/clearance, deforestation, water pollution, ecological damage from acid precipitation and ozone plumes. |
| | Land or water pollution from waste dumping | Pollution of land from dumping of conventional household, industrial and commercial solid wastes and toxic/hazardous wastes. Leaching of toxic chemicals from waste dumps into water. Contaminated industrial sites. Pollution of surface water and possibility groundwater from sewage and storm/surface runoff. |
| | Pre-emption or loss of resources | Fresh water for city, pre-empting its use for agriculture; expansion of paved area over good quality agricultural land. |
| Global | Non-renewable resource use | Fossil fuel use, use of other mineral resources, loss of biodiversity. |
| | Non-renewable sink use | Persistent chemicals, greenhouse gas emissions, stratospheric ozone-depleting chemicals. |
| | Overuse of 'finite' renewable resources | Scale of consumption that is incompatible with global limits for soil, forests, fresh water |

*Source:* Satterthwaite, D (1999) *The Links between Poverty and the Environment in Urban Areas of Africa, Asia and Latin America*, UNDP, New York

problems that are typically associated with poverty to those that are more closely related to overconsumption. Thus, for example, books on environmental problems in low-income cities tend to emphasize the problems in the upper rows of the table (Hardoy et al, 1992), while books on affluent cities focus on those in the lower rows (Nijkamp and Perrels, 1994).

For the purposes of this subsection, smaller selections of urban environmental problem areas are discussed briefly in turn. This selection is summarized in Table 2.3, which classifies some of the better known problems relating to air, water and waste, very roughly, according to their scale. To the extent that the tendencies noted above hold, one would expect the local level problems, such as inadequate household water supplies, indoor air pollution, and unsafe household and neighbourhood waste handling to be most severe in the poorest urban centres. Alternatively, one would expect the indicators of global stress, such as carbon emissions and aggregate waste generation to be highest in the most affluent cities. And finally one would expect the city-scale and regional problems, such as urban river-water pollution, ambient air quality and the improper disposal of collected wastes to have a more ambiguous relation to affluence, perhaps being most severe in the middle-income cities.

## *Water*

### Access to adequate water for health

The two most serious water-related health problems in urban areas are contaminated drinking water and a lack of water for washing, which in urban areas depend on neighbourhood and household conditions. Both are quite clearly more severe problems in conditions of poverty and improve with affluence.[4] Statistical analysis relating national income to inadequate access to safe water in urban areas yields a declining curve similar to that for inadequate sanitation, though somewhat lower (ie a higher share of the urban population has access to safe water at all income levels) (Shafik, 1995; World Bank, 1992). As with sanitation, while the quality of the statistics is open to debate, the overall tendency for access to water to improve with affluence is undisputed.

### Pollution of open waterways

It is far more difficult to identify and compare statistically urban contributions to water problems at the city, regional and global level. River-water quality is affected by rural activities (eg agriculture) as well as urban, but at least it has been studied.

---

4 In many rural and some urban areas water-related insect-borne diseases, such as malaria, are also important. Such diseases also tend to be more severe in conditions of poverty

**Table 2.3** *Urban environmental burdens of different scales in relation to air,*
*water and waste*

|  | Local | City-regional | Global |
|---|---|---|---|
| *Water* | Poor access to adequate water for health needs | River water pollution | High aggregate water consumption* |
| *Air* | Indoor air pollution | Ambient air pollution | Contributions to carbon emissions |
| *Waste* | Poor household and neighbourhood waste handling | Poor disposal of collected wastes | High aggregate waste generation |

* There is no well-defined global environmental burden relating to water, and fresh water is not (yet) globally traded, so water consumption is best treated as a very rough indicator of the contribution to global freshwater imbalances (Shiklomanov, 1997)

These results are commented on below. Of more direct relevance, the introduction of sewerage systems that use water to remove human wastes from the household environment provide a good heuristic example of the shifting of environmental burdens.

There is some international evidence that, like ambient air quality, river-water quality tends to deteriorate with increasing national income, and then improve, for both chemical and biological contaminants (Grossman and Krueger, 1995). The notable exception is total (as opposed to a fecal) coliform, for which counts increased with national income. Also, a somewhat similar study found that river quality, as measured by dissolved oxygen levels, declined monotonically with income (Shafik, 1995).

An example of the displacement of water pollution is provided by the use of water for waste removal. The conventional, sewer-based, response to sanitation problems uses water as the medium to carry faeces away from people's homes. City-regional burdens can result, however, depending on how the sewerage is disposed of. First, there is an increase in water demand when flush toilets are introduced (in any case most sewers cannot operate without large quantities of water). Second, if the sewerage is released in the waterways, the pollution in and around the home is displaced to downstream inhabitants or other water users. If the sewerage is treated (or healthy dry sanitation systems are used (Drangert et al, 1997; Winblad, 1997)) the overall health benefits are likely to be higher, although the sludge must still be disposed of or recycled.

This displacement of urban water and sanitation burdens is illustrated in Table 2.4. Among a cross-section of 70 cities, grouped according to per capita income, the average share of households connected to sewers increases from 26 per cent among the low-income cities to 70 per cent in the middle-income group to

**Table 2.4** *Sewerage connections, wastewater treatment, and water use by gross city product per capita*

|  | Gross city product per capita (1993 US$) | | |
|---|---|---|---|
|  | *<1000* | *1000–10,000* | *10,000+* |
| 1 Number of observations (cities) | 9 | 30 | 31 |
| 2 Average % of households connected to sewers | 26 | 70 | 99 |
| 3 Average % of wastewater treated | 26 | 43 | 93 |
| 4 Estimated average % of faeces released untreated with sewerage | 16 | 42 | 7 |
| 5 Per capita water use (litres/day) | 110 | 210 | 310 |

*Source:* Based on data in United Nations Centre for Human Settlements (Habitat), The Global Urban Observatory, *Global Urban Indicators Database* (Habitat, Nairobi, 1997)
*Note:* These cities are major urban centres in countries for which the relevant data are available, and should not be taken as representative of urban centres generally

99 per cent in the high-income group. The average share of wastewater treated increases from 26 per cent to 43 per cent to 93 per cent. The combined effect of these two monotonically increasing functions on the estimated share of faeces released untreated with the sewerage is first an increase from 16 per cent to 42 per cent, and then a decline to 7 per cent. In effect, sewerage systems are introduced faster than treatment systems, leaving the middle-income cities with the greatest quantities of raw sewerage to dispose of in the waterways. (Some unsewered faeces are also likely to find their way into the waterways, but not in sufficient quantities to reverse the trends.)

## Global water pollution

Turning to global water burdens, many of the relevant tendencies are evident, but it is even more difficult to support empirical generalizations. There is no obvious equivalent to carbon emissions with respect to water – there is no major pollutant known to be putting the sustainability of the global water system under threat. As indicated in Table 2.4, water consumption is highest in the high-income cities, and this undoubtedly reflects some of the same shifts that for other resources would create global burdens. However, in the case of water, consumption is itself not a good indicator of global impacts. There are some water pollutants which, despite the clean-up efforts undertaken in many of the more affluent cities of the world, continue to grow, especially in countries where controls are lax (Shiklomanov, 1997). Moreover, if one were to consider the indirect effects of urban consumption on water systems, the effects would almost certainly be higher in affluent cities, where overall consumption levels are higher.

*Air*

## Indoor air pollution

While statistics on indoor air pollution in urban areas are not widely available, the relationship between urban affluence and exposure to the most significant pollutants is almost certainly similar to that for sanitary facilities: it is highest in poor cities and steadily declining with increasing affluence (Smith, 1993a).

Just as fuel combustion accounts for a large share of outdoor air pollution, it also accounts for a large share indoors, particularly where smoky fuels are burned in poorly ventilated rooms (Smith, 1988). The most health-damaging source of indoor air pollution is probably cooking and heating fires (Chen et al, 1990; Smith, 1993b; Smith et al, 1994). Household fuel choice is often described as an energy ladder, with fuels such as crop residues and firewood at the bottom, followed by charcoal, kerosene, liquified petroleum gas (LPG) and finally electricity (McGranahan and Kaijser, 1993; Smith et al, 1994). Since smoke can be unpleasant as well as unhealthy, and the less polluting fuels are more convenient for most purposes, they are often favoured by wealthy households who can afford to switch. Generally, the higher up the ladder, the less polluting the fuel. There is also a rural–urban dimension to the ladder, with crop residues and firewood being more readily available in rural areas. However, smoky fuels, including coal, are also often used in urban areas, particularly in poor countries (McGranahan and Kaijser, 1993).

Air pollution in and around the home and workplace, where people spend most of their time, is particularly threatening to health (Smith, 1993a). As described in Chapter 5, there are many other serious indoor environmental problems in poor settlements, and in this context the almost exclusive emphasis many researchers place on smoke from cooking fires may be misplaced. Rather, it is in the context of the indoor air-pollution problems that also afflict affluent cities, such as passive smoking, that the dangers of smoky fuels appear so overwhelming. Thus, radon, poor ventilation, pathogens that thrive in air-conditioning systems (causing, for example, Legionnaire's Disease), and dust mites may be significant in the context of the relatively healthy indoor environments of affluent cities. But they cannot compare with the problems related to crowding, damp, insecticide exposure and other hazards often found in indoor environments of many poor urban settlements. Since people spend a great deal of time in these environments, the potential for exposure is especially high.

## Ambient air pollution

Turning to the citywide air-pollution problems, there are at least some indications that the most serious problems arise in middle-income cities. Ambient concentrations of smoke, sulphur dioxide and particulates have generated widespread concern and are comparatively well monitored. There have even been statistical studies of the relationship between urban ambient air pollution and affluence (Grossman and Krueger, 1995; Shafik, 1995). The data for these studies are international databases that underrepresent both small and poor urban centres whose air quality is less well monitored.[5] By and large, however, one would expect their inclusion to accentuate rather than reverse the patterns that have been identified in existing studies.

Overall, the results of these studies conform to the patterns described above for sulphur dioxide. One study found that urban air pollution follows a 'bell-shaped curve' with concentrations of suspended particulate matter peaking at roughly US$3000 (per capita national income *c*1985) and sulphur dioxide at roughly US$4000 (Shafik, 1995). The other (Grossman and Krueger, 1995) found an 'inverted U-shaped' relationship for smoke. Sulphur dioxide was found to follow a similar pattern, but turned up again at very high levels of income (due, perhaps, to a very small number of observations above US$16,000). The turning points for both smoke and sulphur dioxide were around US$4000–5000.

To some degree, the additional ambient air pollution as one moves from poor to middle-income cities could be displaced indoor air pollution. Thus, for example, as people shift from smoky fuels to electricity, there is simultaneously a shift from indoor air pollution to ambient air pollution, if the electricity is generated in thermal power plants. More important, the increasing ambient air pollution reflects increasing transportation and industrial activities taking place in relatively uncontrolled settings, while the later decline relies on policy measures to curb pollution.

Since the decline relies on policy measures, one might expect untargeted pollutants (and particularly those that do not shift with the targeted pollutants) to decline less in affluent cities. Thus, for example, only recently have epidemiological studies underscored the importance of $PM_{2.5}$ (fine particulates with aerodynamic diameters < 2.5 μm), and the US Environmental Protection Agency endorsed annual and 24-hour limits for $PM_{2.5}$ in 1997 (Lippmann, 1999). As a result of such measures, it seems likely that an inverse relation between $PM_{2.5}$ and affluence will become more pronounced in the coming years.

## Contributions to global carbon emissions

Turning to global air-pollution problems, the contributions of affluent cities come to the fore. The results of statistical studies of carbon dioxide emissions indicate

---

5   The sources were unpublished data from the Monitoring and Assessment Research Centre (MARC) in London in one case (Shafik, 1995), and the Global Environmental Monitoring System (GEMS) of the World Health Organization and the United Nations Environmental Programme in the other (Grossman and Krueger, 1995)

that these emissions increase with national income. While no studies have looked at changing urban carbon emissions in particular, several have analysed carbon emissions from fossil fuel burning and cement production (Holtz-Eakin and Selden, 1995; Shafik, 1995), and it is safe to assume that most of these emissions are urban. The more detailed of these studies (Holtz-Eakin and Selden, 1995) did find that emissions increased less at higher income levels. More specifically, there is evidence that in recent years the carbon emissions per unit of economic output has fallen in a number of high-income countries, even as it has increased in low-income countries (Roberts and Grimes, 1997).[6] Overall carbon emissions per capita clearly rise with income, however.

The shift from city-level to global air-pollution burdens is somewhat similar to the shift from indoor to ambient air pollution, although in this case it is the city that is being 'cleaned up' and the activities contributing to global burdens that continue largely unabated. This quite clearly applies to fossil fuel consumption, which is still closely tied to the car and high material consumption levels. The relationship between affluence and carbon dioxide emissions would undoubtedly be steeper if emissions were assigned to the final consumers of the goods and services whose provision led to the emissions (Rothman, 1998).

## *Waste*

### Household and neighbourhood waste-handling

Household waste creates local environmental problems when it is not collected but allowed to accumulate in residential areas. The health threat of household solid waste is less acute than faecal waste, but it is often mixed with faecal material where sanitary facilities are lacking and can also provide a breeding ground for vectors of disease, such as flies and rodents. Uncollected waste can also block the drains, leading to various water-related problems and in some cases flooding.

Like inadequate sanitation, inadequate solid waste removal is a serious problem in low-income urban areas, and collection tends to be better the more affluent the city. This is evident in Table 2.5, where the average share of households without a regular waste-collection service decreases from 38 per cent in the low-income cities to 0 per cent in the wealthy cities. While households without collection services may still find the means to dispose of their waste outside their neighbourhood, a

---

6 Roberts and Grimes define the environmental Kuznets curve for carbon emissions in terms of emissions per unit of economic output rather than the more conventional emissions per capita, thereby identifying a turning-point despite increasing emissions per capita. For the purposes of this discussion, a fall in carbon intensity is not evidence of an Environmental Kuznets Curve which would require carbon emissions per capita to decline at higher levels of output per capita

**Table 2.5** *Waste generation, collection and disposal by gross city product per capita*

| | Gross city product per capita (1993 US$) | | |
|---|---|---|---|
| | <1000 | 1000–10,000 | 10,000+ |
| 1 Number of observations (cities) | 8 | 26 | 24 |
| 2 Average waste generation per household (kg/day) | 1.0 | 0.9 | 1.4 |
| 3 Average % of households with regular waste collection service | 62 | 87 | 100.0 |
| 4 Estimated waste collection per household (kg/day) | 0.6 | 0.8 | 1.3 |
| 5 Average % of waste disposed of in open dumps | 62 | 37 | 0 |
| 6 Estimated waste collected and disposed of in open city dumps | 0.4 | 0.3 | 0.0 |

*Source:* Based on data in United Nations Centre for Human Settlements (Habitat), The Global Urban Observatory, *Global Urban Indicators Database* (Habitat, Nairobi, 1997)
*Note:* These cities are major urban centres in countries for which the relevant data are available, and should not be taken as representative of the urban population in their income class

range of studies in low-income cities have found waste removal to be a serious problem – indeed, far more serious than this particular set of statistics would seem to suggest (Grieg-Gran, 1998).

## Poor disposal of collected wastes

Even if waste is collected, it still creates city-level disposal problems. Open dumping is an obvious symptom, but much depends on what the wastes are, and many landfills, incinerators and other waste-disposal systems create serious environmental burdens in and around the city. As indicated in Table 2.5, the share of waste that is reported to be disposed of in open dumps declines from a high of 62 per cent in the poorest cities observed to 0 per cent in the wealthiest. Since the quantities of waste generated do not vary to the same extent, and somewhat surprisingly are lowest in the middle-income cities, this would seem to imply that open dumping is most serious in the poorest cities.

On the other hand, even in this case, there clearly are opposing forces at work that can create a shift in priorities towards the citywide waste problems as one moves from poor to middle-income industrialized cities. First, there is a sense in which the collection of waste shifts the burden from the localities where the waste is collected to the city as a whole. And as noted above, collection rates are higher in middle-income than in poor cities. Second, the share of putrescible waste, which causes short-term problems in the vicinity of the waste site but no serious long-term disposal problem, is higher in the poorest cities (Cointreau, 1986), while the share of industrial wastes is lower. Using the data summarized in Table 2.5 to estimate very roughly the amount of solid waste collected and disposed of in open city dumps yields far closer statistics: 0.4kg per capita in the poorest cities and 0.3kg in the middle-income cities and 0.0kg in the affluent cities.[7] Assuming that greater shares of waste in the middle-income cities are hazardous or non-degradable, the citywide burden of the middle-income cities could well be larger.

### Aggregate waste generation

The closest thing to an indicator of global contributions to the waste burden is aggregate waste generation, which increases with affluence. While this tendency is quite muted in Table 2.5, statistical studies of municipal waste generation have been conducted, and these studies have found a positive relationship between waste generation and income (Shafik, 1995, for example). Large quantities of urban waste represent a disposal problem for the city. The more important waste burden for affluent cities, however, is that for at least some materials the accumulations of waste reflects the interruption of natural material cycles and their replacement with linear flows. Even to the extent that affluent urban centres can solve their immediate disposal problems, few have shifted towards the sort of clean technologies that might radically alter waste generation.

### *Stereotyping Poor, Middle-Income and Affluent Cities*

The problems of air, water and waste are closely interconnected, and relate to numerous other urban environmental problems. Drawing together and adding to the shifts described above, it is possible to provide a somewhat stereotyped description of three different types of cities. The problems of the low- and middle-income cities are described in more detail in Chapter 3, where the results of studies of Accra, Jakarta and São Paulo are presented.

While contrasts have been emphasized up to this point, it is also important to recognize the similarities in the environmental challenges that different cities face. Partly because of the close interconnections between environmental problems at every level, even in low-income cities, environmental problems tend to be public in nature, complex and multisectoral. It is just that the relevant public is more restricted where environmental problems are more local.

In low-income settlements, local environmental problems are a major cause of disease and death. Inadequate household water and sanitation, smoky cooking fuels, waste accumulating in the neighbourhood, disease-bearing pests: all are major contributors to ill health and mortality, especially among children (World Bank,

---

7 These figures were calculated by multiplying the collection share in each city by the waste generation rate and the open dumping fraction

1993a). Inadequate household water supplies and sanitation are typically more crucial to people's well-being than polluted waterways (Cairncross and Feachem, 1993). There is often more exposure to air pollution in smoky kitchens than outdoors (Smith, 1993a). Waste accumulating, uncollected, in the neighbourhood often poses more serious health problems than the waste at city dumps. Flies breeding in the waste and mosquitoes breading in water sites can add considerably to the local health risks (Chavasse et al, 1994; Schofield et al, 1990). And all of these risks involve closely interrelated local environmental processes:[8] waste clogs the drains, faecal material gets into the drinking water; mosquitoes breed in the water containers, flies breed in the filth and leave deposits on the food, and so on. Virtually everyone living and socializing in the neighbourhood is at risk, but especially women and children.

In middle-income, industrializing cities, increasing wealth will tend to bring improvements in local environmental conditions. Some combination of public, private and collective sector initiatives are likely to have dealt with the worst water and sanitation problems, and most households are likely to have shifted to clean fuels. Housing will be better, at least on average, with less damp, less crowding and better ventilation. On the other hand, industrialization and motorized transport are likely to have added a new menu of environmental burdens, this time falling principally at the citywide or regional level. The pollution of the ambient air and waterways is likely to be higher. The abstraction of ground water may have become so severe that saline infiltration and/or land subsistence is a problem.

In affluent settlements, the most serious local environmental hazards have been displaced or reduced, while existing lifestyles pose major, if often uncertain, delayed and diffuse threats to our life-support systems. Waste, once a problem primarily in and around people's homes and workplaces, now interferes with a range of regional and even global processes. High levels of materials and energy consumption and waste generation, selective pressures on distant ecosystems, new hazards arising from technologies developed to meet the demands of the affluent – these are the stuff of the global sustainability challenge. And just as it is hard to live in a deprived neighbourhood in a poor city in the developing world and avoid the local environmental hazards, so it is hard to live in an affluent neighbourhood in the developed world and avoid contributing to global environmental burdens.

---

8 These processes also have extra-local dimensions (eg if infectious diseases only spread within neighbourhoods, they could not persist), but the threat to residents can typically be contained through measures undertaken locally

## A Simplified Environmental History of Affluent Cities

The underlying relationship between urban affluence and environmental burdens is sufficiently robust to have a historical manifestation. If one looks back to the middle of the last century, most of the now affluent cities of the North had as serious local environmental health problems as virtually any poor city today.[9] Urban living had long been extremely unhealthy, and the rapid urbanization that accompanied rural enclosure and urban industrialization created historically unprecedented levels of urban crowding. Mortality rates in urban centres were far higher than in their rural surrounds (Bairoch, 1988) and urban discontent was harder for the authorities to handle. Indeed, for the 19th century bourgeoisie, there were two 'infectious' hazards that could emerge from the overcrowded and unsanitary back streets of the industrial cities: revolutionary fervour and disease (Shapiro, 1985). For many 19th century commentators, filth, immorality, disease and revolution were all intertwined. Together, they threatened the very basis of society, along with its social distinctions.[10]

### Water and sanitation

Wohl starts his wide ranging account of public health in Victorian Britain with an account of the sanitary problems befalling a London household (Wohl, 1983). The sequence of sanitary insults – fever, stench, forced removal, death of the head of household – reads like a typical story from a community deprived of basic sanitation. However, the household of concern is Royal, and the surviving widow Queen Victoria. Obviously, it was far more hazardous to live in the overcrowded and impoverished back streets of London, than the spacious Royal residences. Nevertheless, the sanitary problems of the 19th century city threatened all strata of society in a way that they rarely do today. Cholera epidemics were a special concern, leading *The Times* in 1848 to dub cholera 'the best of all sanitary reformers' (Wohl, 1983).

In many ways, the sanitary movement was the environmental movement of the 19th century. Indeed, looking back, the sanitary revolution appears as one of the great successes of the industrializing countries of the late 19th and early 20th

---

9 In contrast to the overall trend towards globalization so often remarked on, the burden of poor sanitation has become more localized since the 19th century. In medical terms, epidemics have become less significant relative to endemic disease transmission. Nevertheless, it is fair to say that the sanitary health threat in 19th-century cities arose primarily from local environmental hazards

10 The threat of infectious disease was simultaneously part of the justification for social segregation and influenced urban planning. This was most evident in colonial situations. In colonial Africa, for example, theories of disease were explicitly used to justify recommendations enforcing spatial segregation (Feierman and Janzen, 1992)

centuries. Without it, the multifold increase in productivity that accompanied industrialization would have been less possible, and far less meaningful. While scientists like to claim credit for the enormous health improvements that accompanied the water and sanitation initiatives undertaken in so many cities, it is evident that science was just one small part of the process which transformed living conditions.

Bad sanitation, which then referred to a range of poorly understood environmental hazards rather than just excreta disposal, was increasingly seen as responsible for this urban disadvantage (Wohl, 1983). Prominent scientists studied water, sanitary conditions and health, and reformers in urban centres around the world discussed both the technical and moral aspects of urban sanitary reform (Hamlin, 1990; Ladd, 1990; Luckin, 1986). The topic was even of popular interest in many countries. The General German Exhibition of Hygiene and Lifesaving in 1883 attracted 900,000 visitors over a period of five months (Ladd, 1990). As in environmental discussions today, one of the most heated debates was about the appropriate role for government and whether attempts to impose sanitary improvements constituted an infringement on what we would now call the private sector. There was also concern that the measures taken to improve sanitation were displacing rather than solving the problems.

The poem that Coleridge wrote during a visit to Cologne in the 1840s, below, probably represents the most eloquent questioning of the wisdom of environmental displacement, and yet it also refers to some of the more outlandish scientific approaches to understanding sanitary problems:

> In Köhln, a town of monks and bones,
> And pavements fang'd with murderous stones
> And rags, and hags, and hideous wenches;
> I counted two and seventy stenches,
> All well defined, and several stinks!
>
> Ye nymphs that reign o'er sewers and sinks,
> The river Rhine, it is well known,
> Doth wash the city of Cologne;
> But tell me, Nymphs, what power Divine
> Shall henceforth wash the river Rhine?

Sanitary science at the time of Coleridge's visit had not yet widely accepted the existence of germs. Indeed, the reference to counting stenches and stinks could well be a reference to scientific practice at the time. Many people believed that breathing in evil-smelling fumes caused diseases, and some scientists responded by classifying and counting these smells. Thus, for example, in 1790 Jean-Noël Hallé who held the first chair of public hygiene in Paris, carefully documented the odours encountered along the banks of the Seine, following a request from the Société Royale de Médecine (Corbin, 1994). In retrospect, such practices seem almost ludicrous (though perhaps no less ludicrous than many of the environmental indicators used today will seem in the future).

Coleridge's question to the nymphs of sewers and sinks, on the other hand, resonates with modern environmental sensibilities: it is all very well to use water to carry away urban waste, but who is going to clean up the water? This question, in relation to various environmental media and various wastes, still remains unanswered. It lies at the heart of the search for 'clean technologies' that could pre-empt the need for extensive clean-up or even end-of-pipe solutions by minimizing waste generation and recycling as much as possible (Jackson, 1993; Jackson, 1996).

Some sanitary reforms were also resisted on the grounds that valuable nutrients were lost when human waste was flushed away with water. Many of the early schemes envisaged using water to transport the waste and apply it to agricultural fields. When serious practical difficulties were encountered, however, such attempts at recycling were forgone. It should not be thought, however, that what we now think of as 'sustainability' concerns were ignored. The loss of nutrients was far more obvious than it is today, since farmers had to do without an important source of fertilizer. Even the best known sanitary reformer, Edwin Chadwick, explicitly regretted the loss of fertilizer (see Chapter 3).

Eventually, the sanitary reformers won out, and their initial concerns about environmental displacement were largely forgotten. Replacements for recycled human waste were found, first through natural substitutes and later through chemical synthesis. Somewhat ironically, this involved new forms of environmental displacement, involving far more than human wastes alone. Initially, trade in natural fertilizers increased. In the extreme, the faecal material of seabirds, guano, was shipped in from distant shores, replacing local recycling. In effect, disruptions in local cycles were overcome by tapping more distant ecosystems. By 1913, when synthetic ammonia began to be produced, the recycling of urban human waste in agriculture had already been greatly reduced.

The pressure for sanitary reform also grew as the public nature of the health threats was increasingly acknowledged. While the health problems were far worse in poor areas, the affluent were also at risk. Moreover, the ill health of the poor was itself felt to be a burden on the whole society. Politicians were even concerned that the military strength of their nations was being undermined (Shapiro, 1985). It was gradually accepted by the politically powerful that the burden was indeed public and required a public response.

The sanitary reforms initiated what Joel Tarr has termed 'the search for the ultimate sink' (Tarr, 1996). Indeed, his account of how, over the last two centuries in the United States, solutions for one pollution problem often generated new pollution problems in different localities or in different media, very much confirms the tendencies being examined here. The following paragraphs draw heavily on his presentation, although similar processes of displacement were also occurring in various other parts of the world.

Prior to the sanitary reforms, water and faecal disposal systems in the United States had a local focus. Water came from local sources and faeces were typically disposed of in cesspools and privy vaults. In 1802, Philadelphia constructed the first urban waterworks and by 1880 there were 598 such systems. As people used more water, problems with overflowing cesspools and privies grew worse. Between the 1850s and the 1880s most municipalities in the United States constructed sewerage systems, but these were primarily for stormwater drainage. The transition towards water-carried sanitation systems was promoted by the Sanitary Movement, institutionally grounded in 'the American Public Health Association, the National Board of Health and the multitude of local and state boards of health that appeared in the late nineteenth century' (Tarr, 1996, p11). Efforts to improve sanitation were accompanied by large publicity campaigns designed to change the way that people perceived waste and 'filth'. By 1911 all major American cities had sewerage systems, with most (88 per cent in 1909) of the wastewater disposed of untreated in waterways. Cities were loath to invest in systems that would primarily benefit downstream inhabitants. Instead, the water systems were reworked to cope with sewerage-polluted water from upstream cities. The ultimate effect of this sanitary revolution was considerable health improvement, but badly polluted waterways.

A number of sewerage-treatment plants were constructed in the interwar period with the help of federal funds, but only made a marginal impact. Concern increased, however, as formerly unsuspected health hazards were identified, and new industrial pollutants were added to the water. By the 1960s, the scene was set for a new 'pollution' revolution, and in 1972 the Clean Water Act was passed, calling for zero effluents by 1985. While this goal has still not been reached, improvements have been recorded in many quarters, and hopefully the worst of waterway pollution has passed.

However, as new productive activities are introduced and the science of water improves, new water-related threats continue to emerge. Moreover, the balance between the pollution of water sources and the need to treat water for human consumption remains a delicate one.

## Air pollution

Air pollution has followed a somewhat similar process of intervention and displacement. Ventilation was the crux of public health tactics in late 18th-century France (Corbin, 1994) and probably elsewhere. Air pollution was then considered part of the sanitary threat. Chimneys, of course, had long been used to displace indoor smoke concentrations into the outdoor air. They did not require public action, however. Many of the early governmental efforts to control air pollution targeted smoky fuels in large cities. By 1912, 23 of the 28 largest cities in the United States had smoke-control ordinances, principally aimed at visible smoke from commercial establishments. Such measures missed the domestic consumers, whose use of smoky coal was a major contributor to urban air quality problems. It was not until the 1940s and 1950s that natural gas and oil began to replace coal on a significant scale for domestic heating, as well as industrial, commercial and transport uses.

Most of these shifts had far more impact on the local air-pollution problems than on regional and global problems. Indeed, some measures quite literally displaced the air pollution burdens. Electricity generation distanced pollution from the end-users, providing a clean fuel in the home. Coal-fired plants were located near urban centres, contributing to urban air pollution, although, as electricity grids developed, the distances increased. Further displacement measures were taken when, under the advice of air pollution experts in the 1950s and 1960s, taller stacks were increasingly used by the ore-smelting and electrical utility industries to avoid violating local air-pollution ordinances. By 1963, some utility stacks had reached 700 feet.

Unfortunately, tall stacks not only reduced local exposures, but also contributed to acid-rain problems by allowing pollutants to travel long distances, as well as by propelling sulphur and nitrogen oxides into the upper atmosphere. Here a range of transformations can occur, resulting in acid rain. Acid rain, falling on sensitive ecosystems and even human-made structures, became an important environmental concern in the 1970s.

The 1977 amendments to the Clean Air Act provided the basis for regulating stack height, and concern for acid rain further spurred such technologies as fluidized bed combustion and flue gas desulphurization, as well as the use of low-sulphur fuels. As a result, the emissions of acid precursors from affluent cities and their industrial hinterlands have fallen in recent decades.

As described above, however, affluent cities continue to contribute to greenhouse gas emissions, both directly and indirectly. The history of urban air pollution has much in common with many of the other environmental burdens. The affluent cities of today were almost all dirtier and more unhealthy in the past, with a larger share of their ill health originating from environmental factors. But they are far from environmentally benign today.

## QUALIFYING THE URBAN ENVIRONMENTAL 'TRANSITION'

These stylized accounts capture some important aspects of urban environmental variation and change. Taken in isolation, however, they could be very misleading. They could be taken to imply, for example, that this urban transition is the inevitable outcome of development, or that economic growth can be counted on to reduce local and then citywide environmental problems, and perhaps eventually the global burdens that are now associated with affluence. Alternatively, they focus so much attention on interurban differences that the importance of intraurban variation and urban–rural interactions may be obscured. Thus, before any conclusions are drawn from these accounts, it is important to consider some of the second-order complications.

## Intraurban Variation

In the stylized account of affluence and urban environmental burdens provided above, both affluence and environmental burdens were treated as characteristics of cities. But no city, of course, is of uniform affluence and environmental quality. Indeed, many of the same wealth-related differences that are evident between cities are also evident within cities. Moreover, intraurban variations in affluence, for example, may play an important role in determining how cities respond to environmental issues. Indeed, some researchers have gone so far as to claim that greater equity, all other things being equal, will lead to higher environmental quality (Torras, 1998).

Urban inequality is implicit in most indicators of local environmental burdens which often take the form of shares of the urban population facing what are considered to be unacceptable burdens. Thus, to say that x per cent of a city's population lacks access to adequate water, adequate sanitation or smokeless energy sources, explicitly divides the city into unequal groups. There are also, of course, appreciable inequalities in most affluent cities. Lifestyles and hence environmental burdens vary. The homeless of New York undoubtedly consume fewer resources and impose less of a global environmental burden than the wealthiest residents of New Delhi.

The overall affluence of a city does make a difference, but it is important to recognize that generalizations based on aggregates and averages cannot be assumed to apply at the individual level. In particular, the equity dimensions of urban environmental management must clearly take account of both intra- and interurban differentials.

## The Role of Governance

Despite the attention being given to affluence, the stylized descriptions of urban environmental transition do not capture its political and economic dimensions. They do not explain, for example, the difficulties that most cities face in addressing the environmental burdens that are characteristic of their level of affluence, or why some cities are more successful at managing their environments than others. Poor cities and neighbourhoods almost inevitably face serious local environmental health problems, but even within the same city neighbourhoods of comparable wealth vary enormously in their environmental quality (Bapat and Crook, 1984). Much the same applies throughout the transition: affluence is clearly only one factor that influences environmental burdens. Other factors may include the natural setting, the functional role or the historical context of the neighbourhood or city. But different cities and communities also react differently to the challenges they face. Even to begin to understand this variation, it is important to consider the nature of the political and economic challenge that these environmental burdens raise.

Politically, the groups most at risk tend to be at a political disadvantage, especially the economically deprived in relation to local hazards and the not-yet-born in relation to global burdens. In many cases there are politically powerful groups that have a vested interest in maintaining environmentally destructive activities. But even when this is not the case, it is a political challenge to ensure that such environmental risks are taken seriously in the public arena. And unfortunately, the market mechanisms by which many human needs are met do not function effectively when it comes to most environmental burdens.

Economically, there are externalities and other collective action problems at every level. Households in areas lacking basic services only affect the environmental quality of their neighbourhood marginally, but bear the combined burden of environmental insults from a wide range of sources.[11] Urban ambient air and water have long been used in economic texts to exemplify the economic difficulties posed by public goods, and global environmental goods threatened by affluent lifestyles are even more geographically public in scope.

Moreover, at every level the problems tend to be difficult to perceive directly and involve scientifically complex phenomena. As described in Chapter 3, this even applies to local water and sanitation problems which experts still only understand very partially a century after the peak of the European sanitary revolution. This uncertainty tends to reinforce the political and economic obstacles to action. Poorly understood and economically externalized threats that fall heavily on the politically marginal groups, are easily ignored.

This implies that better and more equitable governance should help to reduce the incidence of environmental burdens at every level of affluence. Differences in governance could explain at least part of the very appreciable variation in environmental burdens that have been observed in cities of comparable affluence. Because of the scales involved, local governance would seem to be more relevant to problems in poor cities and global governance to problems emerging from affluent cities. In practice, however, scales of governance cannot be so neatly circumscribed.

---

11 Even household environmental health problems have a public dimension, especially when they expose people to infectious diseases that can then be spread person-to-person

National (and state) governments often control the possibilities for cities and municipalities to develop the revenue base or receive the proportion of public funds they need to meet local responsibilities for water, sanitation, drainage, rubbish collection and other local environmental problems. National governments are also key actors in global agreements. Moreover, local actions and governance are linked to global processes, and good global governance must be locally grounded. Thus, on the one hand local measures to improve environmental health often depend critically on international finance, and approaches to environmental service provision are heavily influenced by international trends. (The collapse of communism, for example, had a profound effect on attitudes to state provision of water and sanitation in poor cities, although the fall of communism had little or nothing to do with the relative merits of public ownership of environmental utilities.) On the other hand, global agreements to curb greenhouse gas emissions are likely to be very disruptive if their implementation is not based on good local governance.

In short, the form of the urban environmental transition reflects both physical and social processes. Moreover, while the form of the transition can be explained, it is by no means predetermined. With better governance, more effective means for addressing environmental burdens at every scale should be possible. It is not possible, however, to compartmentalize different scales of governance and make clear generalizations about their relative importance to different environmental issues.

## Interscale Effects

In describing the physical outlines of the urban environmental transition, the only interscale effect described was environmental displacement, whereby measures that reduced local burdens create larger scale burdens. Environmental displacement is a serious concern, but there are also instances where reducing local environmental burdens diminishes the larger scale burdens and vice versa. Similarly, deteriorating local environmental conditions can contribute to international or even global burdens.

In relation to water and sanitation, the local conditions that facilitate the spread of diseases locally also increase the risks of epidemics and even pandemics. Research on urban epidemics of infectious diseases at the turn of the last century indicate a complex global pattern, even for diseases whose spread depends on local environments and human interactions (Cliff et al, 1998). The recent cholera pandemic in Latin America would probably not have emerged were it not for deficient water and sanitary conditions in the urban centres of the region (Tauxe et al, 1995), and it is also possible that climate change played a role (McMichael et al, 1996). While the spread of the endemic diseases that now constitute the major share of the water- and sanitation-related disease burden is less easily monitored, it is equally complex and undoubtedly involves interurban infection through human movement (ie not just through water-borne routes, such as water-borne sanitation). Moreover, large concentrations of people living with poor sanitation is, according to some researchers, conducive to outbreaks of new 'plagues' that could spread around the globe (Krause, 1992). Such links between local and larger scale burdens are neglected in the first-order account of the urban water and sanitation transition.

With regard to air pollution, some recent research suggests that household biofuels emit large quantities of methane, an important greenhouse gas. Thus, shifting to 'cleaner' fuels could serve both health improvements in poor households and reduce global warming (Smith and Akbar, 1999). There are also potential complementarities between reductions in carbon emissions and ambient concentrations of particulates. Some researchers have even claimed that hundreds of thousands of lives could be saved annually by climate control policies (Working Group on Public Health and Fossil-Fuel Combustion, 1997). In practice, some measures to curb carbon emissions would reduce ambient concentrations of health-threatening pollutants in cities, while others would not. But what are missing are not technical opportunities for addressing environmental burdens at different scales simultaneously, but the incentives, understandings and equitable institutional settings to ensure that such opportunities are seized.

Alternatively, global environmental burdens will not be felt equally across the world, and low-income urban areas are among the most vulnerable to disruptions. Thus, while global environmental change may not be a priority issue for low-income cities, neither is it only an issue of concern to the affluent who can afford to worry about the distant future.

In short, just as there are opportunities for addressing environmental burdens at every scale, given good governance there are also opportunities for reducing the trade-offs between the different scales.

### Urban–rural Interactions

While some urban–rural interaction is implicit in the stylized accounts above, most of this interaction is expressed in terms of the environmental impacts of urban production or consumption. However, the relation between urban development and rural environmental burdens goes beyond the effects of urban consumption, pollution and waste. Urban developments, for example, have played a major role in the commodification of rural produce and the various responsive transformations in the rural agricultural and natural landscapes.

A recent history of Chicago, from an environmental perspective, provides almost 400 pages of analysis, with virtually no mention of the environmental burdens described in the 'environmental transition' above (Cronon, 1992). Instead, the account centres on, for example, the loss of species diversity in the grasslands as farmers responded to the evolving Chicago grain markets; the decline of the

White Pine forests in response to developments in Chicago's lumber industry; the changing animal stocks and living conditions that emerged through developments in Chicago's meat handling and marketing. Far from being straightforward increases in demand, these shifts involved complex sets of interrelated technical and institutional changes, with Chicago at the hub.

The Chicago grain market, for example, evolved from individually traded shipments to the trading of receipts linked to graded grain elevators, which in turn enabled the emergence of futures markets allowing options on future purchases to be bought and sold. This in turn changed both the rural grain trading system and the incentives placed on individual farms. Very different but equally significant changes occurred with meat and lumber, with implications for a variety of other urban–rural relationships. Many modern cities are centres for similar types of innovation, and some research indicates that such innovation, often in the form of financial instruments that are far removed from physical production processes, are central to the emergence of 'global cities' (Sassen, 2000).

These sorts of urban–rural interactions are beyond the scope of this book. By and large, they do not go against the conclusions that can be drawn from a narrower focus on urban environmental burdens. It is important to recognize, however, that such a focus does not fully capture the environmental implications of urban development.

## CONCLUSIONS

Urban development is so complex and varied that it may seem perverse to draw simple conclusions about the relationship between urban affluence and environmental burdens, let alone draw policy conclusions. Human creations, cities have never been tamed. Outcomes of opportunism, cities are forever being planned. Sites of civilization and wealth, cities are also centres of degradation and exploitation. They embody humankind's greatest accomplishments and its greatest failings, often manifesting them as two sides of the same coin. Cities reflect our capacity to create and adapt to radically new environments, and demonstrate the risks of doing so. And now, even as the share of the world's population living in urban areas is approaching 50 per cent, the city is beginning to seem an anachronistic construct (Borja and Castells, 1997).

Urban development has always created environmental hazards as well as opportunities. Bringing large numbers of people to live together in a small area is inherently problematic. Many of the most notorious diseases, from measles to the plague, emerged and spread once human settlement became sufficiently crowded to sustain them (Cohen, 1989; Mascie-Taylor, 1993). Many of the most ecologically destructive agricultural practices, such as intensive monocultures, only emerged in response to urban demands for surplus production. Crowding people into cities also concentrated waste and pollution. The environmental problems that confronted early urban centres still have modern analogues, even if many lessons have been learned since the early cities rose and fell (Southall, 1998).

Urban crowding also brought a range of social challenges and opportunities, many of which also still reverberate today. Urbanization helped to concentrate political power, often allowing urban elites to exploit the rural hinterlands and at times to create far-flung empires. Urbanization also undermined pre-existing forms of social cohesion. In what was probably the first social theory of urban development, Ibn Khaldûn (1332–1406) described the corrosive effect of urban living on social solidarities in North Africa. This corrosion, he argued, left them open to a new wave of conquest by nomadic tribesmen whose 'asibiya', or group feeling, was strong (Khaldûn, 1981). Both 'urban bias' and 'urban anomie' remain common themes up to the present day (Lipton, 1989).

But many new challenges are confronting today's cities and old challenges are being radically transformed. Cities have never been so varied in their wealth or so closely interconnected economically, socially and physically. Some are critical nodes of the global economy and its information network (Sassen, 2000); others are very local affairs. Many, and not only the poorest, are home to some of the most excluded groups. There has never been such a compelling need to confront the urban challenges globally, or so great a danger that the diversity of urban needs will be neglected. And the global environmental challenge – how to prevent the collective impact of local actions from irrevocably damaging the world's life-support systems – has added a fundamentally new complication to development politics at every level.

Despite these complexities, there are common tendencies worth noting. The principal scale of urban environmental burdens varies with affluence, and it is appropriate that environmental priorities should vary correspondingly. To a first approximation, low-income cities need to focus primarily on local environmental health problems, industrializing middle-income cities on citywide and regional burdens, and affluent cities on global burdens.

This does not imply that low-income cities should be less concerned with environmental issues. Indeed, both the level and share of morbidity and mortality from environmental causes is higher in low-income settlements, gainsaying any attempt to argue that only the affluent can afford to care about the environment.

There are also a number of political dimensions to the fact that the environmental burdens of urban poverty are more localized than those of urban affluence. Perhaps most obvious, it suggests that environmental burdens exacerbate existing inequalities. The poor may burden their equally impoverished neighbours with environmental risks, but the affluent burden an expanding 'public'. Moreover, these differences reveal a political aspect to principles like 'sustainability' and 'subsidiarity'.

'Sustainability' has become the key environmental desideratum, reflecting an increasing emphasis on the part of Northern environmentalists on ecological damage and burdens on future generations. But sustainability is more relevant to affluent than to low-income settings. The evolution of environmental concerns, from an early concern with immediate local burdens to the contemporary concern with dispersed and long-term impacts, has not simply been the result of a better understanding of environmental processes. It has also reflected real changes in the nature of predominant environmental threats that are emerging from conventional economic development. As later chapters demonstrate, sustainability is not a suitable goal with respect to the key environmental health problems threatening the urban poor.

'Subsidiarity', the notion that responsibilities should devolve to the lowest appropriate level, has become a common organizational principle. Thus, it is often argued that environmental problems should be addressed at the lowest appropriate level of social organization. This too raises serious equity concerns. It can easily be interpreted as a justification for removing higher level support rather than increasing local control. Both the history of affluent cities and the contemporary experiences of low-income cities indicate that even local burdens require responses at all levels, not least international. It is also inequitable to let the poor deal with their own problems, while governments and international agencies devote their public finance to the problems of the affluent.

The tendency for global burdens to increase with affluence, however, does create a tension that reaches back to low-income settlements. The 'transition' is not a trajectory that the currently low-income cities can expect to follow. The global pressures are collective, and in effect the ecological space for conventional development is exhausted. Thus, there are good reasons for searching for the means to avoid environmental displacement and preventing global burdens from increasing, even at the lower end of the income scale. But this search must be viewed in the context of the overall responsibilities for global burdens to which low-income residents contribute very little.

# 3

# Urban Water: From Health to Sustainability[1]

This chapter focuses on water and its role in both health and sustainability. The two main sections follow the logic of the transition described in the previous chapter: water and health is examined first, followed by water and sustainability. In this introduction, the importance of not overinterpreting this transition is reiterated.

Somewhat at odds with the notion of a transition from health to sustainability burdens, water-related threats to urban sustainability did not suddenly emerge in the late 20th century, and water-related health problems are not about to disappear in the 21st century. Indeed, many of the 'new' insights of environmentalism reflect the re-emergence of old concepts and concerns that were at least on the sidelines during past environmental debates.

In the 14th century, Ibn Khaldûn placed water for human consumption first in the list of resources whose negligence had made a number of Arab cities of the past 'very ready to fall into ruins, inasmuch as they did not fulfil all the natural requirements of towns' (Khaldûn, 1981, pp238–239). His concern is mirrored in modern texts that describe cities straining the limits of their water supplies (Anton, 1993). Modern technologies, with their much greater capacity to draw on distant supplies, can create larger scale water deficits, but they also create the capacity to sustain cities in the face of more local deficits.

Coleridge's poem about Cologne, given in the previous chapter, was written in the early 19th century, but displays a modern sensibility to the dangers of using water to displace pollution. The ostensibly modern notion that using water to carry away human waste is unsustainable because it interrupts nutrient cycles also had 19th-century precursors: an influential French writer and social activist complained that water-borne sewers interfered with the 'circulus' of nature, and saw this as a major threat to social development (Reid, 1993, pp53–70). In *Les Misérables*, Victor Hugo seemed to favour the arguments of 'modern' environmental

---

1 This chapter is based upon Kjellén, M and McGranahan, G (1997) *Urban Water – Towards Health and Sustainability*, Stockholm Environment Institute (Stockholm), with the permission of the Stockholm Environment Institute

economics, claiming that 'Each hiccup of our cloaca [sewer] costs us a thousand francs. From this two results: the land impoverished and the water contaminated. Hunger rising from the furrow and disease rising from the river' (p 1257 of Signet Classics paperback edition).

If the seemingly modern issues of urban water, nutrient cycles and sustainability have actually been with us for centuries, the seemingly old-fashioned issues of water, poverty and infectious diseases may unfortunately be with us for centuries to come. Reports based on government statistics indicate that in the early 1990s about one-fifth of urban dwellers in the South were without adequate access to safe water and about one-third were without adequate sanitation – and what governments define as adequate may still be far from healthy. There are roughly 3 million deaths every year from diarrhoeal diseases, most of which could probably be averted by water-related improvements. While water-related health problems are likely to remain far more severe in the South, some are beginning to re-emerge in wealthier countries. The 1993 diarrhoea outbreak in Milwaukee in the American Midwest, where more than 4000 were hospitalized after being infected with a parasite in the municipal water supplies, was a challenge to Northern complacency (World Health Organization, 1996).

## WATER AND URBAN HEALTH

### *The Sanitary Movement, Water Science and Water Engineering*

In Chapter 2, it was argued that the sanitary movement was in many respects the environmental movement of the 19th century: it brought attention to hazardous side-effects of urban development; it engaged public figures as well as scientists in debating unresolved scientific, political and moral issues; and it changed the course of urban development. Despite a lack of scientific consensus and considerable pressure to do nothing to interfere with economic growth, a great deal was accomplished, especially in affluent cities. To some degree, problems were displaced rather than resolved, but a health transition was accomplished along the way, and the level of collective action achieved bodes well for the contemporary environmental agenda. On the other hand, this history also raises a difficult question for the environmental movement. Have the 'old-fashioned' problems of water, local sanitation and health lost their prominent place on the environmental agenda because they are less important globally, because our environmental horizons have expanded, or because these 'old-fashioned' environmental problems have been supplanted by environmental problems that are more critical in the affluent parts of the world?

## The sanitary movement and broader environmental concerns

Looking back, it is easy to view the sanitary improvements of the 19th and early 20th centuries as feats of science and engineering, now perhaps rendered less glamorous by an awareness of their broader environmental inadequacies. At the time, one might argue, scientists were just discovering that the routes of disease transmission involved human waste and microbially contaminated water. When engineers devised the means for cutting off many of these routes with piped water, water quality control and sewerage systems, they had to rely on existing science. It was hardly surprising that they failed to consider the consequences of introducing water-borne sewerage on, for example, nutrient cycles. Such sophistication had to await late 20th-century environmentalism.

This interpretation is seriously misleading, as indicated in Chapter 2. Partly because human waste was widely used as a fertilizer, a loss was quickly perceived when it no longer reached the fields. The debates concerning water and sanitary improvement in the 19th century were as wide-ranging as the environmental debates of today. And in any case, many of the major public health improvements were undertaken before the bacterial theory of disease was established, and scientific opinion on the relation between water and health was deeply divided. The theories that lost out in the course of scientific advance were often as supportive of sanitary improvement as those that won. For example, the once reputable scientific view that ill health was brought on by miasmas, a sort of air pollution that could disturb the balance of humours in one's body, was often used to justify efforts to improve sanitary conditions. Indeed, some historians have argued that miasma theory, with its holistic tendencies, provided more support for general cleanliness and the removal of filth, than the bacterial theories that tended to place the emphasis on particular pathogens (Rosen, 1993).

## The sanitary movement and public debate

Furthermore, as indicated in Chapter 2, sanitary improvement in the 19th century was not the preserve of experts that it was to become in the early 20th century. Just as in contemporary environmental debates, scientists were brought in by all sides to justify both environmental intervention and laissez-faire. And at the height of the public health movement, debates about water and health engaged not just scientists and engineers, but a whole panoply of public figures. It was only later, when a conventional approach to water and sanitation had been established, that public interest in such events waned and experts took over most of the key positions. As Hamlin notes, we are again entering a period of uncertainty about water and must again learn to debate water issues in public (Hamlin, 1990). In this context, it is important to take the right lessons from the 19th-century experience.

Ironically, one of the dangers of treating the sanitary revolution as a scientific and technical achievement is that, even as it exaggerates the importance of science in the past, it ascribes an unduly limited role to science in the future. This applies especially to the notion that an understanding of microbial disease transmission brought about the sanitary revolution, and more generally the epidemiological transition away from infectious diseases in the North. Such accounts overstate the significance of scientific breakthroughs such as Snow's famous demonstration in the 1850s that the Broad Street pump in London was the source of a local cholera outbreak, and Koch's successful isolation of the cholera bacillus some 20 years later. They also mask the profound ignorance that remains regarding the transmission and evolution of water-related diseases. Certainly a great deal has been learned, but not so as to provide any easy answers.

### Sanitary improvement as a technical fix

Once economic growth and a set of public health measures, including piped water and sewerage, were found to reduce the incidence of most water-related diseases to comparatively insignificant levels, the motivation to understand them better fell drastically. Debates about which specific measures underpinned the epidemiological transition seemed academic when the whole package was clearly desirable. Moreover, as practitioners find in so many sectors, funding for water and sanitation utilities was easier to justify when uncertainties were ignored. Even people working in the water sector came to believe that giving people clean drinking-water was the key to reducing water-borne diseases.

More generally, piped water and articulated sewerage systems came to be viewed as the technical fix for the urban health disadvantage. For the greater part of this century, the accepted wisdom has been that the urban health-related goal in the water and sanitation field should be to provide every dwelling with piped water and a water closet, or the closest possible equivalent. Indeed, this was very much the premise of the Water and Sanitation Decade (the 1980s), which had as its global target 'to provide all people with water of safe quality and adequate quantity and basic sanitary facilities by 1990' (World Health Organization, 1981, Annex 1, p52).

However, for many urban dwellers in the South, such technical fixes remain as elusive as ever. Public investment in a capital-intensive infrastructure is becoming less rather than more prevalent, and the private sector is unlikely to fill such a large and costly gap. With less costly systems, there is still enormous uncertainty surrounding the long-standing environmental health issues relating to water and sanitation. Once one leaves the areas where water comes out of indoor taps and faeces are flushed away with the press of a button, there is still the need for a systemic approach to environmental health issues involving water. There are numerous local externalities that relate local water supplies with sanitation, insects, waste disposal and a host of community-level environmental problems (McGranahan et al, 1996). There is clearly a need for local collective action, articulated and supported both nationally and internationally, even if there is unlikely to be any single model for organizing local environmental improvement (see Chapter 5). In short, there is a need for a new, less patrimonial, more sophisticated environmental health movement.

## Urban water and modern environmentalism

Northern environmentalists have recently managed to broaden international policy debates to include water and sustainability, introducing a number of complex and poorly understood challenges in the process. It is likely that today's theorizing about sustainability will one day seem as quaint as the miasma theory of disease. Indeed, the notion that filth and impurity give off a miasma that can disturb the balance of humours in the human body is not so very different from the concern that cities disturb the water system and hence the balances of nature. The miasma theory helped to underwrite an active holistic approach to sanitary improvement at a time when reductionist science was in danger of fostering inaction. Sustainability debates are hopefully providing much the same for broader environmental concerns. Unfortunately, however, they are in danger of further marginalizing the environmental health concerns that spurred the urban-based sanitary movement of the 19th century, despite the large numbers of people for whom these concerns are still central.

## Water and Infectious Diseases

Even now, our practical understanding of how best to improve the environment and health situation in disadvantaged neighbourhoods is not much better than our understanding of how best to address sustainability problems globally: it is far easier to make a long list of preventive steps which, taken together, would undoubtedly reduce the environmental health burdens considerably, than it is to demonstrate the importance of particular hazards and prioritize particular measures. Water is critical to the transmission of many diseases. In arguing for the importance of water, it is common to oversimplify its role and overemphasize the significance of contaminated drinking-water. The role of water in washing pathogens away from the path of potentially infected people is probably at least as important as its role in bringing pathogens to people. As a result, in areas where faecal-oral diseases are endemic, how much water people get and how they use it, may be more important than its quality.

There is still enormous uncertainty, however, concerning how faecal-oral diseases are most often transmitted and which interventions are likely to make the most difference. Moreover, the accumulation, flow and quality of open fresh water is critical to the spread of malaria, dengue fever and a variety of other vector-borne diseases. Here too, better quality water is not a sufficient remedy, and if pursued unthinkingly can even facilitate disease transmission. In combating water-related diseases, it is possible to identify a few measures, such as hand-washing and applying oral rehydration therapy, that are sufficiently general and important to advocate widely, but for the most part the simplest solutions come at a very high cost. Overall, while far more could be done on the basis of existing knowledge, a better understanding of these processes could still make an enormous difference.

## Misleading simplification

Consider the selection of quotes provided in Box 3.1. The message is simple and seems to confirm what every world traveller experiences: bad water makes people ill and there is a lot of bad water about. And yet water contamination is only one, perhaps quite small aspect of water-related disease transmission. The statistic of 80 per cent probably derives from the enormous number of episodes of diarrhoea that are estimated to occur every year: about 4 billion in 1995 (World Health Organization, 1996, p24). For someone unfamiliar with the nuances of health statistics this figure is very misleading, since a typical episode of diarrhoea is far less severe than most disease episodes. Nevertheless, diarrhoea is undoubtedly associated with a great deal of morbidity and mortality. Indeed, diarrhoea still competes with acute respiratory infection for the position of principal childhood killer. Thus, the more serious concern is that most of these statements falsely suggest that these diseases are the result of water contamination.[2] In fact, water relates to disease in a wide variety of ways, with water contamination only one of many aspects.

---

### Box 3.1  Misleading Waterlines

*'It has been estimated that as many as 80 percent of all diseases in the world are associated with unsafe water'* (Hofkes, E H, (ed), 1983, *Small Community Water Supplies: Technology of Small Water Supply Systems in Developing Countries*, p9)

*'Clean drinking water is essential for our health: according to the World Health Organisation 80% of all diseases are caused by polluted water'* (Van der Veken, M and Hernandez, I, 1988, *Women, Technology and Development*, p11)

*'An estimated 80 per cent of all diseases and over one third of deaths in developing countries are caused by the consumption of contaminated water'* (UNCED 1992, Agenda 21, paragraph 18.47 )

*'Eighty percent of all disease in developing countries is spread by consuming unsafe water'* (Platt, A E 1996, 'Infecting Ourselves: How Environmental and Social Disruptions Trigger Disease' (Worldwatch Paper 129), p42)

*'Let us not forget that about 80 percent of all diseases, and more than one third of all deaths in developing countries are caused by contaminated water'* (United Nations Environment Programme, News Release, World Water Day, 22 March 1996)

---

2  Despite these quotes, we have not been able to find any official WHO document ascribing 80 per cent of diseases to water contamination.

## Water-related transmission routes for infectious diseases

Table 3.1 presents a classification of water-related transmission routes. With the *water-borne* route, water brings the pathogens that people ingest to become infected – in such cases contaminated water really is the culprit. With the *water-washed* route, people become infected because water failed to carry the pathogens away – it is the absence of washing that is used to define the route. *Water-based* transmission refers to infections whose pathogens spend part of their life-cycle in aquatic animals. Transmission via *water-related insect vectors* refers to diseases spread by insects that breed in or bite near water.

**Table 3.1** *Environmental classification of water-related infections (1), and the preventive strategies appropriate to each*

| Transmission route | Preventive strategy |
|---|---|
| Water-borne | Improve quality of drinking-water<br>Prevent casual use of unprotected sources |
| Water-washed (or water-scarce) | Increase water quantity used<br>Improve accessibility and reliability of domestic water supply<br>Improve hygiene |
| Water-based | Reduce need for contact with infected water[a]<br>Control snail population[a]<br>Reduce contamination of surface waters[b] |
| Water-related insect vector | Improve surface water management<br>Destroy breeding sites of insects<br>Reduce need to visit breeding sites<br>Use mosquito netting |

a Applies to schistosomiasis only
b The preventive strategies appropriate to the water-based worms depend on the precise life-cycle of each and this is the only general prescription that can be given
Source: Cairncross, S and Feachem, R G, (1993)) *Environmental Health Engineering in the Tropics: An Introductory Text*, 2nd ed, John Wiley & Sons, Chichester

## Classifying water-related diseases

The relationship between transmission routes and types of disease is far from perfect, although similar classifications have long been applied to water-related infections. What is presented in Table 3.1 is a variation of the classification developed by David Bradley in the early 1970s, upon which most current classifications are based (White et al, 1972). The original terminology distinguished water-borne, water-washed, water-based and water-related infections, often leading people to conflate the possibility that a disease can be borne by water with the much stronger claim that it is always spread through the water system. In fact, the distinction between water-borne infections and water-washed infections has always been problematic, as Bradley has made very clear:

> *All infections that can be spread from one person to another by way of water supplies may also be more directly transmitted from faeces to mouth or by way of dirty food. When this is the case, the infections may be reduced by the provision of more abundant or more accessible water of unimproved quality* (Bradley, 1980, p12).

Unfortunately, as the quotations in Box 3.1 clearly demonstrate, such qualifications are often neglected, with most cases of diarrhoea and dysentery ascribed to water contamination. The more recent text upon which Table 3.2 is based forgoes elegance to avoid this sort of misinterpretation, and combines the water-borne and most water-washed infections into the more illustrative class of 'faecal-oral' infections.

**Table 3.2** *Environmental classification of water-related infections (2)*

| Category of infection | Type of infection |
| --- | --- |
| Faecal-oral (Water-washed or water-borne) | Most diarrhoeas and dysenteries |
| Other water-washed | Infectious skin diseases and louse-borne typhus |
| Water-based | Schistosomiasis, guinea worm, etc |
| Water-related insect vector | Malaria, dengue fever, etc |

*Source:* Based upon Cairncross, S and Feachem, R G (1993) *Environmental Health Engineering in the Tropics: An Introductory Text*, 2nd ed, John Wiley & Sons, Chichester, where a far more complete listing of diseases can be found

### How much is known about the transmission of water-related diseases?

The tendency to ignore the considerable uncertainty that still surrounds these infections and how they spread often creates the impression that expert opinion is vacillating. The following statement in the World Health Report 1996 illustrates this seeming instability:

> *It was long thought that contaminated water supplies were the main source of pathogens causing diarrhoea but it has now been shown that food has been responsible for up to 70% of diarrheal episodes* (World Health Organization, 1996, p38).

Unfortunately, such statements suggest that the remaining uncertainties are minimal, though with terms like 'up to', any real commitment to accuracy is avoided.[3] In fact, the relative importance of the different routes that faecal-oral diseases can take remains in large part a mystery (and need not always involve a faecal-oral route). Nor is this simply a matter of not knowing in sufficient detail what conditions are like in the more disadvantaged neighbourhoods. Conditions are sufficiently bad in most underserviced neighbourhoods that any number of possible transmission rates could explain a high level of faecal-oral disease. Indeed, experts are often left wondering why the prevalence of faecal-oral diseases is not higher in many neighbourhoods (Drangert et al, 1996).

Flies play a potentially important but largely unknown role in the transmission of faecal-oral diseases (Chavasse et al, 1994). Faecal pathogens are known to flow via ground water from pit latrines to nearby wells, but there is enormous uncertainty in how far is safe (Stenström, 1996). Numerous behavioural patterns can affect the likelihood that people, and especially children, will directly encounter faecal material and ingest it, but these are difficult to identify, let alone prioritize (Boot and Cairncross, 1993; Cairncross and Kochar, 1994).

The paths of transmission that particular faecal-oral pathogens will actually favour depend on a variety of features, such as the infectious dose, persistence and multiplicability in food (Mara, 1996), and some paths may to lead to people who are likely to be immune. The measures that can be taken to prevent transmission also depend on where the transmission takes place, and it can be important to distinguish between transmission within the domestic domain as opposed to transmission in the public domain (Cairncross et al, 1995). Moreover, people may engage in defensive behaviour when the hazards are perceptible, which itself changes the effects of certain hazards and needs to be taken into account when designing policy responses (Alberini et al, 1996).

### Water quality versus water quantity

Looking specifically at the alternatives to improving water quality or improving people's access to sufficient quantities of water as a means of reducing the transmission of diarroheal diseases, there is a good case to be made for claiming that too much attention is given to water quality (Cairncross, 1990). It is difficult to find clear epidemiological evidence distinguishing between the effects of

---

3 Although no source is given, it seems likely that the upper limit of 70 per cent is from a WHO commissioned paper that estimated that 'On the basis of the predicted impacts of controlling transmission associated with poor personal hygiene, and water supply and sanitation, food as a vehicle may contribute to the transmission of between 15 and 70% of all diarrhoea episodes. This range is so wide as to be of little value, but the available data do not permit more precise estimates' (Esrey et al, 1985)

improving water quality and providing better access to water, but while a number of studies have demonstrated the importance of providing more water to poor households, the evidence with respect to water quality is more ambiguous (Esrey and Habicht, 1986).

It has been suggested that one of the reasons that many studies fail to find a significant association between improvements in water quality and diarrhoeal prevalence is that most contamination occurs in the home, while tests for faecal contamination are typically made at the well or tap (Esrey and Habicht, 1986; Huttly, 1990; Lindskog and Lundqvist, 1989). Indeed, a number of studies have documented higher concentrations of faecal coliforms in household water containers than at their sources (Benneh et al, 1993; Lindskog and Lundqvist, 1989).

However, it is far from certain that the contamination that occurs in and around the home is comparable to contamination from outside. A recent and influential study contends that:

*In-house contamination does not pose a serious risk of diarrhoea because family members would likely develop some level of immunity to pathogens commonly encountered in the household environment. Even when there is no such immunity, transmission of these pathogens via stored water may be inefficient relative to other household transmission routes, such as person-to-person contact or food contamination. A contaminated source poses much more of a risk since it may introduce new pathogens into the household* (VanDerslice and Briscoe, 1993, p1983).

However, the empirical evidence in support of these claims is very limited, and the argument itself depends heavily on some behavioural assumptions that one would expect to be culture dependent. If, for example, children play freely in the neighbourhood and drink in the homes of neighbours, then a sharp distinction between in-house and communal water contamination is not convincing (Pickering, 1985).

Most of the complications mentioned up to this point suggest that water quality receives too much attention relative to the role of water in washing away pathogens. Another generally ignored complication – the evolutionary implications of different water systems – suggests a rather different conclusion. In placing obstacles on some of the routes of disease transmission, not only is the rate of transmission altered, but so are the evolutionary pressures brought to bear on the pathogen. It has been argued that interrupting water-borne routes will put in motion evolutionary pressures towards less virulent strains of, for example, cholera (Ewald, 1994). To put it crudely, pathogens that rely more heavily on personal contact lose out if their hosts are immobilized, while those that are water-borne do not. Thus, so the argument goes, eliminating the water-borne route creates evolutionary advantages for strains that are not debilitating. Ewald derives estimates that suggest that taking account of evolutionary pressures would radically alter the benefits ascribed to water purification in Bangladesh, turning it from an uneconomic alternative to a measure costing one-tenth as much per life saved as vaccination. Thus, rather than immunize the potential hosts, one would leave larger scope for less virulent pathogens, to the disadvantage of the more dangerous strains.

Another role that water has to play in faecal-oral diseases lies in their treatment. Dehydration is usually the proximate cause of death in fatal cases of diarrhoea, and can often be treated with water and oral rehydration salts. Initially developed in Bangladesh, this simple measure has been heavily promoted by UNICEF, and it has been estimated that around half of diarrhoeal cases are now treated with oral rehydration therapy (UNICEF, 1996).

## Water and insect vectors

Other than faecal-oral diseases, the most important category of water-related disease is the last: water-related insect vector (see Tables 3.1 and 3.2). Malaria, filariasis, yellow fever and dengue fever are all classified as water-related diseases because their vectors breed in water. Malaria alone kills an estimated 1–2 million people annually, and there are up to half a billion new cases every year, second only to diarrhoeal and respiratory infections (World Health Organization, 1996). The role of water contamination in the transmission of these insect-borne diseases is very ambiguous, however. Indeed, one of the reasons that malaria is typically more prevalent in rural than in urban areas is that most malarial mosquitoes, like humans, prefer clean water. Urban water pollution can actually help to protect residents from malaria, although some malarial species have found urban water niches. The mosquitoes that carry dengue haemorrhagic fever have generally been more successful in finding urban water niches and often breed in household water containers. Such containers tend to be more common where water supplies are intermittent, but are only indirectly linked to water contamination.

Despite the complexity of these various water-related diseases, in affluent cities they are only rarely a problem. While experts may debate exactly how and why this epidemiological transition takes place (Mosley et al, 1993; Smith and Lee, 1993), inadequate sanitation in the broad, 19th-century sense is closely associated with poverty. Poverty alleviation would seem to be one of the most obvious means to achieve improvements in environmental health (Bradley et al, 1991). Indeed, one possible justification for leaving the issues of water, sanitation and health off the environmental agenda is that the solution is poverty alleviation and infra-structure provision, not environmental management. For a variety of reasons, however, such justification is weak at best.

## Localized urban water scarcities

Localized water scarcity is common in many squatter areas and other localities where groups of people are excluded from the use of public water systems and lack the means to develop private facilities. For example, low-income areas in Nairobi, Kenya, consume some 35 per cent of the domestic supply, but account for almost two-thirds of the population. The city's per capita consumption is about 90 litres per day, but only 20 litres per day in low-income areas (and over 200 litres in high-income areas) (Lamba, 1994). In the case of Guayaquil, Ecuador, the average production and supply capacity of the existing facilities would allow each inhabitant an average daily consumption of 220 litres, but daily consumption ranges from an average of 307 litres per inhabitant in the well-to-do parts of the city to less than 25 litres for those supplied by private water-sellers (Swyngedouw, 1995).

While the differences in consumption levels often vary between different geographical areas, reflecting the 'limit' of the piped network, public, private and 'natural' systems can work alongside each other, but still without relieving the poor of their water problems. In Jakarta, where less than 20 per cent of the households have piped water, most households use wells as their main drinking-water source, and over 20 per cent buy drinking-water from vendors (Surjadi et al, 1994). However, the quality of the ground water differs across the city and in some areas high salinity makes this water unfit for drinking.[4] Wealthy households in these areas are more frequently connected to the piped public water supply, while the poor usually buy their drinking-water from vendors. Hence, a majority of the richer households will pay the lower official price, while most of the poor pay a ten times higher price per litre from ambulating vendors.[5]

---

4 The high salinity in large parts of Jakarta is often cited as an example of salt-water intrusion due to the overuse of the aquifer. However, water in these parts of Jakarta may have been brackish for thousands of years and salinity (except in very limited areas) should not be attributed to abstraction (Rismianto and Mak, 1993). Both piped and well water in Jakarta is heavily contaminated with faecal material, and virtually everyone, except a minority using bottled water, boil their water before drinking. This is clearly anthropogenic pollution, but has also been a problem for centuries (Abeyasekere, 1987). On the other hand, chemical pollution is also widespread, at least in the ground water, and is a more recent problem

5 The high vendor prices in Jakarta are often attributed to imperfect competition. To overcome that, an aggressive standpipe investment programme to reduce the distances between neighbourhood taps was implemented in the late 1980s and early 1990s, and the municipal water enterprise permitted all households with a metered connection to resell water starting in April 1990. There are indications of some benefits derived from the deregulation (Crane, 1992; Lovei and Whittington, 1991; Lovei and Whittington, 1993), but vendor prices have remained high. This has been attributed to lack of information to households about the legality of reselling water (which may still make very little difference

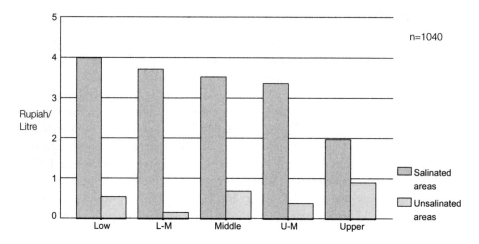

**Figure 3.1** *Average price paid per litre of drinking water in Jakarta, by geographical features and wealth quintiles*

*Data source:* Stockholm Environment Institute and Atma Jaya Catholic University, Household Environment Database, 1991–1992
*Note 1:* The survey was undertaken in Jakarta DKI
*Note 2:* The five wealth groups, of roughly equal size, relate to a wealth index based on the households' tenure of consumer durables
*Note 3:* Mineral water users are excluded
*Note 4:* At the time of the survey there were approximately 2000 rupiah to one US dollar. The average price of water from vendors was 5 rupiah per litre, while the litre price from PAM (Jakarta's municipal water authority) for a household consuming 15 cubic metres a month was about half a rupiah

The average prices paid by different wealth groups in different geographical areas are summarized in Figure 3.1. Poor households in saline areas pay on average almost 4 rupiah per litre, while the richest households in saline areas on average only pay 2 rupiah per litre. In areas with 'potable' ground water, however, the poor can resort to well water which is not paid for, and hence pay less than the average richer person who still is more likely to have a piped-water connection and pay the official price for water (Kjellén et al, 1996). These price differentials reflect the fact that the urban poor are more dependent on the residual natural water resources of their own localities, while the wealthy have come to depend on a man-made system that spreads the burdens over a far broader area.

to the actors on the informal water markets), or it may be that the price of the resold water actually reflects a high scarcity value, indicating that the major problem is the insufficient quantities of water of acceptable quality available in large parts of Jakarta

The situation in Jakarta reflects a somewhat extreme example of a common tendency for the poor to rely on 'secondary' water markets for drinking-water, as they are unable to access the municipal water distribution system directly. That in many parts of the world the poorest segments of the urban population suffer from chronic water scarcity does not just reflect their lack of market command. There is ample proof that poor city dwellers often pay more per litre of drinking-water than the richer urbanites (Bhatia and Falkenmark, 1993; Kjellén et al, 1996; Swyngedouw, 1995; World Bank, 1988). Often, the principal difficulty is to get a water connection, not to pay for the water.

# WATER AND URBAN SUSTAINABILITY

## *Displacing the Burden*

Cities and their citizens cannot sustain themselves by drawing only on the resources within the city boundaries, and with increasing water use, sources further and further afield are often tapped. Similarly, the wastes cannot be absorbed within the city, but are displaced to the surrounding ecosystem. In the quest for new clean water and ways of disposing wastes, cities may appropriate both historical and spatial hinterlands, and through overexploitation or pollution, undermine ecosystems and people's livelihoods far away in space and into the future. The capacity to displace environmental burdens increases with wealth and the development of centralized water supply and sanitary systems. In poor neighbourhoods, inadequate access to water and sanitation has primarily local effects, while integrated urban infrastructure allows better-off segments of the population to draw on a larger resource base, protect themselves from exposure, and displace hazardous or unpleasant pollutants. Middle-income mega-cities often have particularly severe impacts on the regional ecosystem, but the wealthier, often much cleaner, cities in the North may still impose an enormous 'ecological footprint' on global hinterlands. As the environmental transition becomes complete, many of the effects become globalized, contributing, for example, to climate change, which may alter hydrological cycles differentially across the world. As problems of insufficient water quantities and water pollution are transferred from the local to the broader environment, the challenge shifts from one of maintaining human health to one of preserving the integrity of life-support systems for future generations.

## *The invisibility of linear material flows*

Circular material flows cannot be kept within the confines of a city where most of the ground is paved and food production can only take place on a very limited scale. Circular flows extending beyond the bounds of the city are more feasible, but not at all characteristic of existing urban development patterns. The risks associated with linear flows are rarely immediately evident, however. Indeed, the material flows that characterize cities of the post-industrial era are to a large extent invisible to the cities' inhabitants. The overuse of resources and overloading of waste sinks often take place at a considerable distance from the city, and even there, may not become evident until a number of irreversible ecosystem damages have occurred. Many of the most resource- and waste-intensive cities are superficially getting cleaner.

Compounding this visibility problem, tracking the physical pathways of environmental impacts provides at best a partial picture of the environmental effects of a given urban demand. Markets and other mediating institutions also determine the resource repercussions of a given change in demand. In one set of circumstances, for example, by reducing the demands being met by a local reservoir it may be possible to reduce the pressure on distant water bodies. Thus, if there is an overall decline in demand, the reductions may occur at the more costly and distant sources. In another set of circumstances, efforts to reduce the demand on local sources may shift demand, rather than savings, to the more distant sources. Thus, if the overall demand remains constant, savings from local sources may be compensated by increased consumption of the more distant sources. What scenario actually applies depends in part on the physical characteristics of the water system, but even more on the institutional context.

## Urban encroachment on life-support systems

Most of today's cities are located on prime agricultural land or near valuable ecosystems, so even though the estimated land surface dedicated to urban uses is only 1 per cent of the earth's total surface (World Resources Institute, 1996, p58), urban expansion affects the earth's most productive ecosystems. Such losses are serious in nations with limited arable land. Urban expansion also threatens marine and lacustrine ecosystems: 42 per cent of the world's cities with more than 1 million inhabitants are located along coastlines (ibid), and many of them have been experiencing unprecedented growth. There are strong economic pressures to develop coastal areas because of the attraction of shoreline locations, and coastal wetlands have been a particular locus of conversion. Apart from land conversion, nearby urban markets may induce the overexploitation of certain fish stocks or other resources, as well as the outright destruction of natural habitats.[6]

---

6 The draining or filling of marshes is often viewed as beneficial since wetlands may be breeding places for disease vectors such as malaria mosquitoes. Indeed, the elimination of wetlands is an important part of many environmental health strategies. The WHO/UNEP Community Action Program kit for *Insect and rodent control through environmental management* guides the following action: 'In the community: Drain or fill marshes, swamps, puddles, etc.' (World Health Organization and United Nations Environment Programme, 1991)

Cities interact with their hinterlands (and hinterlands interact with their cities – their markets) in a number of ways, many of them highly complementary. However, while natural resources tend to be drawn in *to* the city, the flow of 'wastes' tend to lead *from* the city along different pathways and towards destinations far from their sources. Water, being a major metabolic medium of the urban system, with 60–100 times the rate of the flow of fuel (White, 1994, p125),[7] is an extremely effective means of environmental displacement, but one which virtually precludes the recirculation of, for example, nutrients.

## The history of using water to displace environmental problems

Cities have a long tradition of using rivers, lakes and coastal waters as receptacles for diluting and dispersing wastes. The River Aire, flowing through Leeds in England, was described in the 1840s as follows:

> *It was full of refuse from water closets, cesspools, privies, common drains, dung-hill drainings, infirmary refuse, wastes from slaughter houses, chemical soap, gas, dye-houses, and manufactures, coloured by blue and black dye, pig manure, old urine wash; there were dead animals, vegetable substances and occasionally a decomposed human body* (Wohl, 1983, p235).

The introduction of water-borne sewerage systems, whereby increasingly large quantities of sewage were poured into water bodies, initially without any type of treatment, tended to increase the problems of surface water pollution. At the end of the 19th century, some 50 years after London had embarked on its great sewerage scheme, the Bazalgette's sewers were daily pouring close to 700,000 cubic metres of sewage into the River Thames, constituting about one-sixth of the total volume of the river water. The seeming lack of concern for river pollution may be attributed to the larger concern for the still very high death rates in most Northern cities in those times. This is illustrated by a statement in 1898 by Edwin Chadwick, perhaps the most famous sanitary reformer:

> *Admitting the expediency of avoiding the pollution, it is nevertheless proved to be of almost inappreciable magnitude in comparison with the ill-health occasioned by the constant retention of pollution [ie excrement] in the most densely-peopled districts* (Wohl, 1983, p239).

---

7 The metabolism metaphor has been used to describe cities as parasites that damage their 'host' – the environment (Douglas, 1987; Girardet, 1992). The concept, a variation to an input–output model where resources, through activities, are turned to residuals, can give guidance towards enhancing the complementarity of the city and its host, making the relationship more symbiotic and less parasitic

This view was supported by the fact that, with the extension of the sewerage system, death rates *were* declining, in spite of the increased river pollution. Still, the problems of river pollution were debated, and during the last decades of the past century 'a conviction gradually developed in [the British] Parliament and among sanitary and environmental reformers that the prevention of river pollution should be . . . "an indispensable requisite of every system of sewage disposal which can lay claim to efficiency"' (Wohl, 1983, p243).

The awareness of the need to protect the ambient water quality was not generated by concerns for the health of the public of the polluting cities, but for the threats that severe pollution imposed on the life-support systems of the cities and the well-being of downstream residents. The minutes of evidence of the Royal Commission on the Prevention of River Pollution from 1866 are full of complaints from professional and amateur fishermen that their livelihood or sport was endangered. To impose controls of pollution in those times, as today, raised serious concerns that it might lead to severe economic dislocation. Some steps were taken to form river boards, placing river-pollution control in hands other than those of local bodies, but legislation was ineffective, giving precedence to industrial interests over those of public health and conservation (Wohl, 1983). National legislation, accepted standards of water quality and larger scale sewage treatment would not be implemented until the next century, and the quality of the Thames' water would not be improved substantially until the 1970s.

### The role of centralized systems in displacement

If each household or neighbourhood has to deal with its own human waste problems, the faecal material is unlikely to travel very far (except if there is a convenient stream or river). Faecal pollution burdens are commonly displaced from the home environment through water closets and articulated water-borne sewerage systems, and from the city environment through the lengthening of sewage outfalls or disposing of sewage sludge into the sea or landfills, or to the atmosphere through incineration. Similarly, localized water scarcity within the city may be displaced through the extension of piped water-supply systems. As the central authority assumes the responsibility for providing all citizens with adequate amounts of water, to 'fill the pipes' may entail importing water from faraway systems. While dam construction and water diversions allow urban expansion and stable water use with less regard to hydrological fluctuations, river flows are reduced and water shortages (or pollution burdens) are transferred to downstream riverine habitats.

Where the extension of the centralized systems is limited, so too is the displacement. In many low- and middle-income cities, public water and sewerage systems only serve the more affluent segments of the population, and hence, in many poor neighbourhoods, pollution burdens as well as water scarcity are retained locally.

## From Health to Sustainability Concerns

Poor sanitary environments take their toll on health rather than on the ecological foundations of the city, as described in Chapter 2. Faecal-oral diseases are endemic in densely populated settlements that lack an adequate water supply and sanitation. In better serviced neighbourhoods, ample amounts of washwater help to reduce transmission, and pathogens, most of them in human excreta, are flushed away through a public sewerage system. Where treatment is lacking, pathogens may well appear in ambient waterways, but are less likely to be encountered, especially by households from the polluting areas. In some cases polluted ambient water is ingested, directly or by eating seafood, especially uncooked 'filter-feeders'. There may also be adverse health effects where wastewaters are used for irrigating crops. However, the main impact of urban sewage is on aquatic, not public health.

The release of pollutants from urban areas threatens the ecosystem integrity in numerous ways. Alterations in the levels of dissolved oxygen and nutrients, salinity and acidity change the environmental conditions to which the aquatic life are acclimatized. While it is difficult to identify and assess specific causal relationships that threaten biotic communities, species are lost to extinction, and impoverishment of biotic diversity can lead to less stable and less productive habitats (Covich, 1993). Adverse ecological effects may also affect economic productivity in the short run.

### An extreme example of the displacement of water burdens

Mexico City has evolved as a mega-city in a water-scarce region essentially through the 'successful' displacement of both water pollution and water shortage (see Box 3.2). The mining of ground water and large water transfers allow a per capita use of over 300 litres per day, sustaining 45 per cent of the country's industry and serving 94 per cent of the city's population of over 15 million people (Joint Academies Committee on the Mexico City Water Supply, 1995). The alteration of the natural hydrological system was a prerequisite to the city's expansion. The Valley of Mexico, originally a closed basin, was artificially opened in the 1700s to control flooding. This has also enabled Mexico City to remove its effluents out of the basin. Without this, or some alternative form of displacement, Mexico City's aquifer would have been destroyed by pollution long ago. Still, poverty prevails, and the city has yet to supply all its people with water: 6 per cent of the population – almost a million people – have neither household connections nor neighbourhood standpipes. They are likely to suffer from water scarcity, resulting in greater health risks, but imposing less of a water resource burden. And even among the connected households, average water consumption levels are far less than those of Mexico's northerly neighbours.

## Box 3.2  Mexico City: the Epitome of Regional Environmental Displacement

In the time of the Aztecs, the city of Tenochtitlán was the centre of a large empire that already depended on imported resources, mostly agricultural products appropriated from subordinated groups in other areas. But the water supply system relied only on the immediate surroundings, with aqueducts bringing spring water on to the urbanized island in the saline Lake Texcoco. The valley's drainage used to enter the lake system, and the Aztecs had constructed earth dikes to control flooding and to separate freshwater lakes from brackish ones. In the place of ancient Tenochtitlán is now Mexico City which has gradually overtaken most of the former lakebeds, progressively drained since colonial times, and some hillsides, contributing to soil erosion and increases in flash floods.

Mexico City relied mostly on spring water until the mid-1850s, when the discovery of potable ground water under artesian pressure was followed by a well-drilling surge. Over time, pressure has been lost and many natural springs dried up. With the realization that groundwater supplies were being depleted, construction of an aqueduct to import water from a neighbouring basin was initiated in the 1940s. Today, a quarter of Mexico City's water, or around 16 cubic metres per second, is imported from the Lerma and Cutzamala basins. The total extraction from Mexico City's aquifer is over 55 cubic metres per second (of which 42 cubic metres are used for the city, and the rest for agriculture).

Groundwater abstraction and artificial drainage of the valley have led to land subsidence which over the last 100 years has lowered the central part of the city by an average of 7.5 metres. This exacerbates flood problems and in order to confine storm water, dikes have had to be built and pumping has been required to lift drainage water that used to flow by gravity. Because subsidence rates vary, many structures (including sewers) have been weakened and some buildings lean dangerously, a phenomenon that is made more serious by frequent seismic activity. Since the 1950s, when many wells in the city centre were closed, the subsidence rate in the central area has stabilized at around 6 centimetres per year, but in other areas sinking velocity can be up to 40 centimetres per year.

Mexico City's effluents are carried by the general drainage system and out of the basin through tunnels at the north end of the valley. The dry weather flow is estimated at 44 cubic metres per second, consisting mainly of untreated municipal wastewater. Some 10 per cent of the wastewater is treated, not out of concern for the receiving watercourses, but to enable reuse within Mexico City. The treated water is reused for landscape and agricultural irrigation, groundwater recharge, and industrial as well as recreational purposes, but the sewage sludge is returned to the sewer system.

The environmental and economic burdens of Mexico City's unsustainable water use are only to a limited extent being borne within its boundaries. Water revenues collected in the city account for less than 10 per cent of the government's expenditure for providing the water. Pollution, while also damaging local irrigation and causing algal bloom in Lake Texcoco, is mostly displaced to the Tula Basin (contributing to the spread of parasitic diseases through wastewater irrigation) and eventually to the Mexican Gulf. Chronic water shortages are in great part transferred to the Lerma and Cutzamala basins, from which water is imported. The tapping of ground water beyond its rate of renewal is a way of appropriating 'historical' hinterlands and displacing water shortages to future generations (although it is already hitting back at the city though land subsidence).

*Sources:* 1) Anton, D J (1993) *Thirsty Cities: Urban Environments and Water Supply in Latin America*, International Development Research Centre, Ottawa. 2) Ezcurra, E and Mazari-Hiriart, M (1996) 'Are megacities viable? A cautionary tale from Mexico City' *Environment*, vol 38, 6–15, 26–35. 3) Joint Academies Committee on the Mexico City Water Supply (1995) *Mexico City's Water Supply: Improving the Outlook for Sustainability*, National Academy Press, Washington, DC

## Wealth creation and the appropriation of hinterlands

Because of their ability to innovate, humans are not bound by a carrying capacity defined by existing technology. However, a major component of humankind's 'ingenuity' has been to draw on an increasingly extensive resource base and displace waste to increasingly distant locations or to diffuse it more broadly. In other words, 'From the beginning of the European empires of the sixteenth century to the industrial empires of the present, the richer people in the richer countries have appropriated *global* hinterlands to meet the needs of their increasingly urban citizens' (White, 1994, p57). These developments have accelerated during the last 50 years. As William Rees explains '. . . the five-fold increase in the scale of human economic activity in the post-war period has begun to induce ecological change on a global scale which simply cannot be ignored in planning for human settlements' (Rees, 1992, p122). Larger cities' pull on resources, in these days through trade, may be one of the major historical changes happening to planet earth. The urban-industrial society is displacing resources such as soil nutrients or fossil carbon into the sea and the atmosphere, and mixing some of the more hazardous wastes into toxic cocktails.

## A clean city with a history of water pollution

The cleanest cities of our times are among the wealthiest, with good quality water supplied to both industry and households, and most effluents treated in order not to foul the local or the regional environment. In these cities the epidemiological transition away from water-related infectious diseases has been virtually completed, and persistent environmental problems tend to have poorly understood, indirect or delayed impacts on human health. Many currently very 'clean' cities in the developed world have for long periods of time been releasing polluted water, thus accounting for far more than their share of the build-up of contaminants in the oceans.

Stockholm, Sweden, situated on the boundary between the Lake Mälaren and the Baltic Sea, proudly dubs itself as one of the cleanest cities in the world, at least when it comes to the water environment. Still, the city has passed through a trajectory, maybe less critical, but still similar to that described above for London. For much of the last century, the mortality rate was higher than the birth rate, at least in part as a result of water-related diseases. Then the quality of local ambient waters went from bad to worse with the increased use of water closets, and by the 1930s the waters were considered unhealthy and bathing houses were closed down. The treatment of wastewaters started in 1934, and by the 1970s treatment had been extended so that all wastewater was treated mechanically, chemically and biologically before it was released into the sea. Lake Mälaren, the city's water source, was also regulated to avoid brackish sea-water and (treated) wastewaters to enter from the sea, and upstream sources impairing the quality of lake waters were addressed through cooperation with other municipalities around the lake. As the emissions of phosphorous and oxygen-demanding substances have been considerably reduced, plankton production in the inner archipelago has decreased and water has become clearer. Trout have been restocked, and annual swimming competitions, suspended in the 1920s, were reassumed in 1976.

Stockholm has been successful in addressing the regional impacts on its water system and its immediate water surroundings are remarkably clean. Also, over half the sewage sludge produced is used as agricultural fertilizer, but problems remain relating to the acceptability of this practice (Stockholm Vatten, 1996). While Stockholm may not qualify as a hot spot of obvious pollution to be addressed along the coasts of the Baltic, the emission of nitrogen has remained unchanged and still favours plankton production in the outer archipelago. Much historical pollution remains in sediments. For the Baltic Sea, the more large-scale problems, relating to the long-range transport of pollutants through both water and air, exist in the open sea (*Ambio*, 1990), to which historically Stockholm may be a major contributor.

## Indirect routes of undermining water systems

With cleaner cities and city surroundings, the major challenge is again shifted, now towards the more far-reaching threats of the urban-industrial systems to global ecology. High energy consumption, based largely on fossil fuel, is to a large extent an attribute of wealthy cities in the North – especially those with colder climates requiring extensive heating. This contributes to global climate change whose predicted effects include sea-level rise and increased variability of local hydrological cycles.

The purchasing power of urban elites and the masses of middle-class urban consumers to a large extent dictates which commodities are produced, and even the production processes. As regards diets, urban dwellers generally eat more meat and water-intensive crops. To produce 1 kilo of wheat requires some 500 litres of water, 1 kilo of rice, up to 2000 litres of water, and some 20–50,000 litres of water per kilo of meat. To produce one car consumes (directly and indirectly) close to 400 cubic metres of water (Ehrlich et al, 1973, pp 107–108). Increasing numbers of more environmentally aware and concerned citizens prefer goods that are produced in ways that are less damaging to the ecosystem, but such preferences are not easy to translate into effective demands.

## CONCLUSIONS

The current burden of water-related diseases in urban areas is not, by and large, the outcome of the citywide water supply and pollution problems that threaten sustainability. Low-income urban neighbourhoods and households are more likely to lack water because they cannot access the city's water supplies than because those supplies are limited. A comparatively healthy overall water balance can be accompanied by extremely unhealthy conditions in disadvantaged neighbourhoods. Indoor piping and low water prices may be the rule in one neighbourhood, while residents of a squatter settlement nearby must choose between a heavily polluted stream and extremely expensive water from vendors. Water may be clean in the pipes, but be heavily contaminated by the time it has been carried home, stored and ladled into a guest's drinking vessel. For many of the more disadvantaged urban dwellers, water scarcity and life-threatening water pollution are not future prospects given unsustainable practices, but current realities. Only concerted actions, based on better science, more respect for local knowledge, and politics that create a continuous pressure for improvement, are likely to make significant headway.

Alternatively, a city's water future may be grim even when cheap and reasonably clean piped water remains widely available. Indeed, many of the measures employed to address urban environmental health problems, such as providing low-price piped water supplies and water-borne sewerage systems, can add considerably to the water-environment burden of a city. Thus the water use patterns of middle-income mega-cities are particularly unsustainable, despite the fact that the average prevalence of water-related diseases is likely to be lower than in smaller but poorer urban centres.

As such, the health and sustainability aspects of urban water systems are both important, but worth keeping conceptually distinct. In wealthy cities where piped water and water-borne sanitation are universally provided, sustainability can be a very useful organizing principle for water system improvement. Improvements should not be a threat to health, of course, but it is in the domain of sustainability, more narrowly defined, that most progress needs to be made. Alternatively, in the more disadvantaged neighbourhoods, where water scarcity and quality problems are a serious and immediate threat, the water agenda ought to be developed around a concern for health and welfare. Improvements should be sustainable, but sustainability is not appropriate as an overarching goal, however progressive this may seem.

The shift from water-related health problems to water-related sustainability problems is to at least some degree a process of displacement. This displacement process can be portrayed as an intensification and extension of linear material flows, a major feature of urban metabolism. In the extreme this process could lead to the cumulative loading of waste substances into the sea, the atmosphere and other sinks, eventually undermining our life-support systems and creating a new wave of environmental health problems. As with the traditional environmental health problems, but on a spatially far broader scale, this presents both a physical and an institutional challenge.

Physically, we still understand far too little about the water systems upon which we depend. Institutionally, we have yet to create the incentives to ensure that when we do understand what needs to be done, we have good reason, both individually and collectively, to do it. This is widely recognized in relation to sustainability, but as later chapters demonstrate, it is equally true in relation to traditional water-related health problems. This is no excuse for inaction, but good reason to seek a better understanding of the challenges involved.

# 4

# Shifting Environmental Challenges in Accra, Jakarta and São Paulo

This chapter is about three cities. On the one hand, all are national centres in what have been variously termed 'underdeveloped', 'developing', 'Third World', 'Southern' or, in the latest post-Kyoto terminology, 'Non-Annex 1' countries. On the other hand, they are located on different continents, with very different cultures (or rather mixes of cultures), and rather different natural settings. It may seem perverse to try to relate their environmental differences to affluence and city-size rather than culture and geography, but this makes the patterns that emerge all the more compelling.

Accra is the smallest and poorest of the three, and São Paulo the largest and most affluent. In the light of the transition described in the previous chapters, one might expect Accra to face the most severe environmental burdens at the household and neighbourhood levels, São Paulo to contribute most to global burdens, and Jakarta or perhaps São Paulo to have the worst city-level burdens. This does indeed appear to be the case. Scientific positivists could argue that this proves nothing, inasmuch as the transition itself was conceived after the city studies were complete. The strength of the comparison is not as an empirical test with three observations, however, but as three cases where the relations between affluence and environmental burdens can be discerned, and to at least some extent explained, both within and between the cities.

This chapter draws heavily on the empirical results of the ten years of collaborative research on household and neighbourhood-level environmental problems. Locally available and internationally published secondary data are also employed in order to position the three cities within the context of the urban environmental transition.

The results of the multicity study do suggest that increasing affluence is associated with a shift from local to regional and from regional to global environmental challenges. Many of the worst environmental health problems are those hazards that appear in and around the home,[1] and these are mainly found

---

1 Environmental hazards at places of work may be equally significant, but are not well documented, either in this study or in the international literature.

in the poorest city of Accra, or more specifically in poor neighbourhoods (which are more prevalent in Accra). Serious environmental health risks can be found among the poorest households in Jakarta and to some extent also in São Paulo. However, some of the most striking differences in environmental health risks occur among the more deprived households of Accra, where increasing poverty becomes an immediate risk to health. Moreover, while the economic inequalities in Jakarta and São Paulo may result in the higher wealth ratio between the richest 20 per cent and the poorest 20 per cent in those cities, for a number of the key environmental health indicators the differences are more appreciable between the richest 20 per cent and the poorest 20 per cent in Accra.

In contrast, the citywide problems of securing sufficient resources and waste sinks to support the urban metabolism is far more challenging in the larger and on average much wealthier cities of Jakarta and São Paulo. The urban environmental transition would also indicate that a shift towards global environmental challenges such as climate change should take place. Such contributions (to greenhouse gases) are hard to establish on a city basis, but the national data which are used in this chapter also point towards the fact that the wealthiest city of the three, São Paulo, indeed creates a larger burden on the global ecology than the other two cities. In addition, some of the city-level environmental problems such as ambient air pollution are improving, indicating that São Paulo may have passed the highest point on the 'environmental Kuznets curve' (described in Chapter 2).

## METHODS

This chapter is based on comparable cross-sectional studies of household environmental problems in Accra, Jakarta and São Paulo. The studies were initiated by Stockholm Environment Institute (SEI) and carried out in collaboration with the Department of Geography and Resource Development of the University of Ghana-Legon, the Urban Health Study Group of Atma Jaya University in Jakarta, and Centro de Estudos de Cultura Contemporânea (CEDEC) in São Paulo.

A common and central component of all these studies was a household questionnaire survey, carried out in late 1991 and/or early 1992. In each of the cities, about 1000 households were surveyed on a range of topics, including water supply, sanitation, food habits, pests, pesticide use, solid-waste disposal, indoor air pollution, crowding and related health problems. Each major problem area was assessed in terms of the physical processes and severity, the health risks involved, as well as the residents' priorities and willingness to pay for improvements.[2]

---

2 This chapter only presents selected parts of the multicity study with relation to the environmental transition. Detailed study results have been published elsewhere, both in

The surveyed area for Accra was the city's greater metropolitan area. The Greater Accra Metropolitan Area (GAMA) is composed of the three districts of Accra, Tema and Ga. Accra in the text generally refers to GAMA as regards the household level statistics, and generally to the Accra Metropolitan Area (AMA) as regards internationally published material. It is worth noting, however, that the Ga area accounted for less than 6 per cent of the household sample, and hence has relatively little impact on the summary statistics.

In the much larger city of Jakarta, the survey was limited to the special administrative district that constitutes the national capital of Jakarta, DKI (Daerah Khusus Ibukota or Special Capital District). Hence, Jakarta in the text generally refers to Jakarta-DKI. This is also the area referred to as Jakarta in most secondary sources, both Indonesian and international.

In São Paulo, the survey was carried out in the city (= municipality) of São Paulo, and São Paulo in the text generally refers to this city/municipality. In other publications São Paulo may refer to the metropolitan region of São Paulo, or even the state of São Paulo, both of which have far larger populations (although even the city of São Paulo dwarfs the GAMA's population).

The household questionnaire surveys used similar but not identical survey instruments, as the locally relevant practices, technologies and priorities are sufficiently different that imposing standard questions would have lost much of the important detail. Thus, while the same topics were covered, not all questions are directly comparable. Regarding the household level environmental problems, the survey results from the three cities are used. However, the focus of these three comparable surveys was on the local environmental threats and thus little data on regional or global threats were produced. Hence, the presentation of these environmental challenges below relies on secondary data from locally available planning documents as well as international publications. The major limitation of these sources is that they do not easily allow for comparisons between the three cities. A consequence of this is that the empirical review that follows includes only a limited set of variables and the year of the measurement may differ for different variables.

---

comparative terms and for the individual cities. Comparative presentations include McGranahan and Songsore, 1994; McGranahan et al, 1996; McGranahan and Songsore, 1996; McGranahan, 1998. For Accra, city study results are found in Benneh et al, 1993; Songsore and Goldstein, 1995; Songsore and McGranahan, 1993. Findings from Jakarta are presented in Surjadi, 1993; Surjadi et al, 1994; Surjadi et al, 1995 and those for São Paulo have been published in Jacobi, 1995a; Jacobi, 1995b; Jacobi, 1995c; Jacobi, 1994. In addition, as a follow-on to these three city studies, another scoping study, following the same approach as in those three, has been carried out in Port Elizabeth (South Africa). The findings from this study have been presented in Thomas et al, 1999 and Potgeiter et al, 1999

# THE THREE CITIES IN CONTEXT

As indicated above, the three cities, Accra in Ghana, Jakarta in Indonesia, and São Paulo in Brazil, span three continents and have no obvious cultural similarities. Jakarta and São Paulo are both mega-cities, among the largest urban agglomerations in the world. Accra is considerably smaller and poorer, but, like Jakarta, rapidly growing. Table 4.1 provides summary statistics on the three cities and their respective countries.

## *São Paulo*

The city of São Paulo was established in the 16th century, and coffee exports and waves of immigrants from Europe fuelled its early growth. The later industrial expansion saw a large supply of cheap labour migrating from other regions of Brazil. Most of the industrial wealth of São Paulo was created in the 1960s and 1970s, which is also when the city's growth was most intense. During this period the national economy also boomed, growing at almost 5 per cent per annum. The country's economic performance has been negative during the 1980s, but moderately positive during the first half of the 1990s (United Nations Development Programme, 1998a). The financial turbulence of recent years, however, may bring the trend down.

São Paulo's economy is gradually shifting from its industrial base into services. In 1998 the tertiary sector accounted for almost 80 per cent of the economic activity. The increase in the services sector, however, is not sufficient to absorb excess labour; the unemployment rate is close to 17 per cent. On the one hand, the São Paulo Metropolitan Region is economically the most important area in Brazil, accounting for 18 per cent of the country's GDP and 31 per cent of industrial domestic product (Oliveira and Leitmann, 1994). On the other hand, São Paulo's growth has been accompanied by large health, social and economic disparities (Faria, 1989; Jacobi, 1990; Jacobi et al, 1998).

The figures in Table 4.1 refer to the central districts of both Jakarta and São Paulo, whose populations have stabilized at around 8–10 million people. This is not to say that these urban areas are not growing, but that the brunt of the demographic growth takes place outside the administrative areas of the 'central' cities.

As indicated in Table 4.1, the city of São Paulo has a population of about 10 million, or about 60 per cent of the metropolitan region's 17 million. On the other hand, the São Paulo metropolitan region includes another 38 municipalities and stretches over 8051 square kilometres, more than five times the area of the city of São Paulo. Most of the recent urban growth is taking place outside the city of São Paulo, although both are growing more slowly than past predictions. Recent annual growth rates in the metropolitan region and the city have been 1.4 per cent and 0.4 per cent respectively (EMPLASA, 1998).

The national human development ranking and child mortality is more favourable for Brazil than for Ghana and Indonesia. Although São Paulo can be expected to have an even better position than other urban areas in Brazil, there is considerable variation among the different municipalities surrounding the city of São Paulo.

## Jakarta

Jakarta is situated at the mouth of the River Ciliwung on northern Java, a swampy area that has been populated since ancient times. It became an important city during colonial times. The spectacular growth of Jakarta has, however, mainly taken place since independence from the Dutch, shortly after World War II, at which time the city had a population of about 1 million (Abeyasekere, 1987). In 1995 Jakarta had an estimated population of 8.6 million people (World Resources Institute, 1998). The more extensive metropolitan system known as Jabotabek, which includes Jakarta and neighbouring districts of Bogor, Tanggerang and Bekasi, had in 1990 a population of almost 17 million (Leitmann, 1993).

Jakarta is the capital of Indonesia and its unrivalled political and economic centre. Indonesia's industrial output is mainly based on the extraction of natural resources, including crude oil, natural gas, timber, metals and coal, although some 40 per cent of the population are still engaged in agriculture. Jakarta's rapid population growth during the last part of the century was supported by the very fast growth of the Indonesian economy, averaging 7 per cent between 1985 and 1995. The Asian economy crisis caused severe dislocations, however.

Indonesia has a mixed economy which during the last few years has been rapidly deregulated. In relation to environmental management and services, however, the government has always played a relatively restricted role. Household water and sanitation, for example, have involved large elements of informal provision, even in Jakarta.

## Accra

Accra, with an estimated population of 1.7 million in 1995 (World Resources Institute, 1998), is small in this context, although it still dwarfs other urban areas in Ghana. Over the past hundred years, Accra has grown out of fishing villages and developed into the main trading centre in the country. It is the national capital and the main economic node, but by international standards Accra is a poor city. Almost half the urban population in Accra have incomes below the World Bank's absolute poverty threshold. The poor tend to be concentrated in high-density indigenous settlements and migrant residential areas with poor access to environmental services (Amuzu and Leitmann, 1994).

The overall economic development in Ghana since the mid-1970s was very weak. Following the economic recovery programmes, initiated in the 1980s, many

**Table 4.1** *Selected indicators of city size and national economic and human development*

| Selected indicators of city size and affluence | Accra | Jakarta | São Paulo |
|---|---|---|---|
| 1 Total area (city) (square kilometres) | 420 [a] | 660 [b] | 1577 [c] |
| 2 City population (1995) (millions) | 1.7 [a] | 8.6 [b] | 10.1 [c] (1998) |
| 3 Average annual population growth (1990–1995) (city) | 3.5% [a] | 2.4% [b] | 0.4% [c] |
| | *Ghana* | *Indonesia* | *Brazil* |
| 4 Percentage of national population in largest city (1995) [d] | 27% | 13% | 13% |
| 5 Real GDP per capita 1997 (national) (PPP$) [e] | $1640 | $3490 | $6480 |
| 6 Real GDP per capita among [f] | | | |
| a the poorest 20% (PPP$) | $790 | $1422 | $578 |
| b the richest 20% (PPP$) | $4220 | $6654 | $18,563 |
| 7 HDI (Human Development index) ranking (national) | 133 | 105 | 79 |
| 8 Under-5's mortality rate 1995 (per 1000 live births) (national) | 130 | 75 | 60 |

*Data sources*
1 Accra: Accra Planning and Development Programme, United Nations Development Programme and United Nations Centre for Human Settlements (1992) *Strategic Plan for the Greater Accra Metropolitan Area,* draft, Ministry of Local Government, Accra; Jakarta and São Paulo: Leitmann, J, *Rapid Urban Environmental Assessment: Lessons from Cities in the Developing World, Vol 2,* 1993, World Bank, Washington DC
2 and 3 Accra Planning and Development Programme, United Nations Development Programme and United Nations Centre for Human Settlements (1992) *Strategic Plan for the Greater Accra Metropolitan Area,* draft, Ministry of Local Government, Accra; Jakarta: World Resources Institute (1998) *World Resources 1998–99: A Guide to the Global Environment,* Oxford University Press, New York; São Paulo: EMPLASA (1998) Banco de Dados e Informações sobre os Municípios da Região Metropolitana de São Paulo, São Paulo
4 The World Bank (1999) *1999 World Development Indicators.* World Bank, Washington, DC
5, 6 and 7 United Nations Development Programme (1999). *Human Development Report 1999,* Oxford University Press, Oxford
8 World Resources Institute (1998) *World Resources 1998–99: A Guide to the Global Environment.* Oxford University Press, New York
*Notes*
a Refers to the Accra Metropolitan Area (includes Accra and Tema Districts)
b Refers to Jakarta-DKI
c Refers to the city (municipality) of São Paulo
d Accra, Jakarta and São Paulo are the largest cities in their respective countries
e PPP = purchasing power parity
f Data refer to the most recent year available during the period 1980–1994

economic performance indicators turned to positive values, although employment has declined drastically. Retrenchment programmes in the public sector, associated with structural adjustment programmes, have exacerbated this. Economic growth during the 1990s has been at a rate of around 5 per cent. The mainstay of the economy has historically been agriculture, although it has now been surpassed by the services sector, accounting for some 44 per cent of real gross domestic product (GDP) (United Nations Development Programme, 1997a). The main export products are gold, timber and cocoa.

The three cities are all economic hubs of their respective countries. Thus, the average incomes in the cities selected are higher than those of their respective countries. In the early 1990s, the estimated per capita expenditure in Accra was 50 per cent higher than the national average and that of Jakarta was 130 per cent higher. The economic activity in São Paulo is also considerably higher than the Brazil average. The city had a gross city product per capita of US$8500 in 1998, compared to a national figure of US$4570 (World Bank, 1999).

In spite of the cities' comparative wealth within their respective countries, there is considerable poverty within these cities. The national income is unequally distributed, as is the wealth within the cities. The GDP per capita that is attributed to the wealthiest 20 per cent of the countries' populations is around five times as high as that of the poorest 20 per cent in both Ghana and Indonesia. In Brazil, the ratio is 32:1, indicating much more extreme income disparities. Unfortunately, inequalities tend to increase during times of economic hardship (Ravallion and Chen, 1997) and, given the unstable financial and economic performance of Ghana, Indonesia and Brazil, it is likely that the situation has deteriorated further for the weakest subgroups.

## SHIFTING SCALES OF ENVIRONMENTAL PROBLEMS

As described in previous chapters, many of the most severe urban environmental hazards are found in and around poor people's homes and workplaces. Table 4.2 summarizes some of the indicators of household-level environmental problems derived from representative surveys administered as part of the three-city study. All these indicators involve health risks for either diarrhoeal diseases or respiratory infections, two of the most significant causes of childhood morbidity and mortality. While individually the comparability of such indicators is often doubtful, the overall picture is clear.

Not having a water source at home (row 1) is not only burdensome for women, but also restricts hygiene practices. This afflicts close to half the residents in Accra where, in spite of having an abundant river source, the infrastructure coverage is insufficient to fully cater for the city dwellers' needs. In Jakarta, where the piped-

**Table 4.2** *Household environment indicators in Accra, Jakarta and São Paulo*

| Environment indicator | Accra | Jakarta | São Paulo |
|---|---|---|---|
| | Percentage of sample | | |
| *Water* | | | |
| No water source at residence | 46 | 13 | 5 |
| *Sanitation* | | | |
| Share toilets with > 10 households | 48 | <13 | 3 |
| *Solid waste* | | | |
| No home waste collection | 89 | 37 | 5 |
| *Indoor air* | | | |
| Main cooking fuel wood or charcoal | 76 | 2 | 0 |
| *Pests* | | | |
| Flies in kitchen | 82 [a] | 38 [a] | 20 [b] |
| Number of households: | 1000 | 1055 | 1000 |

*Source:* SEI Household Environment Data Base 1991–1992
*Notes*
a  As observed by the interviewer
b  As perceived by the respondent

water infrastructure is very rudimentary,[3] most households have access to water through private wells. While this water is often not of drinking-water quality, households may still use it for hygiene purposes, and the water quantities that need to be brought from outside the home are thus much reduced. The city with near universal water infrastructure coverage is São Paulo. Nevertheless, residents face frequent supply interruptions because potable water resources in the area are scarce for a city of São Paulo's size, and the distribution system is thus inadequately supplied (Jacobi, 1995a; Kjellén et al, 1996).

High levels of toilet sharing (row 2) often leads to poor sanitary conditions in the toilets themselves, creates more opportunities for faecal-oral diseases to be transmitted between households, and the difficulty of access can lead to open defecation and faeces being mixed with solid waste. The trend for sanitation is the same as for water, with Accra being worst off, Jakarta better off and not a significant problem existing in São Paulo. Toilet sharing is one of the main predictors of childhood diarrhoeal incidences (Benneh et al, 1993).

Without household waste collection (row 3), waste often accumulates in the neighbourhood, providing ideal habitats for flies and rats. While regular household waste collection is the norm in São Paulo, it is rare in Accra. In Jakarta about 37 per cent of the households have their waste collected. With waste collection

---

3 Only 18 per cent of the households in Jakarta are connected to the municipal water supply system (Surjadi et al, 1994)

far from sufficient, refuse generally accumulates in gullies and wastelands in all three cities. Given the much less frequent waste collection in Accra, refuse accumulation tends to take place much closer to where people live and work. Although there is a system of collection from waste points in most residential areas, the collection is erratic and also the legal intermediary dumps often overflow with waste. This also happens in Jakarta, a city that also has problems with waste collection equipment. In São Paulo, the main waste problem relates to final disposal rather than the collection as such.

Where the generally smokier biofuels such as wood and charcoal (row 4) are used without proper ventilation, indoor air pollution may be severe and contribute to respiratory diseases. This is an issue in Accra, but not in the other two cities. This most likely reflects both Accra's smaller size (the rural sources of firewood or charcoal are much nearer) and its lesser affluence (fewer households can afford cleaner fuels). While biofuels are very rarely used in Jakarta, previous studies have shown that biofuel use is common in Java's smaller towns, especially among their less affluent households (McGranahan and Kaijser, 1993).

Flies observed in the kitchen (row 5), apart from providing a general indication of the sanitary state of the household, can facilitate the faecal-oral route of many diarrhoeal diseases. In the survey, this condition was very common in Accra (82 per cent), but less frequent in Jakarta (38 per cent) and São Paulo (20 per cent).

Thus, in every case the indicator improves between Accra and Jakarta, and improves further between Jakarta and São Paulo. The more detailed household statistics confirm this trend. The most obvious explanation for the tendencies observed is the relative affluence of the three cities. Indeed, as indicated in Table 4.3, similar patterns are observed if one looks across different segments of the cities' populations.

Table 4.3 combines intercity and intracity comparisons. The overall tendency is the same as in Table 4.2, with conditions improving between Accra and Jakarta, and improving further between Jakarta and São Paulo. Nevertheless, some of the largest differences are not found between the three cities, but rather between different household segments within the cities.

The largest differences are found between the poorest and the richest wealth quintiles (based on the surveyed households' respective tenure of consumer durables) in Accra. There, about 10 per cent of the wealthiest have no water source in their homes, and some 12 per cent use public toilets (ie share with a large number of other households), compared to 90 per cent and 69 per cent respectively of the poorest households. Because refuse collection from the residence is uncommon in Accra, three-quarters of the wealthier households need to carry their waste to appropriate (or inappropriate) waste-collection sites. Virtually all poor households take care of their own waste in this way. With 38 per cent of the wealthier households mainly cooking with biofuels, it is not unlikely that the

**Table 4.3**  *Household environment indicators in Accra, Jakarta and São Paulo –
intraurban comparisons*

| Environment indicator | Accra | | Jakarta | | São Paulo | |
|---|---|---|---|---|---|---|
| By wealth quintiles[a] | Poorest 20% | Wealthiest 20% | Poorest 20% | Wealthiest 20% | Poorest 20% | Wealthiest 20% |
| | *Percentage of sample* | | | | | |
| *Water* | | | | | | |
| No water source at residence | 67 | 10 | 31 | 3 | 19 | 3 |
| *Sanitation* | | | | | | |
| Share toilets with > 10 households | 69 | 12 | <32 | <10 | <7 | <1 |
| *Solid waste* | | | | | | |
| No home waste collection | 97 | 74 | 52 | 16 | 14 | 1 |
| *Indoor air* | | | | | | |
| Main cooking fuel wood or charcoal | 96 | 38 | 4 | 0 | 0 | 0 |
| *Pests* | | | | | | |
| Flies in kitchen | 96[b] | 51[b] | 52[b] | 21[b] | 50[c] | 10[c] |
| Number of households | 205 | 198 | 208 | 214 | 201 | 187 |

*Source:* SEI Household Environment Data Base 1991–92
*Notes*
a The poorest and the wealthiest 20 per cent groups are derived by dividing the total sample into
five wealth quintiles of roughly equal size, based on an index of the households' tenure of durable
consumer items (ranging from transistor radios to cars)
b As observed by the interviewer
c As perceived by the respondent

individuals having to breathe the smoke are servants or poorer relatives helping
(and residing) in the household.

In Jakarta and São Paulo, where conditions on average are better, the difference
between rich and poor is less pronounced, albeit in Jakarta, the indicators of poor
water and sanitation have frequencies of less than 10 per cent of the wealthy, but
closer to a third of the poorer households. Refuse collection is the area where the
differences are most pronounced in Jakarta, but although there is no home
collection of waste, there are systems of intermediate dumping sites.

In São Paulo there are few household-level environmental hazards that affect
the rich. Indeed, the survey in that city showed that the main concern of the
majority, and in particular of the wealthy, is that of outdoor air pollution (Jacobi,
1995a; Jacobi et al, 1998; Jacobi et al, 1999). Poor ambient air quality is less
localized and is therefore treated and tackled as a citywide problem.

While the poorer households in São Paulo have much worse access to
amenities, the difference is not as large as it is within the other two cities. And it

is definitely not as large as what could be expected from the sheer income inequality, which is exceptionally large in São Paulo and Brazil (Table 4.1). Hence, as mentioned before, although income or relative affluence is a major predictor of the household-level environmental situation, there is much that city authorities and residents can do to improve conditions. In the case of water, the infrastructure coverage in many urban areas in Brazil was extended to far above the Latin American average during the 1970s (Munasinghe, 1992). This expansion was financed through a highly centralized water supply strategy (Vargas, 1995), and of course also contributed to Brazil's external debt. In São Paulo, the expansion was maintained during the 1980s, with increased political scope and pressure to serve favelas (Briscoe, 1993), and the system covers virtually the whole city. During several periods in those days there were no connection fees for poor households. This policy has been abandoned in favour of a more commercially oriented water utility, and connection fees are charged for all new connections.

These indicators of local environmental threats presented in Tables 4.2 and 4.3 give a clue to the health risks and the level of inconveniences that households, and particularly women and children, face in order to secure the necessities of daily life. Still, these problems are suffered by individuals and their close neighbours, with the dominant environmental processes involving local inter-actions, and they do not indicate the level of strain on the city's resource base.

As argued in the previous chapters, the strain placed on a city's resources tends to be less where many people are poor and consumption levels are low. A selection of indicators related to city-level environmental burdens are provided Table 4.4. These indicators are taken from a variety of sources, and some are less comparable than the household-level indicators. Most reflect the pressures rather than the outcomes/impacts, partly because the damage depends heavily on local geography, and tend to be even less comparable. While the differences are in some cases more ambiguous than with the household-level indicators, they do confirm the general tendency suggested and illustrate the extent and manner in which some of the local environmental problems are displaced to the city level. Both aggregate and per capita indicators are presented to separate out, at least roughly, the effects of city size.

Regional water scarcities are an increasing problem globally, and can be particularly acute in the vicinity of large cities where they can lead to sharp increases in the cost of supplying water (Anton, 1993). As shown in Table 4.4, water consumption per capita is about 70 per cent higher in Jakarta than in Accra, and about 60 per cent higher again in São Paulo. Because of their relative sizes, these differences are magnified in the citywide figures. Water consumption increases with affluence both because it becomes more convenient and affordable to use, and because new demands for water develop, such as the use of washing machines and water for washing cars. As noted above, the share of households with water sources in their homes increases from about half in Accra to 95 per cent in São

**Table 4.4** *City-level environment indicators in Accra, Jakarta and São Paulo*

| Environment indicator (metro) | Accra (city) | Jakarta (city) | São Paulo |
|---|---|---|---|
| *Water* | | | |
| 1 Household water consumption (litres per capita per day) | 82 | 138 | 215 |
| 2 Total water consumption (thousand cubic metres per day) | 263 | 1469 | 5017 (metro) |
| *Sanitation* | | | |
| 3 Sewage flow (thousand cubic metres per day) | 46 | 35 | 2400 (metro) |
| 4 Sewage treatment (percentage treated) | 20 | 1 | 26 |
| *Solid waste* | | | |
| 5 Household solid waste generation (kg per capita per day) | 0.4 | 1.0[a] | 1.2[a] |
| 6 Municipal solid waste generation (tons per day) | 1000 | 9000 | 12,000 |
| 7 Percentage of waste collected | 75 | 83 | 90 |
| *Outdoor air* | | | |
| 8 Car ownership (% of households) | 16 | 16 | 33 |
| 9 Mean annual total suspended particulates (TSP) ($\mu g/m^3$ of air) | 137 (1990) | 271 (1990) | 86 (1995) |

*Sources:*

1 Accra and Jakarta: Stockholm Environment Institute Household Environment Data Base 1991–1992; São Paulo: Leitmann, J (1993) *Rapid Urban Environmental Assessment: Lessons from Cities in the Developing World, Vol 2,* World Bank, Washington DC

2, 3, and 4 Leitmann, J (1993) *Rapid Urban Environmental Assessment: Lessons from Cities in the Developing World, Vol 2,* World Bank, Washington DC

5 Accra: Accra Planning and Development Programme, United Nations Development Programme and United Nations Centre for Human Settlements (1992) *Strategic Plan for the Greater Accra Metropolitan Area,* Ministry of Local Government, Accra; Jakarta: Otten, L (1996) 'Integrated Solid Waste Management', *Strategies for a Sustainable Greater Jabotabek,* Jakarta, 8–10 July; São Paulo: CETESB (1998) *Annual Report 1998,* CETESB, São Paulo

6 Accra: Amuzu, A T and J Leitmann, 'Accra', *Cities* (1994), vol 11, no 1; Jakarta: Saleh, D (1996). Discussion topics: 'Strategies for a sustainable greater Jabotabek: Solid wastes management and sanitation sectors', *Strategies for a Sustainable Greater Jabotabek Seminar.* Jakarta, 8–10 July, 1996, and Otten, L (1996) 'Integrated Solid Waste Management', *Strategies for a Sustainable Greater Jabotabek.* Jakarta, 8–10 July, 1996; São Paulo: CETESB. 1998. *Annual Report 1998.* CETESB (São Paulo)

7 Accra: Amuzu, A T and Leitmann, J, (1994) 'Accra', *Cities,* vol 11, no 1; Jakarta: Saleh, D (1996) 'Strategies for a sustainable greater Jabotabek: Solid wastes management and sanitation sectors', *Strategies for a Sustainable Greater Jabotabek Seminar,* Jakarta, 8–10 July; São Paulo: Oliveira, C N E and Leitmann, J (1994) 'São Paulo', *Cities,* vol 11, no 1

8 Stockholm Environment Institute Household Environment Data Base, 1991–1992

9 World Resources Institute (1998) *World Resources 1998–99: A Guide to the Global Environment.* Oxford University Press, New York

*Notes:*

a Includes both household and industrial waste

Paulo, and, as indicated in Table 4.4, the share of households with cars doubles. Many other measures of convenience and water-using devices, such as washing machines, would undoubtedly show similar patterns.

The principal water sources for Accra are the River Densu and the Black Volta, which have the capacity to provide far more water than the current demand. As mentioned before, the demand in Accra is suppressed by the deficient infrastructure coverage.

The citywide impacts of Jakarta's water demands are somewhat difficult to determine. The majority of households in Jakarta use shallow wells, at least for washing. Groundwater salination affects some 40 per cent of Jakarta's residents (Surjadi et al, 1994), and this is often attributed to excess abstraction (Douglass, 1989). However, the salination of the shallow aquifer used by households may be a long-standing natural phenomenon (Rismianto and Mak, 1993), and it is possible that the more serious long-term supply problems lie in the piped-water system. Regardless, overabstraction has increased the salinity problems of the deeper aquifer (Rismianto and Mak, 1993).

Along with better infrastructure and more water-consuming habits and appliances, individual household water use tends to increase with wealth. This is shown by the intraurban comparisons of water consumption in the poorest and the wealthiest groups in Accra and Jakarta (Table 4.5).[4]

The high consumption levels in São Paulo are all met through the piped water system, which is severely straining the city's water supplies. Water scarcity is exacerbated during the dry winter and rationing is applied (Anton, 1993; Jacobi, 1995a). São Paulo is facing severe trade-offs between the competing water uses of

**Table 4.5** *Household water consumption in Accra and Jakarta – intraurban comparisons*

| Environment indicator | Accra | | Jakarta | |
|---|---|---|---|---|
| By wealth quintiles | Poorest 20% | Wealthiest 20% | Poorest 20% | Wealthiest 20% |
| Water consumption (litres per capita per day) | 33 | 90 | 69 | 97 |
| Number of households | 205 | 198 | 208 | 214 |

Source: SEI Household Environment Data Base, 1991–1992
Notes: The poorest and the wealthiest 20 per cent groups are derived by dividing the total sample into five wealth quintiles of roughly equal size, based on an index of the households' tenure of durable consumer items (ranging from transistor radios to cars). Data on water quantities consumed were not collected in São Paulo

4 Figures on water quantities used were only collected in Accra and Jakarta, not in São Paulo

municipal supply, electricity generation and that of waste dilution. The Billings reservoir was built in the 1920s to take advantage of the Serra do Mar drop towards the Atlantic to produce hydroelectric power. The system included a pumping station to take water from the lower Pinheiros River into the reservoir. At that time the river was not yet polluted, but now it contains highly contaminated urban wastewaters and stormwaters, a mixture which is pumped into the Billings reservoir. In order to maintain the municipal water supply, the reservoir has been divided into two parts separated by a relatively permeable earth dam that allows flow in both directions. The smaller part supports the municipal supply, and the larger, lower level part receives the water from the Pinheiros. Pumping continues in the drier season to keep electricity generation going, and during the rains to avoid flooding in the São Paulo municipality (Anton, 1993; Jacobi and Carvalho Teixeira, 1995).

Pollution of the waterways is a serious problem in the vicinity of all three cities. Many of São Paulo's and Jakarta's water-quality problems are related to industrial activity, which is particularly intensive in and around São Paulo. But even faecal water pollution is more of a city-level problem in São Paulo, where the sewerage system reaches some three-quarters of the residents, but 75 per cent of the sewerage is released untreated (Jacobi, 1995a). Forty cubic metres per second of raw sewage and industrial effluent are discharged into the River Tietê which has become almost entirely devoid of oxygen (Leitmann, 1993). Recently, however, investments in sewerage-treatment capacity have increased, and currently some 85 per cent of São Paulo's population is connected to the sewerage network, and up to 50 per cent of the sewage gets treated (SABESP, 1998).

In Accra and Jakarta, where the sewerage systems are negligible, a larger share of the faecal material degrades in the neighbourhoods, where it poses its main risks. However, this does not prevent the waterways of Accra and Jakarta from being very severely polluted with faecal material. Although incidents are sometimes reported (for example, from eating contaminated seafood), ambient water pollution tends to be a more severe problem for the ecology and livelihoods of fishers than for human health. Even among the poor, few people use ambient water for cooking and drinking.

Solid waste generation is difficult to estimate, and the estimates by weight do not indicate appropriately the shift from more organic (and heavy) wastes of poorer households to bulkier wastes with higher contents of plastic and packaging materials among wealthier households. The figures in Table 4.4 nonetheless point towards a trend of less waste produced per person in Accra than in Jakarta, and less waste produced per person in Jakarta than in São Paulo. This is most likely the result of two trends: firstly, the higher the consumption level, the higher the waste production, and secondly, the better the waste collection, the lesser the incentive to limit the amount of waste. Both these factors support the trend.

The city authorities eventually collect most solid waste in the three cities, with a somewhat higher share in São Paulo. Overall, it is the authorities of São Paulo, with its large size, high waste generation and high collection share, which cope with by far the largest solid waste burden. Alternatively, as depicted in Table 4.2, only 11 per cent of the households in Accra and 63 per cent in Jakarta have their refuse collected from the house, and the burden is thus generally borne locally. Households without home collection dump their wastes at collection points, official dump sites, or other, often illegal sites. While the waste that is brought to the collection or dumping sites officially becomes the responsibility of the city authorities, when collection is intermittent, much of the environmental burden is carried by the nearby residents.

The different positions in the 'environmental transition' of the three cities is reflected by the different foci of waste policies and debates in the three countries. In Accra, the focus of improvement tends to involve institutional innovations and investments in collection trucks. In Jakarta, the focus is twofold, addressing the problems of the collection as well as the final disposal sites, including the situation of waste pickers (Surjadi and Handayani, 1998). In São Paulo it is the final disposal of waste that attracts the most attention. The bulk of the refuse is disposed of at the five existing landfills, which are in adequate condition but at the limit of their useful capacity (three to eight years). Incineration, albeit undertaken on a very limited scale, has been a topic of political contention, in particular because of the obsolete technology used.

São Paulo is famed for its poor air quality. Indeed, the city has a history of health warnings due to air pollution from carbon monoxide, ozone and particulates, whereas lead and sulphur dioxide levels have declined with the increased use of alcohol fuel (CETESB, 1995; Hardoy et al, 1992). In the 1980s sulphur dioxide concentrations decreased by over 10 per cent per year and the annual lead average was below the WHO guideline range (United Nations Environment Programme and World Health Organization, 1988). The lowering of sulphur dioxide and lead pollution is a trend that São Paulo shares with most cities in the North, and it indicates that São Paulo is undergoing the 'pollution revolution' depicted in Figure 2.1 on p17. Indeed, initially São Paulo's air pollution was associated with industrial production, but, as the control of point sources has become increasingly efficient, most of the impact on the air quality today is posed by motor vehicles. São Paulo has close to 5 million cars, accounting for a quarter of Brazil's vehicle fleet.

According to Table 4.4, the level of total suspended particulates in São Paulo is below that of Jakarta and Accra, despite the large number of cars and the greater industrial activity. However, in Accra, air pollution problems are mainly concentrated on the industrial areas. Sites with traffic congestion also bring localized problems of airborne lead (ROG/UNDP/UNCHS, 1989). In Ghana and Indonesia, leaded petrol constitutes 100 per cent of the market. In São Paulo it is 0 per cent as no lead is allowed in petrol (World Resources Institute, 1998). This is an indication of how São Paulo has been able to deal institutionally with some of its citywide environmental problems. In Jakarta they may very well be at their peak of ambient air pollution. Apart from having eliminated lead in petrol, the authorities in São Paulo are also dealing with carbon monoxide levels and traffic congestion (Jacobi et al, 1999).

In Accra, outdoor air pollution is not considered a significant problem (Amuzu and Leitmann, 1994). The high levels of indoor air pollution among wood and charcoal users are more alarming (Benneh et al, 1993), indicating that the main concerns for Accra remain in the home sphere. The households' main cooking fuel in São Paulo, electricity, is very clean where it is used (in the home), but its environmental consequences at the (faraway) place of generation may be severe. This may include the destruction of valuable land or the displacement of people in the case of hydropower, or carbon and sulphur dioxide emissions in the case of fossil fuel.

The contribution to global environmental threats is probably best indicated by overall consumption levels. On the one hand, the effects that individuals may have on faraway environments are linked to lifestyles and consumption patterns. The consumption of certain foods or other items may be indirectly very environmentally destructive, depending on how they are produced and transported. Clearly, consumption follows affluence. Another quintessentially global threat, is climate change potentially brought on by the release of greenhouse gases, and in particular carbon dioxide. National figures of carbon dioxide emissions give a hint towards Accra, Jakarta and São Paulo's citizens' contribution to this problem. Per capita emissions are very low in Ghana, with higher values for Indonesia and Brazil (see Table 4.6). These values are far below many of the wealthier countries in the North. For example, the United States releases some 20.5 metric tonnes of carbon dioxide per year (World Resources Institute, 1998).

As with the household-level indicators, the attempt to find quantifiable indicators diverts attention from many of the more unique environmental problems that are characteristic of these cities. All these cities face problems with watershed management, urban-led deforestation and land degradation, and a wide range of

**Table 4.6** *Carbon emissions in Ghana, Indonesia and Brazil*

| Environment indicator | Ghana | Indonesia | Brazil |
|---|---|---|---|
| Carbon emissions from fossil fuel burning and cement manufacturing (metric tons per capita) | 0.2 | 1.5 | 1.6 |

*Source:* World Resources Institute (1998) *World Resources 1998–99: A Guide to the Global Environment*, Oxford University Press, New York

other environmental resources. Moreover, the household environmental problems were shown to vary significantly in Accra, as well as between the cities, so not all residents within a city place the same strain on the city-level environment.

## CONCLUSIONS

In summary, the household environment appears far better in São Paulo than in the other two cities, reflecting higher levels of private affluence as well as organized efforts and ability by the city authorities towards providing infrastructural facilities for the bulk of the population. On the other hand, even on a per capita basis, the levels of activities creating city-level environmental problems are highest in São Paulo, although the effects have been mitigated by somewhat more vigorous pollution-control efforts in some areas, notably air quality.

Jakarta appears at least superficially to have the worst of two worlds environmentally; it faces severe city-level problems, affecting fishing, agriculture and its watersheds (Douglass, 1989; Hardoy et al, 1992), but, due to poorly developed environmental infrastructure, has made little headway towards solving the unhealthy environment in many neighbourhoods. Still, most households are far more affluent than those in Accra, which is reflected in the many private solutions towards improving the household environment (Surjadi et al, 1994).

Accra's residents face the most pervasive environmental health problems, related mainly to the low development of infrastructure to displace the environmental burdens away from the household sphere. Except for localized air and water pollution problems in areas of traffic congestion, industrial sites and lagoons, fishing and agriculture have not (yet) been adversely affected by city activities (Amuzu and Leitmann, 1994).

Hence, the association between affluence and different environmental problems is clear in these cities. The city-level problems, that tend to increase initially with increased affluence, but eventually decrease with even further economic development, are also compounded by city size (which is not independent of economic growth). The main point, however, is not that these tendencies are inevitable. Instead, they are created by human collective action (or non-action). Although there are logical explanations why humans have different abilities and priorities at different wealth levels, the actions that lead to different environmental situations are by no means predetermined. Rather, in order to ensure appropriate environmental management or to support it, it is important to be critically aware of these tendencies and not to risk misdirecting efforts and funds.

# 5

# Organizing Environmental Improvements in Deprived Neighbourhoods: Plans, Markets, Local Collective Action and Beyond[1]

Many of the most serious and health-threatening environmental hazards stem from local sanitary conditions. The importance of these problems has long been recognized. Views on how to resolve them change with disturbing regularity, however. In the following account, three models of local environmental improvement are presented and discussed, principally in the context of sanitation. They are more caricatures than descriptions of accepted approaches. However, in a world where simple messages are often the most potent, these models at times have been more influential and rhetorically meaningful than the more sophisticated positions they caricature. Moreover, the arguments and assumptions explicit in these idealized models are often implicit in accounts of how better governance, freer markets or more local participation are going to improve local environmental management.

The three models are labelled the planning model, the market model and the collective action model, following a similar classification elaborated in the context of rural development (Uphoff, 1993). Table 5.1 summarizes this classification. The three models are built around three different mechanisms of social interaction: bureaucratic organization, which attempts to apply rationality of a higher order to people's behaviour; market processes, which rely on the 'invisible hand' of the market to transform individual preferences into aggregate outcomes; and voluntary association, whereby group decisions are collectively negotiated outcomes.

In a simple version of the planning model, experts, planners and engineers decide how and when improvements are to be made, and public authorities ensure that these improvements are carried out. In the market model, residents' willingness to pay (or work) drives improvement efforts, which are implemented by commercially minded providers or the householders themselves. In the collective action

1 This chapter was conceived and outlined at a workshop in Oxford in 1996, and the authors would like to thank all of the participants for the stimulating discussions, and Sandy Cairncross and Jan-Olof Drangert for useful comments on an earlier draft

**Table 5.1**  *The organizational basis of three approaches to local environmental improvement*

|  | Planning model | Market model | Collective action model |
|---|---|---|---|
| *Principal mechanisms* | Bureaucratic organization | Market processes | Voluntary associations |
| *Decision-makers* | Administrators, engineers, public officials | Individuals, households, vendors, enterprises | Leaders and members of grass-roots organizations |
| *Criteria for decisions* | Policy, and conformity with a plan | Efficiency: maximization of profit or utility | Interests of members and visions of leaders |
| *Guides for behaviour* | Targets, regulations and technical standards | Price signals, incorporating taxes and subsidies | Agreements and accepted goals |
| *Sanctions* | State authority backed by coercion | Financial loss | Social pressure |
| *Mode of operation* | Top-down | Individualistic | Bottom-up |

*Source:* Adapted from Uphoff 1993, p610, which was itself adapted from Esman and Uphoff, 1984, p20

model, neighbours get together and organize their way to sanitary improvement. In the abstract, it is possible to talk of the perfect plan, market or community. Indeed, such utopian visions have proved very alluring. More pragmatic discussions of planning, the market and collective action deal with the obstacles that can prevent plans from being implemented, markets from functioning and communities from acting together in their collective interest. The perfect plan, market or community may still be viewed as ideal, even when the emphasis is on how to achieve second-best in an imperfect world.

These models are politically charged, and at times seem to reflect different visions of how society as a whole should be organized: crudely, the choice between communism, capitalism and some third way (perhaps communalism (Bell, 1993; Crouch and Marquand, 1995)). To put it only slightly less crudely, the planning model could be taken to reflect the vision of the bureaucrat, the market model the vision of the capitalist, and the community model the vision of the grass-roots activist. Partly as a result of these political associations, the attraction of the different approaches tends to follow national and even global political trends. The popularity of the planning model relative to the market model as a means to sanitary improvement, for example, has clearly been affected by the fall of the

Soviet Union, although this fall taught us nothing about the relative merits of planned sanitary improvement.

Putting political associations to the side, the models can also be taken to portray three sectors that coexist in most contemporary societies, and articulate with each other in a variety of conflicting and complementary ways. Indeed, disaggregating further and changing the terminology somewhat, they can be viewed as mechanisms that often operate simultaneously, even within a single organization. For example, a corporation that largely conforms to the market model in its external relations may adopt a planning approach for major parts of its internal organization (adopting, for example, sales targets) and contain many teams and hold many meetings that involve strong elements of voluntary association.

Within the urban water and sanitation systems of many low-income cities, it is also possible to detect different subsectors whose operations correspond more or less closely to one or other of the models. Thus, while public utilities have traditionally adopted a planning approach to service delivery (despite having paying customers), voluntary associations are typically engaged in maintaining or improving sanitation in unserviced areas, and private enterprises compete (or in some cases act as monopolists) in various niches, including water-vending, when economic opportunities allow it.

Both researchers and politicians can easily come to be affiliated with one or other of these models, treating them as competing alternatives rather than as complements. However, there is a growing perception that when the activities of the state, the private sector and the voluntary sector can be made complementary, or even merged, considerable synergies result (Evans, 1996a; Evans, 1996b; Ostrom, 1996). This suggests a different focus for improvement. Arguing over the advantages and disadvantages of plans, markets or voluntary organizations, or trying to improve them on their own terms, may miss the best opportunities. Perhaps attention needs to be paid to how the sectors interact, and to providing mutually supportive environments. This sort of approach is at least implicit in the contemporary jargon of 'enabling policies', 'public-private partnerships' and the like. 'Coproduction' has been used to refer to the creation of goods with contributions from private and public sectors, and sanitary improvement has been cited as a good far more efficiently coproduced than produced within one sector alone (Ostrom, 1996). Thus, for example, the condominial system which has proved to be successful in spreading comparatively low-cost sanitation in several cities of Brazil, works through combining the centralized provision of trunk lines with active local involvement in financing, maintaining and even designing the connections to people's homes (Briscoe, 1993; Mara, 1996).

A further complication stems from the fact that whatever combination of planning, markets and collective action prevails, the most important conceptualization and action often occurs off-stage, in less rationalized arenas. It is not just the competence of the planning, the competitiveness of the markets, the effectiveness of the voluntary organizations, or even the manner in which they combine that determines whether sanitary improvement is achieved. Much depends on social processes, often specific to a particular chronology or conjuncture, whose meanings and evolution bear little relation to formal understandings of public health and sanitation. These processes not only involve local residents, but also the traditional sanitary improvers, including that seemingly calculating professional, the sanitary engineer. Even in extremely bureaucratized situations, sanitary engineers are people who, like everyone else, attach far more meaning to their work than is implied by the requirement that they fulfil a specified set of duties. Often, the difference between success and failure lies less in openly accepted goals and institutional mechanisms, and more in the hidden politics of power and meaning, including, for example, the narratives that sanitary engineers develop out of their daily activities.

The following sections examine the relevance of each of the three models to the practice of sanitary improvement, with particular reference to deprived urban areas. There are three reasons for carrying out this inevitably somewhat artificial exercise. First, as indicated above, practice is often unduly influenced by coherent but simplistic models, which can provide the political clout of the common agenda and the intellectual satisfaction of the easy answer, even when they are not explicit. Many past failures reflect such an influence. Second, when they are made explicit and subject to scrutiny, such models can shed light on the strengths and weaknesses of different strategies and practices. Ideal types need not become utopian visions. Third, at the risk of being misleading, these models can be used to categorize some of the approaches to sanitary improvement, allowing a simplified summary of some recent trends in that improvement.

This chapter does not attempt to synthesize the 'right' approach to local environmental improvement. Historically, the successful sanitary improver has been as much the quirky opportunist as the trained professional or committed activist, and there are good reasons for this. There may be common failures that need to be corrected in a wide range of settings and principles that are relevant to a great many settings, but there is no common solution to be applied.

## THE PLANNING MODEL

Perhaps the simplest version of planned sanitary improvement is that of 'study, plan, execute'. Experts identify the physical dimensions of the problem, a public authority plans for its removal, and a public utility or other implementing agency executes the plan. To the extent that the solution is defined in technical terms, this is a technocratic approach. The planned expansion of water supply and sewerage systems can take this form. Sanitary standards can also be part of a planning approach. These may include, for example, zoning laws, prescribed distances between wells and latrines, technical specifications for latrines and water piping and storage, regulations concerning the accumulation of filth and stagnant water, and other restrictions that at least in principle could be enforced by sanitary inspectors. Prescriptive hygiene education can also be part of a planning approach, inasmuch as an expert decides on the needed change, a public authority decides how it is to be implemented, and the education is basically instructed.

Urban planning for water and sanitation is probably as old as cities themselves. For many, however, the 19th-century sanitary revolution in Europe is the starting point for modern water and sanitary planning. One of the lessons often taken from that experience was that the public sector had to take the lead in planning urban development, especially as it concerned public health. Private enterprises, such as water companies, could not be trusted to provide for public health, and neither could slum dwellers. Efforts on the part of the state to prescribe the intimate details of people's hygiene behaviour never stopped being contentious. However, once state control over water and sanitation infrastructure was achieved, there were few pressures, until recently, to put it back into private hands.

In many Northern countries, as urban planning gained acceptance, water and sanitary planning became increasingly the province of experts. Moreover, the environmental services that were developed and promoted, eventually even in working class areas, made certain norms of private hygiene far easier to maintain. Indoor, piped water connections, flush toilets, water-borne sewerage systems and door-to-door garbage collection: all these technologies complemented the forms of hygiene behaviour being recommended. At their most successful, the technologies helped make it easier to adopt the desired norm than to resist it, at least for people whose pre-existing norms and cultures were those of the technology's centre of origin.

Sanitary improvement efforts in European colonies were often even more top-down than at home. The political and cultural divisions of colonial society compounded the class divisions that complicated sanitary improvement in Europe. Throughout the world urban dwellers were quite naturally more interested in better water supplies, drainage and waste removal, than in prescriptions on how to wash, dispose of faeces, store water, bury the dead and so on. In colonies, however, it was harder to access public funds for infrastructure improvement, and more tempting for the government to blame local practices. These were ingredients for a more contentious sanitary policy. Furthermore, the colonizers were often both unhealthy themselves, and ignorant of the realities of day-to-day life among the colonized. This undermined the credibility and validity of their prescriptions. Nevertheless, sanitary improvement was commonly pursued by colonial governments and local municipalities, as well as by many independent governments in what later came to be known as the Third World.

By the middle of this century, and in many cases long before, sanitary improvement in the industrialized countries was largely seen as a matter of extending known solutions to disadvantaged groups through public utilities, as well as education and regulation. Even the poor urban residents in these countries had come to see fetching water and using outdoor or communal privies as symbols of unacceptable backwardness and deprivation. The technologies and practices promoted were relatively standardized. The planning model was at least tacitly accepted as providing the overall framework for achieving coverage with urban water, sanitation and waste collection. By and large, these 'public services' were assumed to be suitable for planned intervention even within the market-dominated economies of the First World. Private sector involvement was considerable, but not viewed as a driving force or an approach to be encouraged. There seemed to be little reason to curtail state involvement and, in any case, faecal-oral diseases were no longer the prominent health problems they had once been, and the social and political debates over sanitary reform and how it should be organized were muted.

In the Communist and Socialist countries of the Second World, the planning model was, of course, more wholeheartedly adopted. Indeed, applying the narrow criteria of water and sanitation provision, the Second World was relatively successful. At least superficially, planning was well suited to providing basic services, including piped water and, to a lesser extent, sanitation. Even if plans could not always be realized on schedule, and resources were often used inefficiently, there was an epidemiological transition away from faecal-oral diseases as a major cause of death. As in the First World, local sanitary improvement moved off the political agenda. It was the lack of consumer goods rather than environmental services that created political disharmony.

In the emerging Third World of non-aligned, and predominantly low-income countries, a planning model of development was also favoured, and was typically applied to urban water and sanitation even more vigorously than in other sectors. The states of newly independent countries were inclined to view the lack of basic services as a colonial hold over whose redress would require centrally planned investments. For the growing band of Western 'development' experts, imbued with Keynesian economics and the model of the Marshall Plan, state-led infrastructure investment was an attractive means of priming the engine of growth of the 'underdeveloped' countries. Development aid also fostered a top-down approach to sanitary improvement. Urban water and sanitation projects were visible, and their benefits were generally accepted.

Numerous problems arose with the more ambitious post-Second World War attempts at planned urban improvement in Third World cities. Master plans, often multivolumed and replete with engineering details, rarely reconciled the gap between espousing good intentions and detailing how realistic targets could be achieved. In any case, many low-income urban settlements were located in areas where residential development was considered undesirable. In a typical master plan, informal settlements were not so much planned for as planned against or ignored. Often, planners' maps simply omitted large-scale squatter settlements, representing the land as open or undeveloped (Hardoy and Satterthwaite, 1989). Even if their location was not considered objectionable, there is an inherent tension in planning for low-income areas. The minimum level of technology that is politically acceptable often requires economic transfers that are not politically feasible.

While urban master plans are no longer common, a planning approach almost invariably dominates in public water and sanitation utilities (and, it should be noted, many private utilities as well). These are usually in charge of urban piped-water systems and articulated sewerage systems, and often have formal authority and responsibility for less centralized sanitation and public water systems as well. Again, large discrepancies often exist between the stated intentions of utilities' plans and policies, and the manner in which these plans and policies work themselves out in practice.

Especially in poor urban areas, changes in sanitary conditions are often very much influenced by formal government plans and policies, but rarely in the manner outlined in the official documents. For example, the adoption of the principle that an adequate water supply is a basic need which should be made affordable to all, ostensibly promotes the interests of the urban poor. When used as a principle for water-sector planning, however, the 'to all' can easily lose out to the 'affluent', with the outcome being cheap water for the wealthy and short supplies on an open or black market for the poor.

There are a variety of reasons why plans to extend water supplies to low-income urban areas tend to lose out to a pricing policy[2] when the two are in conflict. First, a public utility that keeps prices low, as required by the government, but fails to extend supplies as planned, can still claim to be *striving* to achieve the plan. In contrast, increasing the price of water substantially above the prescribed level can be taken as evidence of deliberate deviation from the plan, even when it is the only means for the utility to finance the planned expansion of the water supply system. Second, when the water tariff is changed by governmental decision, a price increase will have an immediate adverse effect on many, often affluent and politically articulate users simultaneously, and can be taken as a rallying sign for protesters. Extending piped-water connections, on the other hand, is inevitably sequential, and delays affect only small, often poor, groups. This can easily lead to a situation where revenue is forgone due to the price controls, but subsidies are not sufficient to allow system expansion.

---

2 Setting low water prices is often confused with subsidizing water. A subsidy consists of funds paid to the utility to enable them to sell water at a low price. For many utilities, fixed water prices are not fully subsidized, and the utility suffers financially in proportion to the amount of water it supplies at the set prices (Kjellén et al, 1996). This distinction is important inasmuch as some of the most pernicious effects that are typically ascribed to subsidies actually arise when price controls are *not* accompanied by commensurate subsidies

To the extent that controlling a utility's water price reduces the supply of water being made available, the result can easily become higher water prices for those who are forced to purchase resold water or water from alternative sources – typically including the residents of low-income areas. When water supplies at official prices cannot meet demand, the price of water sold on the informal retail market will depend on the quantity supplied and the location of these and alternative supplies, but not the price that the utility charges. In areas where water consumption is already minimal, demand is likely to be inelastic, so even a small decline in supplies can increase prices severalfold (Cairncross and Kinnear, 1991). Thus, if lowering the utility's price also reduces supply and restricts extension of the piped system, existing customers may benefit, but those purchasing on the retail market can end up paying far higher prices for less water. This applies even if the informal retail market is competitive. Often the retail market is non-competitive, raising informal sector prices still further. Moreover, if officials are illicitly capturing part of the excess profits arising from water scarcity, this can create further disincentives to expansion within the utility, reinforcing these inequities (Lovei and Whittington, 1991).

Applying a very narrow planning perspective, the solution to high prices in the informal sector is to extend price controls beyond the utility – to force the private sector to conform to the plan. Selling water at above official prices can be made illegal. Again, however, there are simple reasons why such measures tend to have perverse outcomes, especially when it is water scarcity rather than monopolistic behaviour that is causing the official/unofficial price differential. Putting vendors who sell at market prices out of business can decrease local supplies still further and force consumers on to a black market with still higher prices.

This tendency for low official water prices for connected households to be accompanied by high unofficial prices for unconnected households has been documented for a number of cities (Bhatia and Falkenmark, 1993). It is often cited in arguments in favour of a more market-oriented approach to the provision of water (Serageldin, 1994). Somewhat the same analysis is sometimes applied to the planned expansion of sanitary systems. The analogy between the water and sanitation services is imperfect. When the price-controlled services are not accessible, residents are not as willing to pay for high-priced sanitary services as for high-priced drinking-water. The costs of poor sanitation are more clearly collective than the costs of expensive or inadequate drinking-water. Moreover, the conventional technology of water closets and household connections to water-borne sewerage systems is far more expensive than water connections alone. In very low-income settings, the planned expansion of such systems is likely to be irrelevant.

It is important, however, not to lose sight of the successes that have also been achieved under the banner of planned water and sanitary systems. Under the right circumstances, the goal of affordable water for all can provide a rallying point for rapid improvement in deprived urban areas. A great deal depends on the political and economic context. Much of the rapid extension of water services to the favelas of São Paulo in the late 1970s and 1980s was achieved through a very centralized price-controlled system, but at a time when most of the rest of the city was already served, new sources of finance had become available, and social movements in low-income areas were able to exert pressure on the government (Briscoe, 1993; Kjellén et al, 1996; Munasinghe, 1992).

In many ways, household water connections and sewered water closets are particularly suited to the central planning model of sanitary improvement. As well as being attractive to users, experts can control the system closely. In the more capital-intensive systems, most of the water only leaves the water pipes momentarily before entering the drainage or sewerage pipes. The characteristics of the water/sanitation system can be described technically in considerable detail, the demands on the user are relatively circumscribed and independent of where people reside (as long as they are connected), and, once the system is in place, achieving good hygiene requires comparatively little labour and even less understanding of the mechanisms of disease transmission. A series of simple behavioural norms are what is required of the residents, and the utility can focus on overcoming engineering problems. Indeed, the most obvious attraction of piped water and sewerage is that they can be organized centrally, not that they are otherwise cost-effective (or environmentally optimal).

There are many technologies for providing water and sanitation to deprived urban neighbourhoods that are less costly than household water connections and sewered water closets. Often public standpipes and less expensive sanitation technologies are part of a centrally planned expansion of a public utility, even though most utilities do not feel as comfortable with these technologies. Alternatively, such technologies are often promoted through a more *ad hoc* project approach which, while it may not involve central planning as such, conforms by and large to the planning model. Especially in the post-Second World War period, the project approach to planned improvement received considerable support from development agencies. While current development rhetoric tends to advocate a process rather than a project approach to development aid, it is in large part the operational requirements of aid that created the project approach, and those operational requirements still influence practice.

Projects can be targeted to low-income urban areas, and to some degree this can overcome the problems that arise when low-priced water and sanitation services end up serving only the relatively wealthy. Where water and sanitation problems are serious, as often they are in poor urban neighbourhoods, the need for improvements can seem almost self-evident, particularly to an outsider. Something needs to be done, so it is necessary to work out what the best thing to do is, and to do it. Nobody could object to better water and sanitation. Surely it is just a question of adapting the technical solutions that are so successful in wealthy countries to the local context, perhaps consulting local residents on their preferences at strategic points. There are excellent books outlining the engineering options for sanitary improvement. One includes a 'sanitation technology selection algorithm' which leads one through a maize of questions to the appropriate type of technology (Mara, 1996). It would be easy to get the impression that improving sanitation is very much the sort of activity that can be moulded into projects and replicated widely.

However, there have also been serious problems with the more targeted, project-oriented approach to sanitary improvement. While experiences vary widely, projects too are often usurped by the wealthy, particularly where low-income urban dwellers are squatters or renters, and do not own the land. A project orientation also fosters a short-time horizon. A project is meant to have a beginning, a middle and an end. Projects are sometimes evaluated at completion, but rarely 5, 10 or 15 years later. Project managers, knowing that they will only be held responsible for the situation up to the end of the project, are more concerned to create a system that they can defend as currently operational and in principle capable of being maintained, than one that actually will continue to operate well. The problem of reconciling acceptable sanitation with unacceptable poverty also remains, if not in quite such an acute form as with centrally planned systems.

Whether the planning is integrated or project-based, once one has left the world of household services and entered a setting of multiple shared water sources, scarce public toilets, neighbourhood waste-collection sites, locally maintained drains and the like, planners who are unfamiliar with local conditions have little basis for designing and implementing improvements even when they want to. First, in conditions of poverty people face a range of very serious threats to their welfare, and it is presumptuous of sanitary experts or central authorities to decide unilaterally the level of public resources that should be devoted to sanitary improvement. Second, and probably more important, the operation of low-cost water and sanitary systems depend far more heavily on the local physical and social context than do the more capital-intensive systems.

Many of the behavioural patterns that determine how faecal-oral diseases spread have little to do with sanitation infrastructure, narrowly defined. How children work and play, for example, is not under planners' control. However, when sanitary facilities are rudimentary and medical care is lacking, children's behaviour can be critical to the spread of faecal-oral diseases. Whether children drink water in neighbours' homes, whether they play and defecate in the drains, how far they travel, whether they sleep in separate beds when they become ill: such behaviours not only influence the spread of disease but can determine how effective certain technical improvement efforts will be. Planned sanitary improvement cannot be expected to take account of such behaviour, let alone change it at will. When planners do try to prescribe behavioural change, they often ignore local realities. Mothers are admonished not to let siblings look after their infants, although the loss of income from devoting an adult's time to the task may be an even greater threat to health and welfare. Households are told that they can protect their children by boiling their water, although their children will continue to drink contaminated water elsewhere. Such examples abound.

Local physical specificities also stand in the way of effective planning. In a deprived area, there may be very significant differences in water quality between wells and water taps. A wide range of different technologies are perhaps being employed for both water storage and faecal disposal. Social practices and norms will have developed around the physical architecture of the water and sanitation system. The public tap or well may have become a location for socializing, or a site of conflict.

As a result of all these complexities and constraints, it is difficult for even a well-intentioned planner to decide what water and sanitary measures are needed. Designing and maintaining the physical infrastructure of a low-cost water and sanitation system requires a more detailed knowledge of local physical conditions and social practices than does providing every house with indoor plumbing, water closets and standardized refuse containers to be collected daily. The success of the system depends far more heavily on local practices and contributions. Add to this the fact that residents in deprived neighbourhoods typically have very little political power through which to make planners accountable to their needs, and the planning model as a means to environmental health looks fundamentally flawed.

As described below, the market model and the collective action model have their own problems. Both, however, incorporate local knowledge and priorities more directly into the decision-making process, at least in principle. In the market model, the resident as consumer sets priorities by deciding how much to pay for improvements, while in the collective action model the resident as participant contributes to the group decision. While the current unpopularity of the planning model probably owes more to the poor quality public services in affluent areas than to the lack of services in low-income neighbourhoods, the failure to respond to residents' demands has been central to the overall critique of planned sanitary improvement.

Many planners have recognized of course, the weaknesses of central planning, and most of the literature on planning for local environmental improvement are far removed from the 'study, plan, execute' version of the planning model. Indeed, enabling markets to work and engaging with stakeholders have become standard tasks assigned to planners. Nevertheless, planning does still tend to support narratives that at least implicitly suggest that planners know best, and critics often reinforce these narratives by blaming planners for making the wrong decisions rather than for being so presumptuous as to usurp so much decision-making power.

# THE MARKET MODEL

In the simplest version of market-led sanitary improvement, competing suppliers offer a range of services and technologies, and local residents pay for those that they feel best meet their needs and budget. It is up to the residents to decide whether it is worth buying more water or more food, whether to spend more on improving the structure of the house or the toilet, to put more money and effort into waste disposal or into transportation, and so on. In the idealized vision of the perfect market economy there is little or no role for the state beyond protecting property rights: economic affluence, technological options and residents' preferences determine sanitary conditions. In practice, the market approach to sanitary improvement typically concentrates on increasing the role of market mechanisms, but not to the point of eliminating the role of the state. The more attenuated versions of the market model emphasize getting prices (or more generally financing) 'right' in public utilities, promoting competition where the private sector operates, and privatizing public systems or subsystems when there is no overwhelming reason not to.

Historically, some of the least regulated markets for urban water and sanitation were in the rapidly growing, and very unhealthy cities of 19th-century Europe and North America. The sanitary movement led some of the first incursions on the part of the nascent 'public sector' into the market economy of 19th-century Britain. Whereas patronage and interference in people's private affairs had come to be seen by many as vestiges of feudalism, the sanitary movement was thoroughly modern and underwrote a new form of top-down intervention, ostensibly based upon impersonal science rather than social superiority.

The advantages of free trade were widely proclaimed in many spheres in the 19th century, but the market model (capitalism) was widely seen as a means to economic success rather than public health. By and large, the unhealthy 'masses' of urban poor were the dark side of capitalism rather than the beneficiaries of improved markets. Mortality rates were far higher in urban areas where markets abounded than in the surrounding, more tradition-bound countryside. It would have been a difficult time for even the most ardent market advocates to argue that the urban water and sanitation systems needed a dose of unfettered markets. And while actual sanitary improvements involved far more than planned intervention, the planning model eventually managed to take much of the credit for the sanitary revolution.

In the light of this history, it is somewhat ironic that markets and privatization have recently been promoted as the means to improve access to water and sanitation, and to help ensure the sustainability of the water supply system. Given the very short historical perspective of most policy debates, however, it is not particularly surprising. At the start of the 20th century, recent experience with market failures had helped to convince many that the public sector had to wrest responsibility for water and sanitation from the private sector. Near the end of the 20th century, recent experience with public failures has helped to convince many that the private sector must hold the key to improving water and sanitation. Perhaps the most serious concern looking to the future is that throughout the century an emphasis on the public–private dichotomy tended to suppress institutional innovation. Debates cast in terms of markets versus plans diverted attention from critical questions about how planning and markets interact, how both can be improved upon, and what other institutional forms can and do play an important role. This dichotomy may be less central than it once was, but it is still implicit in the numerous attempts either to defend public sector control (now relatively rare) or promote more private sector involvement (which is still very common).

Numerous different forms of private sector involvement in water and sanitation have been identified (Johnstone et al, 1999). Much of the academic discussion of privatization revolves around different combinations of private and public management and regulation, the characteristics of particular components of water and sanitation provisioning systems, and the appropriate roles for private enterprise and the public sector (Easter and Feder, 1996; Nickson, 1997). In the international policy arena, however, the debate was often reduced to pro- versus anti-privatization, with the pro side more vocal and the anti side relying on entrenched power (which was eroded more quickly than many anticipated).

Among supporters of the market model, 'subsidies' are frowned on and private vendors are typically portrayed as providing an important service whatever price they charge. Public utilities, by way of contrast, are portrayed as being inherently disinclined to take consumers' demands seriously, and inclined towards inefficiency and financial mismanagement. At times, poor residents are granted exception in the pro-market arguments: well-targeted subsidies are allowed. It is often argued, however, that the urban poor are willing to pay the full cost for a good water service, and that this is evidenced by the prices so often paid to vendors and the responses even low-income dwellers give in contingent valuation surveys (see Chapter 6). And if people are willing to pay a price that reflects the true cost for a good water service, so the argument goes, why charge them less? There are better means of providing economic benefits to those in poverty, and unless water is charged at cost, it will be wasted.

Overall, the aspect of the market model that probably received the most support in the early 1990s, before privatization took hold, was cost recovery through user fees, especially with reference to water. Even publicly owned utilities are under pressure to adopt more commercial practices, and indeed some have done so very successfully (Blokland et al, 1999). More generally, it is commonly argued that water needs to be treated as a 'normal' commodity and that more competition is needed in the water and sanitation sector (Crane, 1992, for example).

Many of the arguments in favour of a more market-oriented approach to water have been spearheaded by officials of the World Bank (Briscoe and Garn, 1995; Munasinghe, 1992; Serageldin, 1994; World Bank Water Demand Research Team, 1993), but have been accepted by a large part of the development establishment. Especially in the 1980s and early 1990s, these arguments draw heavily on a somewhat simplistic interpretation of free market economics which became very influential with the resurgence of neoliberalism in the last quarter of the 20th century. As privatization became a reality, however, more practical arguments became necessary.

According to advocates of the market model, the old view that governments must take primary responsibility for financing, managing and operating services is defunct, and a new view is arising that assigns a far lesser role to governments:

*A remarkable consensus has been emerging in recent years for managing water resources and for delivering water supply and sanitation services on an efficient, equitable, and sustainable basis. At the heart of this consensus are two closely related guiding principles enunciated at the 1992 Dublin International Conference on Water and the Environment, which preceded the United Nations Conference on Environment and Development (UNCED – the Earth Summit) the same year:*

- *Water has an economic value in all its competing uses and should be recognized as an economic good.*
- *Water development and management should be based on a participatory approach, involving users, planners and policy makers at all levels, with decisions taken at the lowest appropriate level.*

...

*The new consensus gives prime importance to one central tenet (long familiar to students of public finance) that should underlie the financing of water resources management and water supply and sanitation services. According to this tenet, both efficiency and equity require that private financing be used for financing private goods and that public resources be used only for financing public goods* (Serageldin, 1994, p17).

While the two principles ascribed here to the Dublin conference could be interpreted in any number of ways, those with a market orientation see an attack on subsidies (which do not treat water as an economic good) and central planning (which does not allow decisions to be taken at the lowest appropriate level), and a commitment to use the market except when it would clearly be inappropriate.[3]

Perhaps surprisingly, most of the criteria being proposed to determine when markets are appropriate are, as Serageldin notes, long familiar to students of public finance (Bahl and Linn, 1992). Indeed, they are by and large the same criteria once used to justify government control over water supply and sanitation. An important shift lies in the burden of proof which market advocates wish to place on those who would like to invoke public authorities. There has also been a shift in opinion concerning what ought to be a set of independent empirical questions in favour of those findings which support the market model. Both of these shifts have undoubtedly been facilitated by the failures in existing public sector utilities, combined with the fact that the public sector is generally in a period of retrenchment rather than expansion.

One of the more evident shifts in opinion concerns who is considered to have the requisite knowledge to decide where piped water supplies are needed and what type of water service is appropriate. From the traditional planning perspective, described and criticized in the previous section, it is the health experts and engineers who hold the answers. They are in the best position to decide if a lack of water in any given area is a health threat, and what sort of technical and behavioural changes are needed. From a pro-market perspective, on the other hand, the more serious problem is to make the utilities more responsive to residents' concerns. This market argument is, of course, much more convincing if residents are knowledgeable about health matters, or at least have desires that are consistent with achieving health. The market argument can also garner support from uncertainty in epidemiology: if experts do not know the routes through which diseases are transmitted, why not let residents decide for themselves what improvements are needed? (On the other hand, if residents believe that the government should be responsible for water and sanitation services, the market advocate's respect for local knowledge typically declines, and past planning efforts are blamed for creating a culture of dependence.)

A second shift in opinion has been in the extent to which water and sanitation are perceived to be providing public goods. As indicated in the quotation on the previous page, the market-oriented approach to water and sanitation provision accepts that public funds should be applied to public goods. Economists define a public good as one that, if it benefits anyone, benefits everyone (or at least a restricted 'public'). Public goods are hard to sell on the market, since even those

---

3 Neither market advocates nor detractors need agree with Serageldin's claim that the public goods argument implies a lead role for 'social units' that are at the right scale for the public good in question. Many such 'social units' will not have the legitimacy to claim to act on behalf of the concerned public

who do not buy them will be able to consume them. They are comparatively easy for the public sector to provide, since they are not depleted by overuse. Advocates of planning have tended to view public health, or more specifically the control of infectious diseases, as a public good. By implication, if water and sanitation facilities contribute to public health, they are at least indirectly providing public goods.[4] Market advocates, on the other hand, tend to emphasize the private benefits of water, and really only accept the final disposal of sewerage as posing a public good problem. A systematic attempt at providing a classification is given in the World Bank's policy paper on water resources management (World Bank, 1993b). Serageldin makes a clear case for water being a private good:

> *The provision of water supply to the households carries several benefits. Households themselves value a convenient, reliable, and abundant water supply because of the time savings, amenity benefits, and, to a varying degree, health benefits. Because these "private" benefits constitute the bulk of the overall benefits of a household water supply, the public finance allocation principle dictates that most of the costs of such supplies should be borne by householders themselves. When this is the case, households make appropriate decisions on the type of service they want (for example, a communal tap, a yard tap, or multiple taps in the household). The corollary is that because this is principally a "private good," most of the financing for the provision of water supply services should be generated from user charges sufficient to cover the economic costs of inputs (including both the direct financial cost of inputs such as capital and labor and the opportunity cost of water as an input) (Serageldin, 1994, p19).*

This argument that households should be made to pay the full cost of water has been further buttressed by a shift in position concerning how much even low-income urban households are willing to pay for adequate water services and (more equivocally) adequate sanitation. If it is indeed true that, given the opportunity, people would willingly pay for adequate water and sanitation for selfish reasons, then it is not really necessary to debate whether there are public benefits as well. The evidence for this purported willingness to pay comes from two sources. First, as noted in the previous section, the high prices that low-income vendor users pay for water would seem to suggest a high willingness to pay (Bhatia and Falkenmark, 1993). Second, there have been contingent valuation studies indicating

---

[4] In somewhat different terms, the public goods argument has long been used to defend state-led sanitary improvement. During the 19th-century sanitary movement, poor sanitation was portrayed as a threat to the nation, either directly by undermining the health of the armed forces (Shapiro, 1985, p154) or indirectly by corroding the moral fabric of society (Vigarello, 1988, pp192–201). Poor sanitation was also viewed as a threat to the health of more sanitary dwellers in nearby neighbourhoods (Wohl, 1983)

a high willingness to pay, even in rural areas where it has traditionally been assumed that willingness to pay should be low (World Bank Water Demand Research Team, 1993). Unfortunately, a large share of this research has been sponsored by the World Bank, which was aligned with the market model before the research began.

Neither the argument that local water and sanitation problems involve essentially private goods, nor the argument that low-income urban residents are individually willing to pay the cost for adequate provision, are very convincing to those who are not already inclined to favour the market. It is precisely in areas where there are serious public health problems that neither water nor sanitation provides only private goods (although water is far closer to being a private good in the strict economic sense, which undoubtedly explains the emphasis on water among private sector advocates). Alternatively, while there is no doubt that even poor households will and often do pay very high costs for inadequate water and sanitation facilities, the very minimal level of water and sanitation that, if necessary, residents will pay a high price to achieve does not necessarily ensure public health. In many areas of Jakarta, an often-cited example of high vendor prices, the people who are paying the high prices are buying just drinking- and cooking-water, and have little choice as their ground water is saline. In such cases, high prices do not imply a willingness to pay for wash water, which is critical to health.

The advocacy of the markets has also involved questioning the view that poor urban dwellers have a right to affordable water and sanitation. The issue of rights to particular goods has been the target of a very broad-based free-market critique of government service provision. If people would rather have more food than more water, on what grounds does a government decide that public funds should be devoted to meeting their 'right' to more water? Why not tax these same people less (or provide them with financial transfers) and let them decide what to do with the money? If what is at issue is that the poor deserve more than they get, do they not also deserve to be allowed to choose what they get?[5] While such questions have been debated in a number of contexts, the more telling criticism in many cities of the developing world is that it is not the poor who receive the low-cost services in the first place. But this is really a criticism of planning practice, rather than a defence of markets per se.

Finally, concerns about the monopolization of water have shifted. One of the traditional arguments in favour of public (over private) water utilities is that urban piped-water systems are prone to monopolization. There are significant returns to scale, and once a company has a piped water system in place there are appreciable barriers to entry. Non-piped water supply systems can be very competitive, but if

---

5 Because the free-market argument has become closely associated with a more general criticism of economic support to the disadvantaged, the arguments concerning more efficient means to help the disadvantaged are often neglected

there are only a few point sources, these are easily monopolized. Monopolists tend to supply too little and charge too much. This is an especially serious danger when insufficient water use is facilitating the transmission of infectious diseases, as is the case in many deprived urban neighbourhoods.

The dangers of monopolization are recognized by most market advocates, but they generally argue that regulation rather than public service provision is the appropriate response. A public utility is itself a monopoly and often the state acts to suppress private sector entrepreneurs who arise in competition with a public utility. There is also the danger that public sector employees will attempt to capture some of the monopoly profits that the public utility cannot claim because its prices are controlled. Thus, residents or private vendors can end up having to pay bribes to obtain water connections. The utility may even be inhibited from expanding the piped system if this might eliminate a lucrative black market for water rights (Lovei and Whittington, 1993). Even if the water utility is to remain public, market advocates may recommend promoting private competition as a means of preventing excessive mark-ups by vendors. Thus, where plan advocates tend to interpret the high prices that private vendors charge as evidence that they should be curbed, market advocates tend to interpret it as evidence that there should be more (competing) private vendors (Crane, 1994). Alternatively, the fact that government control of the water system does not have worse effects is sometimes ascribed to the existence of informal, and often black, markets for water in urban areas (Blore, 1989).

In promoting a 'new' more market-oriented approach to water and sanitation, it is common to compare some of the harsher realities of poorly planned improvements with an optimistic vision of what can be done with effective government regulation and competitive markets. The market model comes out looking good in part because the ideal market operates far better than the real planner does. A general disenchantment with planning clearly informs much of the discussion. Subsidies are blamed for the failure of public utilities to extend water to poor urban neighbourhoods, when one could equally well blame the insufficiency of the subsidies (see footnote 2, this chapter). It is assumed that more commercially minded utilities would provide services to low-income households willing to pay the cost, when in many cities far more lucrative opportunities lie in improving services to the wealthy. If the utilities were to adopt a profit-oriented strategy, these improvements could tie up indefinitely the limited capital that is available.

As regards deprived urban areas, many of the weak points of the market model are actually rather similar to those of the planning model. The notion that good water and sanitation are discrete services that can be purchased by households is not so very different from the notion that they are discrete services that can be provided by the government. The complex interconnections which arise in low-income settlements, where services are shared and facilities are scarce, remain just as much of a problem for individualized market solutions as for centralized state solutions. If tenure disputes deter public utilities from providing public services, they also deter individual households from investing in private solutions.[6] To claim that individual households are sufficiently knowledgeable to become the driving force in water and sanitation improvement is not all that much more satisfactory than assigning the role to outside experts: both have valuable knowledge which somehow needs to be brought to bear. And while it may be inappropriate to place responsibility on a distant government, unaware and uninterested in local conditions, it may be just as inappropriate to give full responsibility to private enterprises serving individuals and households who, acting independently through the market, have little incentive to contribute to better neighbourhood conditions.

In practice, of course, private enterprise covers a wide range of very diverse institutional forms. Multinational companies have little in common with informal sector operators, even if both are private enterprises. Ideally, the market determines which is the more efficient for any particular role. But even if the public sector regulates large private utilities, from a local perspective many of the difficulties in engaging with large centralized organizations remain.

At least some of the problems that are inherent in the market and planning models are overcome in the collective action model applied at a neighbourhood level. This third model is explored briefly in the following section. Somewhat analogously to the market model, one of the conclusions is that it is important not to compare the harsh realities of alternative models (in this case market and public failures) with idealistic visions of what communities ought to be able to achieve.

## THE LOCAL COLLECTIVE ACTION MODEL

In the simplest version of the collective action model, residents organize, decide what sort of sanitary improvements are necessary, determine how they are to be achieved, and bring about their implementation. As with the market model, it is the resident's concerns rather than paternal or expert opinions that guide the improvement effort. As with the planning model, however, the resulting sanitation strategy is the articulation of a common agenda rather than the outcome of an 'invisible' hand. When, in the face of government neglect, residents get together

---

6 Tenants as well as illegal and quasi-legal residents are often reluctant to invest in sanitation lest they are evicted or have their rent increased, as are landlords who do not see the advantage for them: theoretically, the landlords can recoup the investment through higher rents, but the price signal is only weakly transmitted to them, if at all (Sandy Cairncross, personal communication)

to build a communal toilet, improve the local drainage or arrange to have waste removed, this conforms to the collective action model. But also, when the residents collectively negotiate with public utilities or other governmental or private sector actors, this can be seen as a more attenuated version of the collective action model.[7]

If, in recent years, the market model has been promoted in opposition to the planning model, variations on the local collective action model have often been promoted in opposition to both the planning and market models. This local collective action model sometimes appears as a recent child of socialist ideals and decentralized politics. Thus, many attempts to 'reinvent' collective action are oriented towards local as opposed to national organization, but attempt to challenge the individualism of the 'neo-liberal orthodoxy' (Crouch and Marquand, 1995). Alternatively, markets and local collective action are often presented as two sides of the New Policy Agenda, which combines market economics with local democracy, and favours NGOs for the provision of services where markets are deficient (Robinson, 1994). But local collective action, and more generally the idealization of small communities, also has a long history.

For many, 'community' has connotations of idealized pre-industrial social groupings, largely autonomous of centralizing states or individualizing markets. For some, it represents a form of social solidarity that goes far beyond expedient association, and that has been undermined by modernization and urbanization (as in Ferdinand Tönnies' pioneering work *Gemeinschaft and Geselschaft*). The term 'community' not only has an intellectual pedigree, but has long been part of the Eurocentric debates about how society as a whole ought to be organized, as well as how low-income settlements should be assisted. The utopian communities proposed by Socialist thinkers such as Robert Owens could be said to involve a community-based local collective action model. Alternatively, paternalistic attempts to assist low-income residents involved a less radical form of community develop- ment, also common in 19th-century Europe.

Many proponents of urban sanitary reform in the 19th century recognized the need to moderate the pursuit of private ends with collective action. As one contemporary put it, 'Private interests are not allowed to interfere with State or municipal development. It is recognized that the welfare of each citizen is best secured by promoting the well being of the community' (Ladd, 1990, p28). By

---

7 In the simple collective action model discussed here, the collectivity that is acting is presented as if it could be based upon expedient association alone. However, in many discussions of communities and local collective action, there is at least the implicit claim that communities can and indeed ought to be much more, and should form part of each member's own identity (Bell, 1993)

and large, however, the imagined community was civil society, or the relatively small elite at the pinnacle of a city's social scale, and the appropriate vehicle for collective action was assumed to be municipal government. The sanitary reforms that eventually won the day were part of a paternalistic agenda that was unlikely to sponsor community empowerment in working-class neighbourhoods as a means of achieving its goals. Some radical communitarians were concerned with sanitary reform, but were never sufficiently successful to have much influence on society at large.

Even when the planning approach to sanitary improvement was at its height, local collective action was often a basis for environmental management in urban neighbourhoods where centralized environmental services and regulations did not reach. But the notion that local collective action should become the motive force for sanitary improvement, displacing, if not replacing, the role of state planning or market forces was not evident. Indeed, when urban sanitary conditions in Europe and America were at their worst, they were often blamed on poor communities' growing incapacity to manage their own environments. Assisting communities to improve their own sanitation was a way of helping to foster the planned sanitary improvement.

In post-Second World War development theory, community development and community participation have taken on a range of changing meanings (Abbott, 1996). For a time, community development was closely associated with modernization theory and treated as a means to mobilize communities to achieve the planned development path. When modernization theory came into disfavour, so did this form of community development. A common criticism of the community development approach was that it failed to redress the lack of power wielded by low-income communities. More radical critics argued that a change in the balance of power was needed, and portrayed community-development programmes as reinforcing existing relations of dependency (despite the explicit goal of most community development efforts to create more democratic processes). However, community participation has continued to be a commonly advocated goal, albeit with participation interpreted in a variety of ways ranging from providing labour or making financial contributions to taking full control over the development process.

As with markets, the perceived failure of the planning model has added credence to alternatives based upon local collective action. For those who subscribe to socialist goals but not statist mechanisms, grass-roots organizations (GROs) have obvious attractions, not only for sanitary but also for other reforms. Simultaneously, local collective action is less threatening to the commercial private sector than central planning. It is possible to envisage NGOs and GROs providing for needs that markets will not serve, in an economy where distribution is primarily a market process. Since, in addition, the opposition between markets and local collective action has had no geopolitical basis analogous to the East–West conflict, the policy debates have been less polarized.

In the environmental field, strengthening or building communities is often portrayed as a means of combating degradation, in contemporary rural (Berkes, 1989) and urban (Douglass et al, 1994) settings. The concept of community is central, for example, to Daly and Cobb's well-known environmental and moral critique of the market model, and the growth oriented industrial economy they believe it has engendered (Daly and Cobb Jr, 1990). Many have argued that regenerating communities is central to achieving sustainable development (Ekins, 1995). A comparatively radical variant of environmentalism is associated with 'decentralized communitarianism' (Harvey, 1996, p180), and the image of ecologically as well as socially self-reliant communities.

In the context of urban development, strengthening communities is often presented as particularly suitable to the development of low-income neighbourhoods. John Turner, best known for advocating self-help strategies, portrays 'building communities' as the best means to pursue housing improvement, given the limitations of state and market-based approaches (Gilbert, 1994; Turner, 1996). More generally, while community participation in urban management is often taken to be desirable everywhere, it is more often portrayed as necessary in low-income communities where both government and private finance is lacking, and more difficult for local residents to control.

Given the emphasis on community participation as regards both environmental management and the development of low-income neighbourhoods, it is not surprising that community participation to address environmental problems in low-income neighbourhoods has received considerable attention (Douglass et al, 1994; Douglass and Zoghlin, 1994; Yacoob et al, 1994). More specifically, community participation is often portrayed as critical to the success of water and sanitation projects as well as more broad-based improvement efforts, and there is a large literature on the topic stretching back a number of years (IRC International Water and Sanitation Centre, 1988; Kemper and Widstrand, 1991; Wijk-Sijbesma, 1979). In the water and sanitation field, community participation is typically considered particularly suitable for rural and low-income urban settlements.

There are a number of features that can make local collective action seem an obvious organizational choice for sanitary improvement in poor urban neighbourhoods. First, and for the reasons outlined above, sanitary improvement in disadvantaged neighbourhoods can be characterized as a spatially localized public good, requiring a local public response. Second, local knowledge about environmental conditions and existing practices is particularly relevant where centralized services are lacking. Also, for many local water and sanitation problems, good communication and principled negotiation within the neighbourhood could serve to share knowledge locally, to direct attention to the right problems and to reconcile different interests. And more generally, local participation is desirable from a range of political perspectives. These potential advantages of local collective action for sanitary improvement are examined in turn below.[8]

Only a few of the sanitary burdens in contemporary deprived urban neighbourhoods seriously impinge on the rest of the city, let alone more distant human settlements. Epidemics are the obvious exception. Historically, epidemics have pushed urban sanitation on to the centre of the urban policy arena since they make even localized sanitation problems a potential threat to all social groups. Contemporary epidemics have much the same impact, but the major sanitation-related health problems are now endemic diseases. The burden of endemic faecal-oral diseases is more restricted to deprived urban areas and of less concern to the urban elite. Within the deprived urban areas, however, they still constitute a major threat to public health.[9] In terms of a public sector/private sector opposition, this would seem to justify public sector involvement. Since the public threat is spatially more localized, however, it is an even better justification for local collective action. Moreover, if the public involved is comparatively small, the obstacles to collective action should be fewer (Olson, 1975). Just as local common property regimes have been recognized increasingly as a potentially viable alternative to either state control or private ownership as a means of managing rural resources (Berkes, 1989), so local collective action is being increasingly recognized as an alternative means to pursue local environmental management in urban neighbourhoods.

In addition to involving at least some public goods and localized externalities, environmental services in low-income areas are often public in the sense of being used by many households. Standpipes, wells, toilets, waste-disposal sites and bathing facilities are often shared. While this does not rule out private ownership and market mechanisms, it can add considerably to the transaction costs. Whether these facilities are developed and maintained appropriately can depend very much on the ability of local residents to organize and act together in their collective interests. This may involve residents in a communal house, residents of a particular block or neighbourhood, or particular groups within a neighbourhood. Regardless, it is commonly assumed that a more cohesive community will be in a better position to manage these public facilities. More generally, the large differences

---

8 In the context of development projects, a number of additional advantages are often ascribed to community participation, with participation defined to include local contributions of either labour or finance. However, such forms of participation do not involve collective action, and the arguments are more akin to those made in defence of the market model

9 To the extent that sanitary conditions affect the manner in which pathogens spread between cities and evolve over time, sanitation remains a public health problem for all groups that are significantly at risk from faecal-oral diseases. According to some researchers, these effects are potentially very significant and need to be taken seriously (Ewald, 1993; Ewald, 1994; Krause, 1992)

observed in the environmental conditions of low-income urban neighbourhoods is often ascribed to the residents' ability to act together in their own collective interests (Bapat and Crook, 1984).

Even when services are provided by the public or private sector, there are complex public dimensions on the receiving end, particularly if the services are rudimentary. Ben Okri's fictional account of a conflict between a nightsoil (human faeces) collector and local residents illustrates nicely the complexity of the social relations involved:

*Some children from a nearby house took to mocking one of the nightsoil men. He was the clumsiest of the lot. He carried a very big bucket and he staggered and weaved and made strange snorting noises. The children made fun of him in songs. When he stopped and faced them and made his strange noises to drive them away they ran to their home and disturbed the elders who were engrossed in their drinking and their arguments. After a while the children went back and tormented the nightsoil man and threw stones at him. One of the stones hit the bucket and made a hollow sound. Omovo avoided treading on it.*

*The nightsoil man stopped again. His eyes blazed and his neck was strong and sweat poured down his forehead. He snorted angrily and tried kicking up sand at the kids, but he staggered, cried out, steadied himself with a phenomenal and pathetic effort, and the children laughed even louder. Omovo wanted to shout at the children. But before he could, the exasperated nightsoil man brought up his free hand, in which was a short broom, then he proceeded to flick the contents of the bucket at the children. They ran, screaming and laughing in innocent wickedness. The nightsoil man followed them. The terrible load wobbled on his head.*

*The elders, who had been drinking, spitting, unmindful of their children's mischief, looked up and saw the grim apparition. One of them shouted: 'Hey, what's wrong with you?' 'Wetin you want?' cried another.*

*The elders got up. The nightsoil man chose his moment. With the awkward and sometimes wicked dignity that comes with such labours, the nightsoil man struggled, snorted, and then deposited the bucket right in front of the elders, in admonishment for the bad training of their children. The effect was staggering* (*Dangerous Love*, Ben Okri, pp266–267).

There are, of course, limits to the notion that since sanitary problems are public locally, they ought to be made the responsibility of local institutions. Neither people nor pathogens act within well-defined boundaries. To the extent that there are physical boundaries, the spatial congruence of the physical and institutional dimensions is hard to achieve, even on the local scale. Socially identifiable communities are unlikely to correspond to particular 'drainage districts' (and indeed need not be spatially organized at all). Although it is possible to distinguish between the public and domestic domains in the transmission of disease (Cairncross et al, 1995), in neither domain is transmission tightly bounded.

A simplistic interpretation of the notion that community institutions can take responsibility for community-level sanitary problems inevitably ignores the complex range of boundary problems that arise in relation to local water and sanitation problems (Kolsky, 1992). However boundaries are defined (including even non-spatial boundaries for intralocal responsibilities, such as responsibility for managing public toilets), externalities will arise within the community. And if the boundaries are between spatially designated communities, inevitably there will be spill-over effects, involving human waste, water and the movement of people that mean that one community's health depends in part on the sanitary conditions in nearby communities. Such externalities help to explain why wastewater treatment always lags behind drinking-water treatment (ibid).

If these boundary problems are to be addressed, some sort of higher level organization is likely to be necessary. There are institutions, including customs relating to sanitation and child care, that extend over quite large geographical areas but do not involve any higher level authority or organization (indeed, the spread of ideas and customs is in many ways analogous to the spread of infectious diseases (Sperber, 1996)). Even more formal community-based organizations often have a scattered membership. But these diffuse forms of what, at a stretch, could still be termed collective action, do not form the basis for a model of sanitary improvement. Overall, local collective action could conceivably address many, but by no means all, of the public goods/externalities problems associated with sanitary improvement.

The second argument in favour of local collective action noted above is the importance of local (often tacit) knowledge and the assumption that local collective action will be based on this knowledge. Again, this applies especially where there is very little infrastructure or household-level services. In deprived urban neighbourhoods, there are a wide range of questions to which local knowledge can be brought to bear: where it would be most convenient to site a public tap and how it should be designed, whether people want and would use a public toilet, whether children are defecating in the open or playing in the drains and if so how they could be prevented from doing so, how solid waste should best be handled, and so on. Some of the relevant issues relate primarily to local preferences and practices that an outsider would typically be ignorant of. There may also be environmental hazards that outsiders simply would not think of, but which are self-evident to a local resident.

Even strong supporters of the community model must accept that scientific knowledge has added a great deal to our ability to understand and address sanitation problems. An advocate for a somewhat attenuated community action model can accept this, but argue that to the extent that this knowledge is practical, it needs to be put into the hands of the community. Thus, rather than having planners attempt to access local knowledge to improve their plans, communities should access scientific knowledge to improve their collective action. Yet again, this is particularly critical in areas lacking centralized environmental services. Someone with piped water and a flush toilet can be given a few simple hygiene rules to follow, but such rules are hard to adapt to the far more varied and hazardous conditions in most deprived urban areas where there are different water sources of varying quality and accessibility, a range of possible (often recycled) containers that can be used to store water, various types and locations of latrines, numerous possible waste-disposal practices, and so on.

Simultaneously, the discussion and negotiation involved in local collective action should in principal allow both the local and the scientific knowledge held within the community to be shared. This is, arguably, an advantage over the market model where people and households act individually, or the planning model where central authorities take the key decisions. And what is shared may include an understanding of the perceptions and priorities of other community members. This should reinforce appropriate local norms and institutions that are suitable to the local specificities, both physical and social.

As with many of the arguments for central planning and markets, while these practical arguments do point to certain advantages of local collective action, they do not demonstrate that it should be the primary basis for sanitary improvement in deprived urban areas. It would undoubtedly be advantageous if scientific knowledge could be combined with local knowledge, and put in the hands of local residents. It would undoubtedly be a good thing if communal facilities and sanitation measures reflected a locally negotiated consensus or compromise. But such goals are difficult and time consuming to achieve. There is no reason to assume that they will automatically result from simply giving communities more political space. Thus, not surprisingly, the more ardent advocates of the local collective action model also strongly favour local empowerment on broader political grounds.

To caricature the local collective action advocate once again, her/his position is that residents of deprived urban areas are the politically as well as economically disadvantaged, so measures that transfer power from the state or commercial interests to such localities improve societal equity. While the planning model reinforces the power of the state, and the market model divides the residents and allows decision-making power to follow economic resources, local collective action lets local residents take control. More generally, the local collective action model at least superficially corresponds to what has been termed 'bottom-up', as opposed to 'top-down' development strategies, with all the political connotations that entails.

Unfortunately, as widely recognized in the literature on community participation, government neglect and even manipulation can parade as a purposeful devolution of control to communities. Indeed, the lack of public funds for public service provision has been an important force acting in support of a regressive variant of the local collective action model for sanitary improvement. Especially in Africa, but also elsewhere, recent decades have seen increasing pressure put on government budgets. For a national or local government that is unable to finance even minimal services for a large share of its citizens, there is an obvious attraction in having local residents organize and undertake their own sanitary improvements (provided these efforts do not involve simply displacing the problems on to neighbouring communities). This can become very inequitable, particularly when participation is treated as especially suitable to disadvantaged areas or groups.

Allowing communities to participate in deciding how things are to be done can easily slide into attempts to have low-income communities organize and finance services that are subsidized in other parts of the city. Similar complaints can be levelled against attempts to increase the participation of particular groups within the community, such as women. Simplifying the participatory message runs the risk of 'overburdening already very busy people, and focusing exclusively on women may exclude other categories of residents with untapped resources and time' (Vaa, 1995, p9). Clearly, this is not the intent of most advocates of participation, but it can be the effect of the participatory approach.

There have been numerous attempts over the years to draw a sharp distinction between 'true' participation leading to empowerment on the one hand and 'false' participation involving manipulation on the other (Abbott, 1996). However, this has not eliminated the problem noted in the previous paragraph, and if applied generally is in danger of misrepresenting sincere attempts to improve the sustainability and effectiveness of development projects. As many critics of the community development strategy of the 1950s and 1960s noted, it is not really possible to determine whether a particular organizational form is empowering without reference to the broader political context within which the actors are situated. This still holds and, as Desai notes, one 'basic problem is that many ideologists of participation want politics without politics' (Desai, 1994, p169). But if, as the more politically oriented advocates suggest, true community participation requires profound changes in societal power relations, then the justification for developing the approach with respect to sanitary improvement is lost unless it can become part of a broader process.

At least within the formal arena, the best hope for a more broad-based application of the local collective action model still lies in the NGOs and GROs which have come to play a significant, though still quite limited, role in urban development. Unfortunately, their record has been mixed. Many of the most redoubtable proponents of the NGO sector recognize the importance of 'biting the magic bullet' and paying more attention to making NGOs more accountable, although how and to whom is still hotly debated (Edwards and Hulme, 1995).

A related problem for any simple model of local collective action is that providing external support for local collective action runs the risk of seriously distorting it. If it is by pleasing outsiders that NGOs and GROs are the best able to survive, then it is doubtful whether they should really be described as being based on *local* collective action. On the other hand, there will never be the perfect community, acting autonomously and in unison, any more than there will ever be the perfect market or the perfect plan, perfectly implemented. So when things go wrong, it will always be possible for the true believer to lay the blame on the fact that communities were not sufficiently empowered (just as planners typically can lay the blame on the fact that the plan was imperfectly implemented and neoclassical economists can lay the blame on market imperfections). Thus, while ostensibly local initiatives can be seriously manipulated by external (or minority) interests, it is difficult to distinguish unacceptable manipulation from inevitable deviations from the ideal.

In sum, as with planning and markets, it is easy to envisage local collective action contributing to sanitary improvement (and having a number of other benefits), but difficult even to imagine it becoming a motive force to which planning and markets would be subsumed. Moreover, the very fact that many of the perceived advantages of fostering local collective action are political rather than specific to the sanitary field is indicative of the importance of the political context within which the improvements are being pursued.

## HYBRID MODELS

It is tempting to conclude that the best means to organize sanitary improvement is to find the appropriate roles for the state, markets and local organization, and to develop a hybrid model. Markets and private enterprise could be given free reign where externalities and public goods problems were minimal. Infrastructure with high returns to scale or prone to monopolization could be heavily regulated (and perhaps even owned) by the central government. The appropriate levels of government could intervene to correct externalities within their scale of operations (eg city government dealing with intraurban externalities). GROs, with the assistance of NGOs, could help to fill the gaps and ensure both that the state fulfils its responsibilities and that the private enterprises do not attempt to gain monopoly or political power.

In short, each sector should build upon its strengths and become complementary rather than competing contributors to sanitary improvement. In contemporary jargon, the state would become 'enabling' (Serageldin et al, 1995b), there would be 'private–public partnerships' (Lewis and Miller, 1987; Serageldin et al, 1995a) and simultaneously community participation would be promoted. Ultimately, the strengths of the various sectors would not only be combined, but they would engage in coproduction, create 'synergies' (Evans, 1996b; Ostrom, 1996) and tap a range of 'win-win' opportunities.

As a critique of much existing practice, there is a great deal to be said for taking a hybrid approach that explicitly recognizes both the weaknesses and strengths of states, markets and voluntary associations. It must also be recognized, however, that these strengths and weaknesses depend on the physical, institutional and cultural contexts within which the institutions are operating. Moreover, even just considering these three institutional forms, it is difficult to construct an abstract hybrid model that is likely to gain the sort of support that has accompanied the planning model, the state model or the voluntary association models in their heydays.

Bowles and Gintes' attempt to propose a 'realistic' utopia for the economy as a whole is grounded on the relative strengths of the state, markets and communities, and in many ways comes close to a hybrid model (Bowles and Gintes, 1998). They note that in a world of perfect information, virtually any institutional form would be able to operate efficiently, but that without perfect information various coordination problems can undermine efficiency. From this viewpoint, the comparative efficiency of different institutional forms can be related to the manner in which they stimulate or suppress the release of relevant information. Many of the advantages and disadvantages discussed in previous sections can be expressed from this perspective.

From an information perspective, the comparative advantage of the state is in its ability to define and enforce rules, especially when at least some informed people have the incentive and ability to provide evidence when those rules are broken. But states have great difficulties accessing private information held by producers and consumers: producers asked to contribute according to their abilities have the incentive to hide them, while consumers allocated benefits according to their needs have the incentive to exaggerate their needs. And of course the public, and especially the less affluent public, often has great difficulty ascertaining the intentions and preferences of actual or prospective state officials, even in democracies.

Markets are perhaps unrivalled in their ability to call forth relevant information on (even anonymous) producers' and consumers' preferences: under most conditions, misrepresenting one's preferences on the market is self-defeating. But they are notoriously silent when it comes to impacts that are external to the market (as is the case with many environmental impacts), as well as being prone to create great inequalities of wealth.

Communities, and especially stable or closely interacting communities, are perhaps unique in their ability to develop flexible and informal rules or norms of conduct, based at least in part on the intimate knowledge of each other's concerns and behaviours. But when it comes to interactions with 'outsiders' or voluntary associations among more anonymous actors, serious coordination problems are likely to arise.

In elaborating their 'real' utopia, Bowles and Gintis argue that it should be possible to redistribute wealth and yet improve efficiency by engaging in redistributions that recognize these different strengths and weaknesses (more fully elaborated in their paper), and thereby reduce coordination problems even as they reduce inequalities. The three redistributions they focus on involve giving workers more ownership of productive capital, giving residents more ownership of their housing, giving children more rights to their parents' income, and giving parents and their children vouchers with which to finance their choice of schools.

One could apply a similar logic to local environmental improvement. It would also seem to argue for owner-occupancy of residential units that are open to market provisioning of environmental services, yield to the state a regulatory and redistributive role (perhaps working in close cooperation with local institutions), and give a central but circumscribed role to community-based organizations, especially in neighbourhoods with close interaction.

Clearly, much depends on the technologies involved, however. Articulated sewerage systems, for example, are better suited to planning than septic tanks or pit latrines since it is easier to develop and enforce well-defined rules for articulated sewerage systems. Thus, on the one hand the choice of appropriate institutional forms cannot precede the choice of technologies, but on the other hand the choice of technologies inevitably emerges from the institutional setting. Indeed, this is at least a partial explanation for why technological and institutional advocacy tend to go together.

If organizing for sanitary improvement were a question of creating the relevant local, city and national organizations from scratch, it might be reasonable nevertheless to develop a hybrid model that is tailored to institutional strengths and weaknesses (more fully elaborated, of course). In practice, however, sanitary improvement always takes place in the context of existing institutions that do not conform closely to any of these ideal types, even in combination. Taking the context into account typically means forgoing any model or best practice, simple or hybrid, except perhaps as a rhetorical device. Moreover, if one looks beyond the water and sanitation sector, networked production has become successful precisely because of its flexibility (Castells, 1996). This flexibility, which is undoubtedly critical in relation to local environmental improvement, is unlikely to be achieved within a fixed institutional framework.

One of the more convincing and yet simple accounts of how local environmental improvement needs to be organized in a particular city comes not from a social scientist but from an architect with local organizational experience. In *Understanding Karachi*, Arif Hasan examines many of the difficulties that the residents of Karachi face in improving their local environments, especially in the less affluent areas (Hasan, 1999). Having worked as an architect in Karachi since 1968 and been principal consultant to the renowned Orangi Pilot Project since 1982, he has an intimate knowledge of the issues. A common theme throughout is the need to face up to local realities and improve on them, whether they involve Mafia-like property developers, legally questionable transport operators or socially concerned NGOs. In almost every sector, provisioning takes place largely outside the formal planning process, often in contravention of the law. But in almost every case there are lessons to be learned from the informal providers, and in some cases there are practices worth emulating. Many of the principles touched on in this chapter are evident in his analysis, but rather than being used to promote a particular model, they are used to develop the sort of understanding that governments, private enterprises and voluntary associations can all learn from.

Overall, while institutional analysis (and social science generally) has a great deal to contribute to our understanding of how to pursue sanitary improvement, this contribution should not be expected to include accounts of best practices or models to follow. Simplification can be very useful for the analytic purpose of understanding the mechanisms whose operation would be obscured by considering all realistic details of potential importance. But such realistic detail must be taken into account in considering any site-specific improvements, and the importance of the local context makes most prescriptive generalizations very suspect.

# 6

# Techniques for Assessing Local Environmental Problems in Deprived Neighbourhoods[1]

Understanding neighbourhood conditions can play an important role in urban environmental management, especially when environmental services are lacking and new approaches are being debated. Most important understandings emerge informally, not from research and evaluation, but from social discourse, interaction and reflection. Indeed, as indicated in the previous chapter, the relative strengths of institutions like markets derives from their ability (or inability) to elicit information. Scientific research has greatly increased our understanding of environmental issues, but its practice takes place at some remove from environmental decision-making. Various assessment procedures have been developed, drawing on informal understandings and science to provide more directly relevant contributions, both to particular decisions, and to inform public debate.

This chapter describes and evaluates three research methods for assessing some of the environmental problems facing low-income households and communities:

1   broad-spectrum household surveys;
2   participatory rapid assessment;
3   contingent valuation.

As part of the study upon which this chapter is based, the techniques were applied on a small scale in Jakarta. At least superficially, the broad-spectrum survey is particularly suitable to broad-based planning, participatory appraisal to NGO initiatives, and contingent valuation to utility pricing decisions. However, while it is useful to recognize these associations, it is equally important not to be overly bound by them.

---

1 This chapter is a revised version of a paper which first appeared as McGranahan, G, Leitmann, J and Surjadi, C (1998) 'Green grass and brown roots: Understanding environmental problems in disadvantaged neighbourhoods', *Journal of Environmental Planning and Management*, vol 41, no 4, pp505–518

Good information can be instrumental in helping government officials and others to determine what needs to be done. In areas where piped water connections, sewers, electricity and reliable refuse collection are unattainable luxuries, it is particularly important that priority-setting is well informed. The opportunity cost of devoting scarce resources to less-than-critical improvements can be a great deal of human suffering. Moreover, a government that is developing a sound strategy for low-cost environmental management requires, in many ways, a better understanding of local conditions than does one that is able to afford capital-intensive infrastructure. Much the same applies to the user: for its own protection, a household using a pit latrine, storing water in a bucket and cooking with wood needs to be better informed of risks than does a household using a sewered water closet, drinking good quality tap water that is continuously available and cooking with electricity.

Good information can not only help motivated reformers to make the right decisions, but can also help to provide the right motivation. Environmental management is as much a political as a technical process. Decision-making almost inevitably involves discussion, conflict and compromise. Generally, discussions and debates based on faulty or inadequate information are more likely to result in faulty and inadequate decisions. Moreover, poorly understood problems are more easily neglected; consequently, economic resources may be diverted to better documented but less important problems. When information is lacking, the problems of the least vocal and typically most needy segments of society are likely to be ignored or misrepresented in policy debates.

In short, good information is critical at every level for effective improvements in household and neighbourhood environments. It is needed by the households and communities who are most exposed to risks. It is needed by delivery agencies that supply water, remove wastes and provide sanitation. It is needed by the health authorities involved in primary healthcare activities. It is needed by those inside and outside government who are involved in settlement improvement. And it is needed in order to develop an effective and coordinated strategy for the numerous actors involved.

The three research methods examined in this chapter represent three very different approaches to assessing the environmental problems facing households and communities, but still only cover a small part of the range of approaches available. The three techniques are all action-oriented and rely on interviews, discussions and simple observations, rather than on sophisticated physical tests. Thus, they exclude more comprehensive scientific evaluations. On the other hand, they are at least somewhat formalized and thus, as noted at the start, exclude some of the most important means of exchanging relevant information: through the schooling system, the media, informal connections, and the daily work of local residents, activists and government officials.

The empirical basis for this chapter is a study that included the application of each of these techniques on a small scale in Jakarta. Each application was designed both to illustrate the technique and to meet the needs of a local client: the broad spectrum survey was used to assist the slum upgrading agency with implementation; the participatory rapid assessment was used by a local NGO to prepare a neighbourhood-level programme; and contingent valuation was used by the water utility to help plan service expansion. These experiences were not meant to be model cases but rather examples that illustrate the strengths and weaknesses of each approach. A more complete account of this study is also available (McGranahan et al, 1997).

## BROAD-SPECTRUM HOUSEHOLD SURVEYS

Sample surveys can be used to collect, simultaneously, a broad spectrum of data on household and neighbourhood environments and related health conditions in an urban area. The focus here is on household surveys, relying on questionnaires administered by enumerators with little or no background in the environment or health. Of the three approaches under consideration, this is the most conventional. It is the approach one would expect a government statistics office to adopt, for example, were it given the task of collecting information on household environmental conditions. On the other hand, improvements in information technology are radically changing the manner in which such information can be used. Coherent data sets, capable of being analysed from a variety of perspectives, are beginning to displace pre-structured tabulations of statistics. Over time, this should greatly facilitate environmental analysis, for which intersectoral relationships are of central importance. It could also allow a far smaller number of high-quality household surveys to provide a far richer source of information than the multitude of household surveys that are conducted now.

Historically, most surveys of household and neighbourhood-level environmental problems have focused on public health issues. Sample surveys eventually came to play an important role in sanitary reform and the largest share of recent household surveys covering local environmental conditions have generally been conducted from the perspective of human health.

In Jakarta, 200 randomly selected households were surveyed in two neighbourhoods, only one of which had benefited from upgrading (via the Kampung Improvement Programme or KIP). Interviewers were trained and a questionnaire was pre-tested. The questionnaire included modules on household members; health; water; sanitation; pests; food; air pollution and housing; and household characteristics. In each household, the principal woman was interviewed.

The survey results illustrated some very appreciable differences between these superficially similar (and almost contiguous) neighbourhoods. The indicators

**Table 6.1** *Comparing survey results across two neighbourhoods*

| | Not upgraded (N = 100) | Upgraded (N = 100) |
|---|---|---|
| a *Drinking-water source* | % | % |
| Well | 5 | 0 |
| Hydrant | 5 | 0 |
| Vendor water | 89 | 77 |
| Piped water | 1 | 17 |
| Mineral water | 0 | 6 |
| **Total** | **100%** | **100%** |
| b *Bathing-water source* | **%** | **%** |
| Well | 96 | 75 |
| Piped water | 1 | 20 |
| Vendor water | 3 | 5 |
| **Total** | **100%** | **100%** |
| c *Type of toilet facility used most* | % | % |
| Aquaprivie | 18 | 77 |
| Drop toilet (over canal) | 59 | 8 |
| Other | 23 | 15 |
| **Total** | **100%** | **100%** |
| d *Sharing of toilet facility used most* | **sample %** | **sample %** |
| Shared toilet | 76 | 26 |
| e *Waste collection* | **sample %** | **sample %** |
| No collection at house | 47 | 7 |
| f *Dumping behaviour* | **sample %** | **sample %** |
| Dump most waste in fields or streams | 34 | 3 |
| g *Presence of pests* | **sample %** | **sample %** |
| Flies usually in toilet | 49 | 10 |
| Cockroach seen in last two days | 75 | 55 |
| h *Pest control (used regularly)* | **sample %** | **sample %** |
| Mosquito nets | 53 | 18 |
| Spray insecticides | 42 | 78 |
| i *Principal cooking fuel* | **sample %** | **sample %** |
| Kerosene | 94 | 59 |
| Liquefied petroleum gas | 5 | 40 |
| j *Cooking location* | **sample %** | **sample %** |
| Separate kitchen | 52 | 62 |
| h *Consumer durables* | **sample %** | **sample %** |
| Colour television | 68 | 88 |
| Refrigerator | 22 | 65 |
| Motorized vehicle | 26 | 45 |

covering sanitary facilities, water sources, solid-waste handling, pest and pest control and indoor air quality, were in almost every case substantially better in the neighbourhood where the KIP had been, and the differences were statistically significant in most cases. A small selection of illustrative results is presented in Table 6.1.

The survey also indicated that while neither neighbourhood was poor by Jakarta's standard, the private wealth was considerably higher in the post-KIP neighbourhood, suggesting that its environmental amenities were probably not due to the government programme alone. On the other hand, the combination of private purchasing power and public squalor was precisely the sort of evidence that a planner could use to justify the need for a public improvement programme: quite clearly the market was more effective in providing consumer durables than neighbourhood amenities.

## PARTICIPATORY RAPID APPRAISAL

In the field of rural development, 'rapid' appraisal procedures became popular in the 1980s as a sort of compromise between academic research and policy consultancies; between lengthy research studies on the one hand, and quick unstructured appraisals by experts on the other. The results of studies conforming to traditional academic criteria of acceptability are often too delayed or qualified to be of much use in policy making or project selection. The recommendations arising from short visits by experts, rarely more than superficially familiar with local conditions, are often timely and to-the-point, but ill informed.

Rapid appraisal techniques attempt to draw on local understandings of local conditions, and yet provide a systematic analysis and structured presentation of information. Many of the techniques associated with the participatory appraisal approach, which gained popularity in the 1990s, developed out of the rapid rural appraisal techniques (Chambers, 1994). However, rapid appraisal more broadly defined is extremely old. Indeed, techniques employed in the 19th century, including Chadwick's famous assessment of environmental health conditions among the working class in Great Britain (Chadwick, 1965), actually bear more resemblance to rapid urban appraisal than to modern survey efforts.

'Participatory' is at once a more ambiguous and a more emotive qualifier than 'rapid'. 'Participant observation' has long been used by anthropologists and others to refer to an approach wherein a researcher participates in the activities of those being studied. In participatory rapid appraisal, however, it is the local residents who become active participants in the research. In principle, the participation of local residents should help overcome the common tendency to neglect local knowledge and priorities. Simultaneously, there is an implicit assumption, or in some cases explicit goal, that local participation in research will increase direct local control over the development process – that, for example, having played an active part in studying their water and sanitation problems, residents will be in a better position to determine what is done to resolve them.

While participatory rapid appraisal (PRA) has rural origins, there is growing interest in urban applications, especially concerning poverty and environmental management. A recent review has found a great deal of urban PRA-style activity in low-income areas (Mitlin and Thompson, 1995). Moreover, some practitioners have found that urban dwellers are more willing to talk, and to challenge and explore convention than their rural counterparts.

The participatory appraisal in Jakarta was undertaken in four neighbourhoods where Save the Children Indonesia was contemplating initiating new activities. PRA teams of three to seven people from outside and inside the community were formed. The PRA began with reconnaissance where neighbourhood officials were visited, the exercise was explained and cooperation was secured. Then, the teams were formed and trained in participatory techniques using an Indonesian manual similar to that developed by Theis and Grady (Theis and Grady, 1991). Finally, semi-structured interviews with key informants and individual community members from different social groups were held, followed by focus group discussions to ascertain environmental priorities.

The PRA process gave a very different snapshot of two settlements from the survey. Unlike the results of the survey, it would be difficult to say which neighbourhood was better off, either economically or environmentally. However, a great many differences both between and within the neighbourhoods were found, a number of which would not have been detected in surveys. Even with regard to water quality, where expert knowledge is often considered indispensable for any sort of judgement, there was considerable opinion: the water from wells in one part of one neighbourhood was considered dark, metallic and irritating to the skin; the water from a deeper well controlled by a bath-house owner was of better quality, although somewhat salty, and usually available year round; the yellowish smelly water from another set of wells was felt to be contaminated by old tannery wastes, and so on. Some of the environmental problems were simply so specific to the locality that one could never expect to capture them in a standardized survey: when a local paint factory unblocked the drains, they would leave the sludge to dry and it would blow around the neighbourhood (apparently in the wake of the PRA the factory agreed to modify its procedures). However, some of the insights provided could easily help a more conventional survey effort: for example, the PRA found that many of the poorest residents rented unregistered rooms that would normally be missed by a standard survey without the addition of some targeted questions.

# CONTINGENT VALUATION OF ENVIRONMENTAL 'GOODS'

Contingent valuation takes an unmistakably economic perspective. It originated as a tool of environmental economics, a means of assigning monetary values to environmental amenities. Economists often diagnose environmental problems as symptoms of market failure. In crude terms, the orthodox economic explanation for why pollution and other environmental disamenities are often excessive is that there are no efficient markets for them. If polluters had to go out and buy the right to pollute from those affected, pollution would have a (negative) price and at least in theory would not be overproduced. Many of the more damaging forms of pollution would become too expensive. Even if a market cannot be set up, economists commonly argue that the polluters should be made to pay the equivalent price through, for example, pollution taxes. But since there is no market price for the pollution, how can the amount they should pay be calculated? One possible way is to ask those affected (at least in the present generation) what price they would agree to if there was a market for the pollution. This is essentially what the contingent valuation method (CVM) attempts.

Most often, contingent valuation is applied because some physical aspect of the environmental amenity in question prevents efficient markets from developing in the private sector. Many environmental benefits, such as clean air, are public goods. A public good cannot be sold because it can only be supplied simultaneously to large numbers of beneficiaries: provision cannot be restricted to those who pay. Since benefits received cannot be linked to individual payments made, potential beneficiaries have little incentive to pay anything. Yet they may well value the good highly, and might have been willing to pay a high price for the good if the supply actually did depend on their payment. At least in Europe and the United States, valuing public goods has been the principal object of CVM. The now classic text of contingent valuation is entitled *Using Surveys to Value Public Goods: The Contingent Valuation Method* (Mitchell and Carson, 1989). CVM is not the only means of valuing public goods. In some cases, the loss of a public good is reflected in lost income (eg lower fish catches) or other changes in market behaviour. But in cases where the public good provides what has been termed a 'passive-use' or 'existence' value, CVM may be the only means available to estimate the value.

Somewhat surprisingly, the principal uses to which contingent valuation has been put in urban centres in low-income countries have had little to do with valuing public goods. Rather than being concerned with the failure of private entrepreneurs to respond to public demands, they have tended to be concerned with the failure of the public sector to respond to private demands. This is in part a reflection of the times: with the resurgence of market liberalism, public failures have become more likely to attract attention. But the failures have been very real.

In many urban areas, environmental services, such as water and sanitation, are priced below cost. One traditional justification has been that the lower prices allow households to receive the service who could not otherwise afford it. However, state-run utilities have been more successful at keeping prices down than at meeting demand. Indeed, keeping prices down, when the subsidy fails to make up the full revenue shortfall, can prevent the utility from being able to finance the extension of the piped water system. As a result, it is often only the relatively wealthy households who benefit from the partial subsidies. Poor households may actually suffer as a result of the price controls. For example, they may be willing to pay the full cost of a water connection, but not be given the option of having piped water at all. Much the same could be said of other services.

Used carefully, contingent valuation studies can provide information that is helpful to providing better services to wealthy and poor. However, it is important to recognize that contingent valuation does weight the preferences of the affluent more heavily (since they have a greater ability to pay). Moreover, when contingent valuation is used to value the private benefits of water or sanitation provision, it is effectively ignoring the public benefits. These omitted public benefits will tend to be a higher share of the value of water and sanitation in low-income areas where inadequate water supplies facilitate the spread of infections diseases and threaten public health.

In Jakarta, a contingent valuation survey was conducted among 200 households in two neighbourhoods where the water utility (PAM) was intending to offer piped water in the near future. The survey instrument included a description of what is hypothetically being offered, questions on the respondents' willingness to pay, and questions on relevant household characteristics. Two versions of the survey were employed to test for possible bias. At the start of the interview, it was stated that the survey was not a formal offer from PAM and at the end the actual PAM water prices and connection costs were described so that respondents would not confuse the hypothetical values with an actual offer.

The CVM survey did not manage to uncover the relationship between the price of water and people's willingness to connect to the piped system. Indeed, the results suggested that for the relevant range of prices, other factors, such as wealth and existing water source, were far more influential in determining whether someone would connect. Moreover, both the quality of the water service and the presence connection charge made a significant difference.

A sizeable (but realistic) connection charge was found to inhibit lower income households in particular, and if the connection charge was transformed into a monthly payment, the difference between the responses of wealthy and poor households was greatly reduced. Thus, for example, only 37 per cent of the poorer half of the respondents wanted to connect even to a reliable water service if they had to pay a connection cost, as compared to 62 per cent among the wealthier households. However, if the connection charges were transformed into a series of payments adding to the monthly bill, the rates were 67 per cent and 79 per cent respectively. This kind of finding, if reproduced on a larger scale, is of considerable importance for a government or utility that is attempting to ensure that public health does not suffer due to water scarcity at the household level. A CVM survey does not prove that people really will connect under these circumstances, but it provides results that should be taken seriously.

## COMPARING AND CONTRASTING DIFFERENT METHODS

The three research techniques described above typically serve somewhat different purposes. They are also commonly associated with somewhat different development paradigms. Broad-spectrum household surveys are often linked to government programmes and projects, and more generally a technocratic approach to development. Participatory rapid appraisal is often applied by NGOs, and associated with the advocacy of grass-roots, decentralized development efforts. Contingent valuation, as applied in the water and sanitation field, focuses on pricing decisions and could easily be seen as a tool of market-oriented economists. The applications in Jakarta fit these stereotypes, at least superficially.

Table 6.2 summarizes the different techniques along with their associated approaches to development, somewhat exaggerating their differences. The purpose is to make more explicit some of the connections between the methods and presumptions about how environmental management ought ideally to take place. As indicated in the first row of Table 6.2, the sample survey is far older and more established than either contingent valuation or participatory appraisal. The sampling theory upon which sample surveys are based was developed mostly in the first half of the 20th century, by the end of which most of the simple forms of presenting survey data had also been developed. The challenge of applying this technique to local environmental problems is a difficult one, but raises few new methodological problems. Being well established confers a certain respectability to the sample survey, but also reflects a somewhat outdated approach. Certainly this applies to top-down planning with which the sample survey is often associated. As noted above, however, improvements in information technology could create new opportunities for the sort of broad-spectrum sample survey discussed here.

The more recent vintage of the contingent valuation and the participatory assessment is at once part of their attraction and a reason to be cautious in their application. Both contingent valuation and participatory appraisal are evolving rapidly, and have attracted many committed researchers who are uncovering new aspects and applications. For the new initiate, this can be both exciting and disconcerting.

For contingent valuation, the most academic of the three techniques, new methodological findings appear every month in economics journals, but their form

**Table 6.2** *Comparing stereotypes of three environmental assessment techniques*

|  | Broad spectrum sample survey | Participatory appraisal | Contingent valuation survey |
|---|---|---|---|
| *Major development* | 1920–1950 | 1980– | 1960– |
| *Dominant discipline* | Statistics | Anti-disciplinary | Economics |
| *Prioritized quality* | Empirical | Political | Conceptual |
| *Typical research centre* | Statistics office | NGO | University |
| *Main target audience* | Planners/project managers | Residents/project managers | Policy-makers/ utilities |
| *Look for solutions in* | Government programmes | Grass-roots initiatives | Improved markets |
| *Dominant paradigm* | Modernist | Post-modernist | Neo-liberal |

is comparatively esoteric, and the implications for non-specialist application are often far from clear. In effect, the novelty of CVM remains somewhat of a barrier to widespread application. Even strong advocates of contingent valuation are doubtful of the possibility of developing simple protocols for applying CVM on a routine basis. It is still possible that future research will cast serious doubt on the reliability of the technique, at least in its current form. However, as the approach matures, and the lessons of experience are distilled, it may become far easier for new practitioners to apply CVM.

Participatory appraisal is also in a phase of rapid development, and if the past is anything to go by, new developments are likely to be accompanied by new labels, suggesting an ever newer genesis. Partly because of the purposefully non-specialist nature of the PRA approach, new developments in PRA often have a relatively popularized form. Unlike contingent valuation, PRA is not intended to be applied by experts, and its novelty is less of a barrier to routine application, at least on a small scale. Experience on applying PRA through larger scale programmes remains scanty however.

As indicated in rows 2 and 3 of Table 6.2, the research base for the three techniques tends to be rather different. The sample survey and the questionnaire approach are closely associated with statistics, which is often treated as a discipline, although it is not associated with a particular topic of study. The emphasis is put on empirical rigour, with the data very much centre stage. Many other disciplines draw on statistics, but for the most part the statistical procedures remain comparable. A statistical approach is relatively easy to adopt in multidisciplinary studies combining some of the more empirically oriented disciplines. While surveys are administered by a variety of different organizations, large-scale applications are often undertaken by specialized organizations, such as statistical offices.

Participatory appraisal is sometimes associated with anthropology, but this is more because of a common interest in local perceptions than because of any methodological affinity. Generally, PRA is against expertise and highly respectful of what local people know or can learn for themselves. Implicitly at least, this sets PRA against the established disciplines, not simply in the sense of being multi-disciplinary, but in the sense of being anti-disciplinary. Somewhat paradoxically, PRA requires its own type of expertise, although not the sort of expertise that involves long periods of formal education. The personal–political relationships between the outside researchers or facilitators and the local participants are central to PRA. Forced to choose, a PRA advocate is more likely to compromise the quality of their statistics or the rigour of their arguments than the quality of their relationship to the community. While governments and research institutions do undertake PRA, it is NGOs, that often adopt a self-avowedly participatory approach to action, that are the most common users.

While sample surveys can easily be used in multidisciplinary studies, and PRA could claim to be transdisciplinary, CVM is clearly wedded to economics. The desire to express people's preferences in monetary terms reflects an economic perspective. Even more rooted in economic orthodoxy is the assumption that people have well-defined and consistent preferences, and that the difficulty is getting them to reveal these preferences in the absence of a market. CVM studies are often very concerned with the extent to which their results are consistent with economic theory, and there is considerable emphasis of conceptual coherence. Unlike PRA, there is little concern with the researcher–resident relationship, and while empirical rigour is considered desirable, few allowances are made for the fact that people often find it difficult to define their preferences in the form that economic theory suggests. While the World Bank has been heavily involved in the CVM studies in the water and sanitation sector, economics departments in universities are the more common research establishment conducting CVM studies, and even the World Bank studies have typically been headed by university researchers.

The core audiences and action orientations of the techniques, summarized in rows 5 and 6, follow quite closely from the research bases. Sample surveys from statistical offices are typically designed in response to requests and funding from the government (or international donors). The sort of information a broad-spectrum sample survey provides is very much the stuff of government reports and situation analysis. A statistical summary of environmental conditions puts the researcher or planner in the position of judging the severity of environmental problems. Most of the information collected typically pertains directly to physical factors. This is the sort of information that many physical planners want. Existing physical conditions can be compared with acceptable conditions. If current conditions are not acceptable, it is up to the planner to determine how to get from here to there.

PRA attempts to help people to define their own environmental priorities. Residents are meant to participate in the research with a view towards participating in the improvement process. Rather than have planners decide what the environmental priorities are, or have policy-makers consult local residents on how much they value different environmental amenities, residents, ideally, are given control over the environmental assessment process itself. This makes the residents the ideal audience, although in practice it is often project managers or local activists who initiate and use much of the information.

A CVM survey attempts to ascertain how much people would be willing to pay for environmental amenities if they could be purchased on the market. The severity of an environmental problem is judged not by its physical features, but by how much people would be willing to sacrifice to eliminate the problem. This is the sort of information needed by policy-makers or commercial enterprises that wish to manipulate prices and supplies, and to ensure that currently suppressed demands for environmental amenities can be met in the future (in economic jargon, to correct market and public failures).

Viewed in these terms, one can detect elements of the different paradigms, summarized in line 7 of Table 6.2, within which these techniques fit best. The broad spectrum sample survey fits within a modernist perspective and a positivist philosophy of science. Facts are by and large treated as neutral, with knowledge progressing by contrasting hypotheses and theories with the facts, and rejecting the hypotheses and theories that the facts do not corroborate. Society too progresses in a relatively straightforward fashion through the application of knowledge. While many statisticians and other users of sample surveys are not positivists, the practice of statistics typically conforms at least superficially to the positivist model.

PRA fits better with a post-modern perspective, given its emphasis on the personal–political dimensions of research, its respect for non-scientific knowledge, its attempts to allow for multiple perspectives, its implicit critique of unilinear models of development, and its scepticism towards both empiricism and meta-theories. By and large, the philosophical foundations of PRA are only beginning to be developed, but those beginnings suggest an explicit rejection of the positivist philosophy of science (Pretty, 1995).

CVM places too much emphasis on popular perceptions over expert judgement to fit the modernist vision of science leading societies ever onward. On the other hand, rather than having the post-modern orientation of PRA, its intellectual foundations lie in neoliberal thinking, with its predilection for markets and free choice. This applies especially to the use of CVM to help identify public failures in the form of public services that the state does not provide, despite the fact that people would be willing to pay the full cost.

To simplify drastically, the broad-spectrum sample survey is the tool of the planner, contingent valuation the tool of the private sector advocate, and participatory appraisal the tool of the grass-roots activist. It might seem that even in choosing how to gather information on local environmental problems, one is implicitly choosing how they ought to be dealt with. But the planner, the market and local collective organizations are all important to local environmental management. While there are serious political conflicts of interest involved, environmental assessment should not be reduced to a question of who gains and who loses power.

## LESSONS FOR PRACTITIONERS

Caricatures can be dangerous, when overextended. The fieldwork in Jakarta indicated that each of these techniques can provide important, and in many ways complementary, insights. A broad-spectrum survey can be an invaluable means of monitoring local environmental changes and providing a benchmark against which to measure planned improvements. Contingent valuation can provide critical insights that are relevant to a utility attempting to provide services more efficiently or equitably. Participatory assessment can help to support grass-roots initiatives. And each technique also provides information of relevance to other audiences.

Even if each technique is associated with a different approach to environmental management, and perhaps even a different world-view, they can all be simultaneously contributing to better local environmental management. Indeed, the tools do not simply assist the actors in the sectors they tend to favour, but can serve to hold them accountable. The broad-spectrum surveys are not just a tool of government, but a tool for evaluating government programmes. The same holds for PRA, which can be a tool in evaluating the performance of NGOs and CVM, which has been used to provide a damning indictment of public service utilities.

Table 6.3 compares the instrumental strengths of the three techniques, with categories designed to give roughly equal weight to the strengths of each technique. The broad-spectrum survey is the most effective at monitoring changing conditions across a whole urban area or set of urban areas. Participatory appraisal is constrained by the difficulties of organizing PRA exercises across a wide area, and the difficulty of combining information from different appraisals if the local residents really did participate in determining what information would be collected and how. Contingent valuation does not really examine conditions and is not suited to examining more than one or two carefully defined problems. For somewhat similar reasons, the broad-spectrum sample survey is best suited for providing databases for planning purposes.

Participatory appraisal is clearly the best suited to actually establishing a basis for local participation in environmental management. Both the broad-spectrum survey and the contingent valuation survey do generally extract information only for use by others. Participation is also credited in the table with being the best at identifying obstacles to environmental improvement. This is perhaps debatable,

**Table 6.3** *Comparing instrumental strengths of sample surveys, participatory appraisal and contingent valuation*

|  | Broad spectrum sample survey | Participatory appraisal | Contingent valuation survey |
|---|---|---|---|
| *Monitoring changing conditions* | Very useful | Less useful | Less useful |
| *Providing database for planning decisions* | Very useful | Less useful | Less useful |
| *Identifying obstacles to environmental improvement* | Useful | Very useful | Useful |
| *Establishing basis for active participation* | Less useful | Very useful | Less useful |
| *Conducting economic evaluation of an improvement* | Less useful | Useful | Very useful |
| *Pricing environmental services* | Less useful | Less useful | Very useful |

but can be one of the most important advantages of PRA in informing outsiders. Both the broad-spectrum survey and contingent valuation can be used to evaluate obstacles, but by and large only if they have already been identified. PRA is more open to new perspectives, and hence to new insights into why environmental problems are allowed to arise and persist.

Contingent valuation provides information that can be compared directly with costs in an economic evaluation of a particular environmental improvement. In comparison, the information from a broad-spectrum survey or PRA is only indirectly related to economic benefits. Similarly, CVM provides information that is directly relevant to pricing policy, whereas the other techniques provide more contextual information. These features make CVM more appropriate when there are one or two clearly defined improvements being considered.

There have been some attempts to combine the different techniques into single studies. Some rapid appraisal efforts have successfully combined the more flexible aspects of surveying with the less participatory aspects of PRA (Collier and Santoso, 1992; Scrimshaw and Gleason, 1992). However, it is important to recognize that in some situations it is inappropriate and even damaging to merge these techniques. This is particularly evident where participation is itself a goal: imposing the demands of CVM or sample survey methods on a participatory assessment often undermines the participatory process. Combining CVM and PRA also poses serious practical problems: CVM requires information which may be well defined within economic theory, but which is often difficult to express in commonsensical terms. Yet the flexibility of PRA is lost if detailed questions are provided. Much the same applies when sampling techniques and codable surveys are imposed. Alternatively, the appropriate sample for a broad-spectrum survey of conditions is unlikely to be the same as that for a CVM survey, and the questionnaires are unlikely to combine well. Certainly there will be cases where fruitful combinations can be designed, but it should be recognized that in many cases the total will be less than the sum of the parts.

An alternative means of combining the different approaches is to apply them in parallel, but only as the needs and opportunities arise. Thus, for example, assume that a government or large NGO intends to initiate in a local environmental management programme in the city of Pollutia, having had some success in nearby Degradia. Information on existing conditions is generally lacking. After contacting a number of GROs, they agree to assist in conducting PRAs in three neighbourhoods that are considered to reflect different varieties of deprived settlements. After these initial PRAs, and while some new activities are being pursued in the initial neighbourhoods, a broad-spectrum sample survey of 1000 households is undertaken. This provides baseline data for the programme, is used in an assessment of how representative the different PRA neighbourhoods are, and provides critical inputs to a stakeholders' meeting held the following year. Water emerges as a key local environmental issue in a hilly region to the south where wells run dry in the summer. A contingent valuation survey is undertaken and reveals that residents are willing to pay the cost for piped water. And the story continues.

This is, of course, a fairy story. In the real world, a series of difficult-to-predict problems will arise, disrupting, shifting and possibly reversing the process. Perhaps one of the GROs will turn out to have no roots at all. Perhaps the sample frame for the survey will turn out to be unusable, the quality control system will break down and the enumerators will find that it is easier to fill in the questionnaires in the comfort of their own homes. Perhaps the results from the CVM will indicate that residents are not willing to pay the cost of piped water, despite serious public health problems. However, the likelihood that a given assessment effort will fail, or that the results will be ignored or misused, cannot be discussed in the abstract but only in context.

Ultimately, proposals to undertake assessments based on one of these three techniques, or any other, must be judged on their own merits. In general terms, it is possible to describe some of the possible uses to which a technique can be put, to identify potential pitfalls commonly encountered, and to discuss relative strengths and weaknesses. In the end there is no substitute for sound judgement, good practice and the active support of good governance, whichever technique is used to understand the environmental problems of deprived neighbourhoods.

# 7

# Gender and Local Environmental
# Management in Accra[1]

Women and children typically spend more time in and around the home than adult men, and are therefore especially likely to be exposed to household and neighbourhood-level environmental problems. This chapter examines the gender dimension of local environmental management in Accra, relating this in turn to household wealth and the environmental hazards that children face. It provides a qualitative account of the gender division of labour in and around the home and a quantitative analysis of some of the environmental risks that women and children are exposed to, and their possible health effects.

The previous chapters by and large treat the household as a single unit. This chapter illustrates some of the dangers of ignoring gender and age distinctions within the household. The results also demonstrate that the urban transition described in Chapters 2–4 can itself have a gender dimension, as does organizing and evaluating environmental improvement.

The gender aspects of the local environment are strongly conditioned by affluence. It is of special relevance to environmental management in low-income cities, and particularly their more disadvantaged neighbourhoods, since, as described in Chapter 2, the most serious environmental problems of such areas tend to be concentrated in and around people's homes.

Age is also an important conditioning factor. While gender discrimination often asserts itself early, among small children it need not be linked to environmental management and exposure to environmental hazards. Thus, while it is to be expected that low-income children will be especially at risk from local environmental deficiencies, it is an open question whether young girls will be more at risk than boys.

The following analysis of household environmental management in Accra adopts a gender perspective, but retains a complementary focus on age and

---

1 This chapter is based on Songsore, J and McGranahan, G (1998) 'The political economy of household environmental management: Gender, environment and epidemiology in the Greater Accra Metropolitan Area', *World Development,* vol 26, no 3, pp 395–412, with permission from Elsevier Science

affluence. The main body of the chapter starts with a qualitative account of gender and age divisions of labour, drawn from research in selected low-income neighbourhoods. These divisions are the outcome of the micropolitics of power within the household and neighbourhood, but also reflect broader social processes and struggles. This qualitative appraisal then provides the basis for interpreting the quantitative analysis of environmental burdens and risks which employs the results of the questionnaire survey and physical tests undertaken in the GAMA as part of the multicity study referred to in previous chapters.

The qualitative discussion is based on a series of in-depth interviews and focus group discussions. This fieldwork was conducted in the low-income neighbourhoods of Nima, Ashaiman, Mamprobi, Jamestown and Old Ashaley-Botwe. These five areas covered the different residential sectors where low-income households live in the metropolis (see Table 7.1 on p139). In each neighbourhood, five women living in compound housing units were interviewed in-depth, and focus group discussions were held with selected women's and men's groups or associations.

Within Accra's households, women are usually formally subordinated to a male household head, despite having considerable responsibility and in some cases autonomy. Away from the home and the workplace, environmental management typically becomes a public responsibility, administered primarily by men, themselves working in hierarchically structured organizations. The qualitative analysis indicates, however, that between what men at least perceive to be the private arena of the household and the public realm dominated by the state, are a number of niches where women play important roles that are to some degree an extension of their household responsibilities. They typically work together to manage the environment of the house compound and are considered primarily responsible for maintaining the spaces between the compounds. They are usually responsible for the children who move from place to place. And of course even in-house environmental management depends heavily on public infrastructure, such as water pipes and connections. All of these topics are picked up and developed further in the quantitative analysis.

The quantitative analysis draws on the results of the study of household environmental problems in the GAMA, referred to in Chapter 4, and undertaken prior to the in-depth interviews and focus group discussions. The main findings and detailed methodologies of the broader study have already been presented elsewhere (Benneh et al, 1993). The quantitative data are from 1991–1992, and are based on a representative sample survey of 1000 households, and physical tests of water quality and exposure to air pollution for a subset of 200 of these households. The questions were put to the principal homemaker within each household, who was most often a woman, and covered a broad range of environmental problem areas including water, sanitation and hygiene, pests, housing problems, indoor air pollution, food contamination and solid waste. Health problems were ascertained through two-week recall questions asked of the principal homemaker, and covering diarrhoea and symptoms of acute respiratory infection among children under six years of age and respiratory problems experienced by the principal homemaker. The water tests were for faecal coliform, both at source and in household storage containers if applicable. The air tests monitored women's exposure to particulates and carbon monoxide while they were preparing a meal.

The quantitative results confirm and go beyond the observation that adult women, on account of their household responsibilities, bear an inordinate share of the environmental health burden within the domestic sphere. A household's wealth (or indirectly its class position) plays an important mediating role in determining the constellation of environmental hazards faced by the principal woman homemaker of a household. Nevertheless, several of the more serious environmental hazards, ranging from exposure to smoke from cooking fires, to pesticides from home spraying, to cross-infection from the children, are clearly linked to the gender division of labour described in the qualitative section. Among children, the qualitative discussion indicates that girls and boys are treated differently. However, while the quantitative results clearly indicate that for children under six, the environmental correlates of poverty pose appreciable health risks, their severity bears no obvious relation to the sex of the child. While age helps to determine which health problems are most severe for both men and women (Stephens et al, 1994), the age trajectory of environmental hazards is gender-dependent.

The following sections focus on existing environmental conditions and micropolitics, but it is important to recognize that the context within which gender relations are defined is changing. Two processes in particular should be kept in mind. First, national and even global changes are affecting the economic opportunities for men and women in Accra differentially. Second, the women's movement is affecting the ways in which gender relations are perceived and acted upon. These processes are changing power relations in the home, and were recurrently referenced in the interviews and focus group discussions (Songsore and McGranahan, 1996).

It is also important to recognize 'that the household is *not* a closed, autonomous unit or separate sphere' (Varley, 1994, p120). Beyond the household, networks of solidarity and other social and economic exchanges exist between household members, on the one hand, and other extended family members, neighbours and community residents, as well as various community and state institutions on the other. Nevertheless, the household and other local socio-spatial constructs are of considerable importance to both environmental management and disease transmission (Cairncross et al, 1995). The internal relations and systems of mutual support are rather complex, and unique to individual households, neighbourhoods and subcultures. However, as a general rule there is considerable asymmetry in the roles and responsibilities that men and women play within the home.

Both women and men in the areas studied portray the man as the normal head of the household, whether in a nuclear unit consisting of man, wife and children or in the multigenerational extended family. This is consistent with other research findings: 'There are many instances where a wealthy woman owns the "marital" house and supports the family – husband included – yet the authority figure in the house remains the man' (Aidoo, 1985, p25). This authority is not undisputed, however. Indeed, there is a growing incidence of female-headed households resulting from marital instability (Fayorsey, 1992–1993; Fayorsey, 1994).

Both women and men also viewed declining economic opportunities for men as contributing to changes in household relations; however, while men tended to perceive a threat to their authority in the home, women emphasized their own increasing responsibilities. The women's movement and associations promoting greater gender equality are clearly influential in Accra, at the very least in determining how changes in gender relations are interpreted. Men were inclined to perceive the promotion of women's rights as a threat to their power in the home, and in the extreme a danger that, as one put it, 'women will become men and men will become women' (Songsore and McGranahan, 1996, p6). Studies in other African cities have shown that women with independent incomes have a long, slow struggle to increase their power in relation to men, whereas a loss in income often implies a rapid decline in influence because of the loss of 'bargaining power' with men over a range of issues affecting themselves and their households (Kanji, 1995; Kanji and Jazdowska, 1995). The situation in Accra would seem to be consistent with this finding.

Overall, despite changing gender relations, the women's environmental responsibilities described in the following section have gone largely unchallenged. Government-supported service delivery has lessened some of the women's burden, at least among the more affluent households. However, the women themselves see very little role for the government in improving some of the environmental problems which affect them the most, such as indoor air pollution. This reflects an important gender-related challenge in local environment and health improvement. Orthodox policy tools are designed for a public sector that deals primarily with problems that extend physically as well as socially into the public sphere. In much of the world, traditional gender roles place burdens upon women within a decentralized but male-dominated private sphere. Some writers have suggested that women are currently in the process of leading a transformation within the private sphere that is analogous to the democratization of the public sphere (Giddens, 1992). Whether such a transformation is taking place is debatable. It is clear, however, that inflexible gender roles and an over-reliance on orthodox public policy can make it difficult for women to manage the household environment efficiently, let alone allocate responsibilities in an equitable manner.

# GENDER AND AGE DIVISIONS OF LABOUR IN HOUSEHOLD ENVIRONMENTAL CARE: A QUALITATIVE ACCOUNT

Most respondents were apt to stress that women as principal homemakers do practically every household task, very much like the proverbial 'hewers of wood and drawers of water', to satisfy men's needs and the needs of the household. In most low-income communities, female children are normally by their mothers' sides, assisting them in their household work from about age seven onwards. Their assignments, depending on their age, tend to include washing utensils, participation in meal preparation, sweeping and the washing of clothes. They also go on short trips to the market to buy needed items while others do petty selling to help generate some income for the family's sustenance. Child labour, especially for girls, is very common in most low-income areas, as children carry out petty trade before and after school hours. The mother's burden can easily become a young daughter's – a sacrifice rarely demanded of boys. School drop-out rates tended to be high in these communities, again especially for the girls.

Even male children are sometimes pressed into petty selling. Additionally, they do such chores as fetching water, dumping waste and running errands. However, boys were considered a second-best choice among the interviewed households. In most cases, boys, like adult males, were out of the house and thought to be 'playing'; older male children were especially likely to be out and about. As the saying goes, 'like father like son'.

## Managing the Home Environment

The principal environmental management tasks normally performed by women include cleaning the home, toilets and bathrooms; washing clothes; fetching water and buying or fetching domestic fuel for cooking; going to purchase food items and other household needs from the market; cooking food, serving meals and cleaning the dishes. In all these activities they may be exposed to serious environmental health risks. Not all environmental caring roles are necessarily undertaken by the principal female homemakers. As revealed by in-depth interviews and focus group discussions, a complex division of labour often exists between wife and husband, wife and especially female children, wife and housemaid or foster-child, wife and mother-in-law or sister-in-law, etc. These vary according to the household composition, stage in the demographic cycle, wealth, type of employment of adults and whether the principal female homemaker is also the principal 'breadwinner'. This variation notwithstanding, women generally take their role as carers for the home environment and as wives and mothers most seriously.

The social norm is for women to do the unpaid physical work and the men to pay the bills – rent, electricity bills, water bills, toilet charges – and to provide money for the upkeep of the family, which in local parlance is called the 'chop money'. Men may undertake, in addition, such occasional tasks as setting traps for mice, killing dangerous reptiles such as snakes that may stray into the home, protecting the household from neighbourhood violence and undertaking minor repairs to the building or the room. While it is becoming the general practice for women to help pay the bills on behalf of impecunious male heads of the household, very few men help in performing the routine household chores on behalf of overworked women.

There are ideological and cultural barriers keeping men apart from these activities. The rather derogatory term 'Kotobonku' is the label given to men who undertake household chores. In the past, the refusal to wash a man's clothes by the wife was sufficient reason for a divorce. Most married men considered it derogatory to scrub bathrooms or wash cooking utensils. Even unemployed men may consider it beyond their dignity to help their wives with household chores. Some men do not even have the elemental courtesy of picking up the bucket from the bathroom after they have washed with water carried to the bathroom by women. This prevailing attitude would appear to be strongest among the poorer uneducated men, although it is in such households that the environmental management burdens for the women are particularly acute.

## Caring for Children, the Elderly and the Ill of the Household

For those female principal homemakers with infants and children, caring for the home also includes feeding, bathing and clothing the child. It is the mother who has to keep close watch over the children, monitoring their health state, worrying when they fall sick and taking them both to healthcare providers and to school. The mother, together with the grandmother and female siblings, is the child's entertainer, playmate, educator and socializer. All these activities entail a heavy demand on the woman's labour time and often stand in conflict with other domestic tasks and income-generating activities. As in most cultures, 'the idealization of the institution of motherhood as all-powerful, strong and caring brings with it the implication that mothers alone have full responsibility for child-bearing and all the related household caring and domestic work' (O'Connell, 1994, p37).

The household head is traditionally responsible for taking care of the household in general. Therefore he/she is responsible for sick people in the home. Male heads of the household may exercise this leadership by deciding on the type of healthcare institution to visit or the form of treatment such sick people should have, as normally they are those who pay the bills. Women in their turn physically nurse sick children and adults (especially elderly people) while increasingly they also contribute towards paying the health bills of members in most low-income households.

As one woman respondent in a focus group for this study remarked: 'It is the woman who takes care of the sick man, and the man too takes care of his sick wife. There are some men who do not bother about their sick wives. Women cannot do the same. They are always full of pity for their husbands'. Women are not only exposed to communicable diseases when other household members become ill, but often they feel the weight of their responsibilities very heavily, adding to an already stressful life.

## Managing Communal Areas in House Compounds and Neighbourhoods

In low-income neighbourhoods where the majority of Accra's population is found, the most popular dwelling type is the single-storey traditional compound house. Several nuclear households normally occupy this either as a collection of extended family members or as a group of individual tenants who do not have any blood relations and who often come from different backgrounds. Over the years, a nexus of informal arrangements has developed for managing communal areas and facilities within the house compound and in the neighbourhood. It is this internal architecture of house compounds more than kinship networks that determines the institutional arrangements for managing shared facilities and spaces. These include the courtyard in the compound house and the immediate surroundings, the in-house shared toilet, kitchen and bathroom. It also includes mechanisms for sharing out electricity and water bills among all members who share the same meter.

A gender division of labour is evident, as women play a critical role in maintaining good hygiene and sanitation within these communal areas. Women are responsible for cleaning shared kitchens, bathrooms, courtyards, toilets and the immediate environs of the house. Arrangements for joint management are often negotiated between the principal female homemakers from each household within the house compound. Among many tenant households a fairly rigid roster is prepared, indicating days or times during which each female principal home-maker is on call for keeping the commons clean. Similar arrangements are found where nuclear households belonging to one extended family live in a family house compound, although these are sometimes more informal and voluntary in nature.

Each house compound has its rules of hygiene practice laid down by the landlord or his caretaker who is often an old trusted tenant for rental units. In the case of family house compounds these are often laid down by the head of the family who, in most cases, is not a woman, although women carry out the implementation. Bachelors who do not have female dependents are exempted from these feminine duties. Rules can be very rigid where resident landlords or landladies share the house compound with tenants. In one such case the following rules were laid down and they were to be observed by all tenants. Persistent violation could cause the eviction of the tenant:

- Women are responsible for managing the communal areas.
- Noisy quarrels between tenants are not allowed.
- The courtyard has to be kept clean.
- No loud music is permitted.
- No domestic animals are to be kept.
- Too many visitors are not allowed for any household.
- By 11pm the main gate leading from the house compound to the outside is locked. Any person hoping to be late in arriving home has to make arrangements with the sons of the landlord to open the gate after that hour.

In the very crowded house compounds in Jamestown, where the open courtyards have been reduced to mere passageways through infilling with the construction of wooden shacks to serve as additional accommodation for family members, the codified rules of hygiene behaviour for every house compound also included the following:

- No spitting is allowed on the ground.
- No defecation is allowed on the ground by children, except in chamber pots.
- No urination is permitted on the walls.

Although these norms exist in neighbourhoods where non-communal houses and less crowded communal house compounds prevail, they are less rigorously enforced since every household has at least a small private area in front of the room in the courtyard where household activities such as cooking take place. Very often, the level of enforcement depends on the knowledge of good hygiene behaviour and the degree of cooperation among householders. As a general rule men only come into the picture intermittently. When there is the need, men may weed around the compound or desilt gutters. They help to resolve conflicts between households due to misunderstandings between children or women.

Elaborate arrangements also exist in individual house compounds for settling electricity bills among individual householders using a shared meter. The bulk electricity bill is shared out using what in most areas is called the 'point system'. A point is defined as an output flow that a household uses, eg points are awarded for bulbs, refrigerators, fans, electric irons, heaters, television sets, etc. A weighted system is employed whereby electric appliances such as irons, heaters and stoves are given two or three points each as the case may be. On a few occasions the rate is the same for all households or based on household size. Owners of the meters, often resident landlords, are in the habit of shifting much of the cost of electricity consumption to other householders. Similar arrangements exist for sharing water bills from an in-house standpipe. In most cases the owner charges co-residents monthly fees or else they pay by the bucket.

Although there is no specific legislation targeting women, very often it is the woman responsible for the day's house compound chores who is held accountable when sanitary inspectors come around. Where fines are levied for dirty surroundings, these may be paid by the specific household on duty or all the resident households contribute to pay the fine. This depends on the negotiated arrangements in the particular house compound. Many environmental externalities exist (eg noise pollution, smoke pollution, effluent pollution, smell nuisance and flies) and are the cause of interhousehold tension despite the informal arrangements.

Where pan latrines exist in house compounds, women are only responsible for their cleaning, leaving the responsibility of daily or weekly removal of the human excreta to a hired conservancy labourer, invariably male. If he defaults, it is the men in the house compound who have to dispose of the waste at a sanitary site (or household members resort to a public latrine until the contents are emptied by the hired conservancy labourer).

The more difficult areas to manage are the environmental niches between house compounds and the commons within the neighbourhood. This is because of the widespread practice of illegal waste dumping and open defecation, or the disposal of black polythene bags filled with human excreta. This often happens under cover of darkness. For example, in some parts of Nima people have to wake up at 3am to visit the community toilet in order to avoid over an hour-long wait in the toilet queue in the morning. It is such long queues and pressures to answer nature's call, together with the door nuisance of these facilities, that often compel these desperate actions in deprived communities (Benneh et al, 1993).

At the community or neighbourhood level, institutions of the metropolitan authority or the community-based organization (CBO) assume management of the communitywide facilities where they exist. Men are usually engaged and paid from the charges levied on households. Women and children do carry waste to the dumping sites or containers and, like everyone else, use the public toilets. Women's influence drops sharply at this point as formal institutions manned by men begin to assert themselves. Women in general were less aware of neighbourhood by-laws than those set at the household and house-compound levels. Some recalled by-laws concerning unauthorized waste dumping, open defecation and the need for good sanitation around the house. They were less conscious of the responsibilities and duties that the metropolitan authorities and utility agencies had in their communities for the delivery and maintenance of services. Perhaps as a result of the poor representation of women at these higher policy-making levels, they are unable to shape policy in response to both their practical and strategic gender needs with regard to environmental management at the household level.

# GENDER, CLASS AND THE HAZARDS OF MANAGING THE LOCAL ENVIRONMENT: A QUANTITATIVE ANALYSIS

## Gender Roles and Responsibilities within the Domestic Sphere

The degree of exposure of an individual or a household to environmental hazards within the home is mediated by the socio-economic status of the household, as well as the gender, age and economic position of individual members. As such, the gender division of labour can be seen to form an important basis for understanding urban environmental health problems at the household level.

About 73 per cent of the thousand representative households surveyed in Accra were male-headed, the remaining 27 per cent being headed by women. Other studies have shown that households formally headed by women have been on the increase in Ghana and now constitute about 29 per cent of all households (Lloyd and Gage-Brandon, 1993, p7). Over half (54 per cent) of all female-headed households had no adult men in the household.

Table 7.1 shows the intraurban distribution of such female-headed households across different residential sectors in the GAMA. These residential sectors were used to stratify the sample and represent a spatial classification of the city on the basis of density, wealth and the preponderance of indigenous 'Ga' residents. There is a marked clustering of female-headed households in the indigenous Ga enclaves where women exhibit a much greater autonomy and often live separately from their husbands (Aidoo, 1985). These indigenous areas include the high-density indigenous sector (HDIS), medium-density indigenous sector (MDIS) and rural

**Table 7.1** *Percentage of households within each residential sector that are female-headed*

| Residential sector | Households in subsample | % Female-headed |
|---|---|---|
| High-density indigenous sector | 170 | 45 |
| Low-density high-class sector | 20 | 5 |
| Middle-density middle-class sector | 50 | 18 |
| Low-density middle-class sector | 110 | 25 |
| Low-density newly developing sector | 30 | 20 |
| Middle-density indigenous sector | 115 | 43 |
| High-density low-class sector | 455 | 19 |
| Rural fringe sector | 50 | 32 |
| Total | 1000 | 207 |

*Source:* Stockholm Environment Institute and University of Ghana, Household Environmental Data Base, 1991

fringe (RF) where 45, 43 and 32 per cent respectively of all households were female-headed. All other residential sectors had percentage scores well below the average for the city.

Overall, female-headed households tended to be appreciably poorer than the male-headed households. This is illustrated in Table 7.2 which presents the share of female-headed household in five groups of roughly equal size, classified according to the wealth of the households.[2] The tendency for female-headed households to be economically worse off has been noted in discussions of the feminization of poverty (Vickers, 1991), and is not at all peculiar to Accra. The average household size of the male-headed households was 6.2, while for female households it was 5.4. The difference in size is very slightly less than the 'missing' male household head.

**Table 7.2** *Relationship between gender of household head and class location of household (%)*

| Class | Male-headed | Female-headed |
|---|---|---|
| | col % | col % |
| Low | 77 | 84 |
| Medium | 17 | 13 |
| High | 6 | 3 |
| Total | 100 | 100 |
| (Subsample size) | (730) | (270) |

*Source:* Stockholm Environment Institute and University of Ghana, Household Environmental Data Base, 1991

Irrespective of the gender of the head of the household, women played the dominant role in environmental management within the household. Overall, 95 per cent of all households had women as the principal homemaker, with a mere 5 per cent of all households surveyed having a male as the principal homemaker. These were either bachelors living alone or hired male domestic servants and cooks often within very wealthy households. Most middle-income households tend to employ other females as homemakers. To put it another way, the data revealed

---

2 Five wealth categories, each containing roughly 20 per cent of the sample households, were constructed on the basis of an index computed from household ownership of consumer durables (Benneh et al, 1993). Thus, while the residential sectors refer to where the household lives, the wealth groups refer to features of the individual households. While this wealth grouping is intended to be relevant to discussions of class and poverty, there is no suggestion that the groups *constitute* classes or that poverty is *defined* by the absence of consumer durables

that only 4 per cent of the 730 households that were male-headed had the household head also playing the role of principal homemaker. By contrast, about 90 per cent of the 270 households that were female-headed also had the head of the household playing the role of principal homemaker.

Women as a group therefore bear the primary responsibility of managing the household environment. But on account of their class location, they may be confronted with an entirely different array of environmental hazards, and rich women may be in a position to transfer these burdens to poor working-class women and men hired by the household. Some of these differences are illustrated in the following section.

## Household Wealth and the Environmental Burdens of Women

The key areas being considered in this section relate to water and sanitation; insect vectors, pests and insect-control methods; and indoor air pollution and housing problems. Statistics summarizing environmental conditions are presented for five wealth groups of roughly equal size. The results illustrate the extent to which the environmental burdens on women become more severe with the declining economic position of the household. They also illustrate shifts in the niches within which these environmental problems are encountered and managed locally. For a wealthy minority, most of these problems involve household technologies and services. The poorer the household, the more likely it is that the women must cope with the potentially conflicting interests of other households that share the technologies and environmental services. Even if the technologies and services were not otherwise inadequate, such conflicts would create difficulties for environmental management, especially in conditions of rapid change.

### Water and sanitation

Women and children, who are responsible for water collection and its use for laundry, cooking and domestic hygiene, suffer most if supplies are contaminated and difficult to obtain. Table 7.3 shows a close relationship between wealth and access to potable water and sanitary services. In the case of water (A), most rich households have in-house piping, which is typically connected to overhead storage containers. The poorest households rely mostly on water vendors, communal standpipes and other less convenient water-supply sources that not only give rise to water hunts during periods of water shortages and supply interruptions, but also necessitate the in-house storage of water in drums and other containers that can easily become contaminated (Benneh et al, 1993).

One can also infer from B, C and D of the table that women in wealthy households who have access to exclusive household flush toilets do not have to face the hazards of collecting child faeces found in the household environment or cleaning a household and neighbourhood environment in which accumulated waste

**Table 7.3** *Access to water and sanitation by wealth quintile of household (%)*

| | | Wealth quintile | | | |
|---|---|---|---|---|---|
| *A Water Source* | 1–Poorest | 2 | 3 | 4 | 5–Wealthiest |
| | col % | col % | col % | col % | col % |
| In-house piping | 6 | 17 | 26 | 49 | 78 |
| Private standpipe | 16 | 28 | 35 | 30 | 12 |
| Communal standpipe | 21 | 8 | 6 | 4 | 3 |
| Vendor | 49 | 41 | 29 | 15 | 7 |
| Other | 7 | 6 | 4 | 3 | 1 |
| Total | 100 | 100 | 100 | 100 | 100 |
| (Subsample size) | (205) | (187) | (210) | (200) | (198) |
| *B Toilet facility* | 1–Poorest | 2 | 3 | 4 | 5–Wealthiest |
| | col % | col % | col % | col % | col % |
| Flush toilet | 7 | 17 | 30 | 47 | 77 |
| Pit latrine | 72 | 54 | 45 | 24 | 12 |
| Pan latrine | 15 | 25 | 22 | 28 | 8 |
| Other/none | 6 | 4 | 2 | 2 | 3 |
| Total | 100 | 100 | 100 | 100 | 100 |
| (Subsample size) | (205) | (187) | (210) | (200) | (198) |
| *C Toilet sharing* | 1–Poorest | 2 | 3 | 4 | 5–Wealthiest |
| | col % | col % | col % | col % | col % |
| Not shared | 6 | 14 | 18 | 31 | 65 |
| Share with ≤10hh | 20 | 21 | 28 | 39 | 19 |
| Share with >10hh | 69 | 62 | 51 | 28 | 12 |
| No response | 5 | 3 | 2 | 3 | 5 |
| Total | 100 | 100 | 100 | 100 | 100 |
| (Subsample size) | (205) | (187) | (210) | (200) | (198) |
| *D Outdoor defecation*[a] | 1–Poorest | 2 | 3 | 4 | 5–Wealthiest |
| | col % | col % | col % | col % | col % |
| No | 53 | 74 | 72 | 77 | 88 |
| Yes | 48 | 26 | 28 | 23 | 12 |
| Total | 100 | 100 | 100 | 100 | 100 |
| (Subsample size) | (205) | (187) | (210) | (200) | (198) |

*Source:* Songsore, J and McGranahan, G 1993. 'Environment, wealth and health: Towards an analysis of intra-urban differentials within the Greater Accra Metropolitan Area, Ghana', *Environment and Urbanization*, vol 5, no 2, pp10–34
a Refers to reported outdoor defecation by neighbourhood children

and human faeces are often intermixed. By contrast, women in poor households have to manage household and neighbourhood environments that are characterized by faecal contamination and filth from waste accumulations and sullage. The poor rely most heavily on crowded communal or shared pit latrines. As a result of the crowding of these sanitary facilities, open defecation is often practised by neighbourhood children.

The women who act as the principal household environmental managers in poor communities face numerous health hazards as a result of the inadequate water supply and sanitary services. Their management tasks are compounded by the need to work with technologies and services that are shared with other households, and often under the control of men. Thus, for example, while the women are responsible for childcare and the toilet habits of their children, it is typically the men who manage the communal pit latrines.

## Insect vectors, pests and insect-control methods

Women as environmental managers have to cope not only with inadequate water supply, poor sanitary conditions and accumulations of waste, but also with pests and insect vectors such as the flies, mosquitoes, rats and cockroaches that find their habitats in poor crowded household and neighbourhood environments. These pests are implicated in the transmission of various communicable diseases such as malaria and various diarroheal diseases. Malarial mosquitoes breed in undrained accumulations of water, and flies are prevalent in kitchens, toilets, cesspools and uncovered household refuse containers.

Table 7.4 indicates some of the burdens that poor households have to face with regard to insect vectors and other pests. Apart from mosquitoes that appear to be cosmopolitan in distribution, with perhaps higher concentrations around the periurban zone, all the other pests investigated showed a marked concentration in poor households. Women in wealthy households and their children face fewer risks from pests, in part because they can afford more effective self-protection, such as full screening and aerosol pesticides. The mosquito coils that are more common in the poor households give rise to air-pollution problems. Women in especially poor households have to face additional problems related to indoor air pollution, crowding and other housing inadequacies. While these are important problems in their own right, the crowding and inadequate housing also help to make the pest problems even more of a collective problem.

## Indoor air pollution, crowding and other housing conditions

While the availability of adequate potable water, sanitation services and solid waste-disposal facilities are of critical concern to the central government and the metropolitan authorities, the same cannot be said of air pollution. This is in part due to the low level of industrial development. There is a virtual absence of chemical

Table 7.4  *Relationship between wealth, pests and pest-control methods (%)*

| | Wealth quintile | | | | |
|---|---|---|---|---|---|
| *A Flies in kitchen at* | 1–Poorest | 2 | 3 | 4 | 5–Wealthiest |
| *time of interview* | col % | col % | col % | col % | col % |
| None | 4 | 7 | 11 | 21 | 49 |
| Few | 43 | 60 | 65 | 64 | 47 |
| Many | 32 | 22 | 14 | 12 | 4 |
| Very many | 21 | 11 | 10 | 4 | 2 |
| Total | 100 | 100 | 100 | 100 | 100 |
| (Subsample size) | (205) | (187) | (210) | (200) | (198) |
| *B Cockroaches in* | 1–Poorest | 2 | 3 | 4 | 5–Wealthiest |
| *house* | col % | col % | col % | col % | col % |
| Never | 5 | 10 | 9 | 8 | 9 |
| Occasionally | 12 | 16 | 20 | 15 | 31 |
| Often a few | 28 | 31 | 26 | 34 | 30 |
| Often many | 55 | 43 | 46 | 44 | 30 |
| Total | 100 | 100 | 100 | 100 | 100 |
| (Subsample size) | (205) | (187) | (210) | (200) | (198) |
| *C Rats enter house* | 1–Poorest | 2 | 3 | 4 | 5–Wealthiest |
| | col % | col % | col % | col % | col % |
| Never | 10 | 16 | 23 | 25 | 40 |
| Occasionally | 19 | 31 | 21 | 26 | 33 |
| Often | 16 | 16 | 22 | 19 | 12 |
| Every night | 56 | 38 | 34 | 30 | 15 |
| Total | 100 | 100 | 100 | 100 | 100 |
| (Subsample size) | (205) | (187) | (210) | (200) | (198) |
| *D Percentage using* | 1–Poorest | 2 | 3 | 4 | 5-Wealthiest |
| *selected insect-control* | sub- | sub- | sub- | sub- | sub- |
| *methods* | sample % | sample % | sample % | sample % | sample % |
| Full screening | 22 | 37 | 52 | 70 | 82 |
| Mosquito nets | 6 | 8 | 10 | 7 | 9 |
| Mosquito coils | 58 | 47 | 51 | 44 | 26 |
| Aerosol pesticides | 14 | 27 | 43 | 51 | 68 |
| Pump pesticides | 6 | 9 | 12 | 12 | 16 |
| Traditional methods | 7 | 3 | 4 | 2 | 2 |
| At least one | 81 | 84 | 93 | 97 | 96 |
| Total does not add | | | | | |
| (Subsample size) | (205) | (187) | (210) | (200) | (198) |

*Source:* Stockholm Environment Institute and University of Ghana, Household Environment Data Base, 1991

and heavy industries, which are often major polluters. Ghana's gold-mining activity, which produces excessive sulphur dioxide and arsenic trioxide, are located in other towns in the interior (Songsore, 1992).

Within the home environment, the picture is different. Women and children are sometimes exposed to high levels of indoor air pollution from cooking fires, particularly when wood and charcoal combine with poor ventilation and crowding. Table 7.5 shows the relationship between wealth and indoor air pollution and housing problems.

The use of inefficient fuels such as charcoal and woodfuel is particularly common in poor households. Small-scale industries operated by poor women in the home and neighbourhood environment such as fish smoking, pito brewing and local food manufacture, add to the risks of indoor air pollution. Most poor households do not have the luxury of a separate kitchen, often cooking in the open air where the risks of exposure may be reduced. Also, since poor households live in poor neighbourhoods where other households are likely to be cooking with smoky fuels, for them smoke exposure from cooking fuels also becomes a collective problem that is very difficult to manage.

It is in poor households that crowding reaches the most alarming proportion (C). Other problems common in poor households relate to leaking roofs and, to a lesser extent, mould and dampness (D). Having discussed the variety of environmental hazards that women in poor households have to face, the next section addresses in more detail the problem of women's exposure to emissions from cooking fuels.

### Exposure to Emissions from Cooking Fuels

The results presented in Table 7.5 suggest a fuel transition as one moves from poor to wealthy households with woodfuels being replaced by LPG and electricity in wealthy households. This shift from woodfuels to LPG and electricity, often described as the 'energy ladder', is a noticeable feature of urban households in many circumstances (Benneh et al, 1993; McGranahan and Kaijser, 1993). However, there is a high stability in fuel-use patterns in the GAMA. For example, 85 per cent of households had been using their principal cooking fuel for more than five years, with somewhat higher percentages among wood and charcoal users.

The predominant source of in-house air pollution is fuel combustion. As such, many of the relevant pollutants are the same as those outdoors: sulphur dioxide, carbon monoxide, nitric oxide, nitrogen dioxide, polycyclic organic matter, and particulates generally. In addition to the composition of the pollutants, the degree of health damage is related to the exposure situation, concentration, the time extent of exposure, and the physiological and psychological status of the individual. Many of the emitted compounds also have chronic long-term effects on health. The exposure of women in the GAMA to respirable particulates and carbon monoxide show a wide variation in relative risk depending on the cooking fuel used.

**Table 7.5** *Relationship between wealth and indoor air and housing problems*

| | Wealth quintile | | | | |
|---|---|---|---|---|---|
| **A Principal cooking fuel** | 1–Poorest col % | 2 col % | 3 col % | 4 col % | 5–Wealthiest col % |
| Do not cook | 1 | 2 | 1 | 0 | 2 |
| Woodfuel | 22 | 7 | 5 | 2 | 3 |
| Charcoal | 74 | 81 | 83 | 66 | 35 |
| Kerosene | 3 | 8 | 8 | 8 | 4 |
| LPG | 0 | 1 | 1 | 21 | 47 |
| Electricity | 0 | 2 | 2 | 3 | 11 |
| Total | 100 | 100 | 100 | 100 | 100 |
| (Subsample size) | (205) | (187) | (210) | (200) | (198) |
| **B Cooking locations** | 1–Poorest sub-sample % | 2 sub-sample % | 3 sub-sample % | 4 sub-sample % | 5–Wealthiest sub-sample % |
| Separate kitchen | 10 | 14 | 23 | 51 | 77 |
| Multipurpose room | 12 | 11 | 12 | 7 | 4 |
| Communal room | 2 | 4 | 4 | 4 | 1 |
| Cooking hut | 21 | 10 | 12 | 5 | 4 |
| Veranda | 27 | 33 | 29 | 20 | 17 |
| Other/open air | 59 | 53 | 55 | 45 | 27 |
| Total does not add | | | | | |
| (Subample size) | (205) | (187) | (210) | (200) | (198) |
| **C M²/person in most crowded sleeping room** | 1–Poorest col % | 2 col % | 3 col % | 4 col % | 5–Wealthiest col % |
| <2 | 16 | 13 | 9 | 4 | 7 |
| 2–4 | 55 | 56 | 54 | 51 | 27 |
| 4–6 | 16 | 17 | 22 | 25 | 27 |
| 6+ | 12 | 14 | 15 | 20 | 39 |
| Total | 100 | 100 | 100 | 100 | 100 |
| (Subsample size) | (205) | (187) | (210) | (200) | (198) |
| **D Problems with building** | 1–Poorest sub-sample % | 2 sub-sample % | 3 sub-sample % | 4 sub-sample % | 5–Wealthiest sub-sample % |
| Dampness | 8 | 6 | 7 | 8 | 5 |
| Leaking roof | 67 | 49 | 40 | 32 | 23 |
| Mildew/mould | 8 | 6 | 4 | 4 | 3 |
| Total does not add | | | | | |
| (Sub-Sample size) | (205) | (187) | (210) | (200) | (198) |

*Source:* Stockholm Environment Institute and University of Ghana, Household Environmental Data Base, 1991

## Exposure to respirable particulates when cooking

A subset of 199 women was monitored for respirable particulates (RSP) and carbon monoxide (CO). These women wore portable pumps with filters for about three hours, spanning the time spent cooking a meal. The particulates collected for this period were measured and the results were used to calculate the average concentration of respirable particulates in the vicinity of the women's faces during the period.

Table 7.6 shows the average concentrations of RSP ($ug/m^3$) in three groups of fuel users. Wood users were subject to the highest average concentrations, followed by charcoal users with kerosene, LPG and electricity users (who were lumped together because of small sample size), experiencing far lower average concentrations. Analysis of variance indicates statistically significant differences in exposure to RSP among the three fuel-user groups ($p = 0.002$), although, as indicated by the standard errors, there was considerable variation within each fuel user group. According to WHO guidelines for outdoor air, the mean daily concentration of total suspended particulates (TSP) should not exceed 150–230 $ug/m^3$ more than seven days per year. In view of this, these levels appear to be disturbingly high, especially for wood and charcoal users.

**Table 7.6** *Average concentrations of RSP ($ug/m^3$) in three groups of fuel users*

| Wood | | | Charcoal | | | Kerosene/LPG/electricity | | |
|------|------|------|------|------|------|------|------|------|
| Mean | SE | n | Mean | SE | n | Mean | SE | n |
| 587 | 94.0 | 21 | 341 | 34.4 | 122 | 195 | 55.0 | 24 |

*Source:* Benneh, G, Songsore, J, Nabila, J S, Amuzu, A T, Tutu, K A, Yangyuoru, Y and McGranahan, G (1993) *Environmental Problems and the Urban Household in the Greater Accra Metropolitan Area*, Stockholm Environment Institute, Stockholm.
*Note:* SE = standard error

Since women in poor households are more likely to use wood (especially those in the RF who engage in subsistence fuelwood foraging) together with charcoal as their principal fuel, one can safely conclude that poor women face the highest exposure to these respirable particulates with possible short- and long-term health damage. Part of the difference in exposure may come from fuel combustion by neighbouring households.

## Exposure to carbon monoxide during cooking

Carbon monoxide, which is emitted from cooking fires, can also be injurious to health depending on the concentration of the gas in the inhaled air, duration of exposure, respiratory volume, cardiac output, oxygen demand of the tissues and the concentration of haemoglobin in the blood. Table 7.7 shows the average

**Table 7.7** *Average concentration of CO measured as dose units (ppmh) and calculated time-weighted averages (ppm) in three fuel-user groups*

| Wood exposure (ppmh) | | | Charcoal | | | Kerosene/LPG/electricity | | |
|---|---|---|---|---|---|---|---|---|
| Mean | SE | n | Mean | SE | n | Mean | SE | n |
| 24.1 | 9.1 | 24 | 33.1 | 2.9 | 137 | 3.8 | 1.1 | 32 |
| *Concentration (ppm)* | | | | | | | | |
| Mean | SE | n | Mean | SE | n | Mean | SE | n |
| 7.5 | 3.0 | 24 | 11.0 | 1.0 | 137 | 1.2 | 0.4 | 32 |

*Source:* Benneh, G, Songsore, J, Nabila, J S, Amuzu, A T, Tutu, K A, Yangyuoru, Y and McGranahan, G (1993) *Environmental Problems and the Urban Household in the Greater Accra Metropolitan Area,* Stockholm Environment Institute, Stockholm

exposures and the time-weighted average concentrations for the three groups of fuel users. Charcoal users were most exposed to CO followed by wood users and finally the group of fuel users consisting of kerosene, LPG and electricity. About 6 per cent of the charcoal users were exposed to an average CO concentration greater than 25ppm, the UNEP–WHO guideline value for one hour of exposure (Benneh et al, 1993, p70).

There are a number of other pollutants whose exposure levels can be expected to be correlated to exposure to CO or particulates. Overall, the exposure monitoring suggests that smoke from cooking fires is a matter of some concern.

### Environmental Risk Factors and Selected Health Problems among Women and Small Children

The analysis of the female principal homemakers presented below suggests that many of the more critical risks they face, at least in relation to respiratory problems, are closely tied to their gender role. Without looking at the environmental health problems away from home, it is not possible to make any general statements about the overall environmental health risks that men and women face. It is evident, however, that women have a special interest in a good local environment, not only for the sake of their children, but to protect their own health.

The analysis of diarroheal and respiratory problems facing boys and girls under six does not indicate any statistically significant difference in the environmental health problems they face. Instead, the health of both is closely related to environmental hazards in and around the home, which are far more severe in conditions of poverty. The risks that children face are not independent of gender relations. As indicated in earlier sections, gender relations are central to how these environmental risks are managed locally. However, the results are consistent with the hypothesis that at early ages gender discrimination within the household is not health threatening.

### Respiratory problems among the principal women of the household

A large number of environmental factors and predisposing conditions influence the prevalence and severity of respiratory infections and common respiratory problem symptoms such as sore throats and coughs. Although the survey was not designed for epidemiological analysis, many of the relevant factors and conditions were covered. These include indicators of smoke exposure (eg smoking patterns, cooking practices, cooking fuels, cooking location and ventilation, and the use of mosquito coils), crowding, damp and poor hygiene, as well as the age and socio-economic status of the woman.

Table 7.8 summarizes the results of three logistic regression models of respiratory problem symptoms reported by the principal woman of the household. The environmental risk factors included in the basic model, which has already been presented in an earlier report (Benneh et al, 1993), are those with coefficients found to be statistically significant with at least 95 per cent confidence. Environmental variables that have not been included because of a lack of significance were the use of a cooking hut, principal cooking fuel, observed evidence of dampness, and selected water and sanitation variables also included in the analysis of diarrhoea. The wealth quintile of the household and the age of the woman were entered as control variables, but were not statistically significant and are not

**Table 7.8** *Logistic models of approximate relative risk of respiratory problem symptoms among principal women of household*

| Factor | Basic model | | Model identifying female-headed households | | Model identifying households with sick children | |
|---|---|---|---|---|---|---|
| | *Odds ratio* | *95% confidence interval* | *Odds ratio* | *95% confidence interval* | *Odds ratio* | *95% confidence interval* |
| Uses pump-spray insecticides | 3.5 | 2.2–5.6 | 3.4 | 2.2–5.5 | 3.4 | 2.1–5.5 |
| Water interruptions are common | 1.6 | 1.1–2.3 | 1.6 | 1.1–2.3 | 1.4 | 1.0–2.1 |
| Roof leaks during rains | 1.5 | 1.1–2.2 | 1.5 | 1.1–2.2 | 1.5 | 1.0–2.1 |
| Always cooks indoors or on veranda | 1.4 | 1.0 . 2.0 | 1.4 | 1.0–2.0 | 1.5 | 1.0–2.1 |
| Number of cigarettes smoked per day | 1.1 | 1.0–1.2 | 1.1 | 1.0–1.2 | 1.1 | 1.0–1.2 |
| Household is female-headed | | | 0.9 | 0.6–1.3 | | |
| Child in house has respiratory symptoms | | | | | 3.5 | 2.0 - 6.2 |

Number of observations = 939

presented. Respiratory problems were identified through a two-week recall of tracer symptoms including sore throat, persistent cough and hoarseness, which could reflect a broad range of respiratory problems including chronic conditions. The summary results of the logistic regressions are odds ratios, which are estimates of the approximate relative risk associated with the factor in question (Armitage and Berry, 1994). Thus, for example, the basic model estimates that always cooking indoors is associated with a 40 per cent increase in the likelihood (or more precisely the odds) of having had respiratory problem symptoms in the last two weeks.

Most of the environmental variables in the basic model could be interpreted as indicators of suspected risk factors for respiratory problems, such as smoke exposure, dampness, poor hygiene and pesticide exposure. It is important not to overinterpret individual coefficients. Environmental risk factors are closely interrelated, and the variables may be acting as indicators for a variety of more difficult-to-measure factors.

What is particularly interesting from a gender perspective is that two of the four environmental risk factors – the use of pump-spray insecticides and cooking indoors – are not only features of the home environment, but linked to the woman's role as principal homemaker. Even dampness and poor hygiene are more relevant to women than to men because of the greater time they spend in the home. Smoking is relatively uncommon among women (only 35 women smoked at all), but is both the only significant factor that is not an environmental risk encountered in and around the home, and the only one that is likely to be higher among men.

It is also notable that while most of the environmental burdens discussed in the previous sections clearly fall more heavily on poor women, those that are indicated as risk factors in respiratory problems are more mixed. The use of pump-spray insecticides is somewhat less common in very poor households, and smoking has not become a poor person's habit, as is increasingly the case in wealthy countries (Benzeval et al, 1995). Leaky roofs and water-supply problems are clearly associated with poverty. Overall, the relationship between risk factors and wealth is somewhat ambiguous, while women in wealthy and poor households alike clearly face environmental hazards on account of their gender role.

The second model includes a variable identifying female-headed households. This variable is not significant, and its inclusion does not alter the other coefficients appreciably. While being a household head undoubtedly influences the activities of women, it does not add significantly to the explanatory power of the basic model. It is worth noting, however, that the use of pump-spray insecticides in the home is only 6 per cent in female-headed households as opposed to 13 per cent in male-headed households, which is itself a statistically significant difference. A possible explanation is that women dislike spraying in part because of the respiratory irritation, but that it is the men who purchase and promote the use of insecticides. Unfortunately, this possibility was not explored in the questionnaire.

The third model includes a variable that identifies households with small children under the age of six who have had symptoms of acute respiratory infection within the past two weeks.[3] The estimated odds ratio for this variable implies that having a sick child is associated with a 3.5-fold increase in the likelihood that the woman will report that she herself had a respiratory problem symptom. Somewhat surprisingly, the other coefficients are not greatly affected. While there are different interpretations that could be given for this high odds ratio, one obvious possibility is that the women contract a significant share of their respiratory illnesses from their children. As indicated above, caring for sick children is one of the traditional female tasks. These results are similar to those found in the companion survey in Jakarta (Surjadi, 1993, p82).

### Diarrhoea and respiratory problems among small boys and girls

Very much in contrast to the situation with adults, among small children it is hard to identify environmental hazards which impinge on girls in particular. However, particularly for diarrhoea, which is more of a health problem for small children than for adults, the environmental risk factors are closely associated with poverty.

The results of two logistic models of diarrhoea among children under the age of six are presented in Table 7.9. The procedures followed were similar to those described above for the analysis of respiratory problems among adult women.[4] In the basic model, the large number of environmental factors with high odds ratios is striking. However, in this case the factors are almost all clearly related to poverty, while they bear no obvious relation to the gender of the children at risk. The second model corroborates the hypothesis that the gender of the child does not determine how susceptible they are to household environmental hazards. A variable identifying households with a girl under six years old was insignificant, and the model estimates that whether there is a girl makes no difference to the likelihood of having a sick child.

---

3 A variable identifying whether there were any children under the age of six was also included to ensure that the association attributed to having a sick child was not confounded with an association with having a child, whether sick or not. It was not statistically significant, however

4 In this case the dependent variable is whether there is a child under the age of six in the household who has suffered from diarrohea (more than three loose stools in a 24-hour period) in the past two weeks. Only households with children under the age of six were included. Environmental variables on the following were omitted from the basic model owing to their lack of significance: water source, type of toilet facility, location of water source, dirty toilet floor, open storage of leftover food observed, many flies observed in the toilet and crowding. The control variables included but not presented (none were statistically significant) were the wealth group, the number of children in the household, and the education level of the principal homemaker

**Table 7.9** *Logistic models of approximate relative risk of diarrhoea among children under the age of six*

| Factor | Basic model | | Model identifying female children | |
|---|---|---|---|---|
| | Odds ratio | 95% confidence interval | Odds ratio | 95% confidence interval |
| Use pot for storing water | 4.3 | 1.7–11.1 | 4.3 | 1.7–11.1 |
| Water interruptions are common | 3.1 | 1.4–6.6 | 3.1 | 1.4–6.6 |
| Share toilet with >5 households | 2.7 | 1.2–5.8 | 2.7 | 1.2–5.8 |
| Purchase vendor-prepared food | 2.6 | 1.1–6.2 | 2.6 | 1.1–6.2 |
| Open water-storage container | 2.2 | 1.1–4.3 | 2.2 | 1.1–4.3 |
| Outdoor defecation in locality | 2.1 | 1.1–3.9 | 2.1 | 1.1–3.9 |
| Many flies in food area | 2.1 | 1.1–3.8 | 2.1 | 1.1–3.8 |
| Do not always wash hands before preparing food | 2.0 | 1.1–3.8 | 2.0 | 1.1–3.7 |
| The child (or one of the children) under six years old is a girl | | | 1.0 | 0.6–1.9 |

Number of observations = 500

Somewhat similar findings emerge with respect to respiratory problems among young children.[5] Most of the significant variables identified in Table 7.10 are closely associated with poverty. Only the first and third might be suspected of being related to the gender of the child. However, while older girls help their mothers more than boys do, as discussed in previous sections, the variable identifying whether children under six are commonly present during cooking does not vary significantly with the gender of the children. Of the 224 households with only boys under the age of six, 26 per cent often have a small child with them while cooking, while for the 182 households with only girls under the age of six, the percentage was 23. Also, most of the households where crowding is severe have only one room, and while older boys may sleep elsewhere, young boys and girls would seem to be equally present. The second model also indicates that the presence of a female child does not add significantly to the basic model. Indeed, the second model estimates a (statistically insignificant) decline in the likelihood of having a child with symptoms of acute respiratory infection among households with girls.

---

5 The respiratory problem symptoms were experienced within the preceding two weeks, and included an episode of rapid and difficult breathing. Again, only households with children under the age of six were included. Environmental variables that were not included due to a lack of statistical significance were: use of cooking hut, use of pump-spray insecticide, principal cooking fuel, observed evidence of dampness, and selected water and sanitation variables. The control variables included but not presented (none were statistically significant) were the wealth group, the number of children in the household, and the education level of the principal homemaker

**Table 7.10** *Logistic models of approximate relative risk of acute respiratory infection (symptoms) among children under the age of six*

| Factor | Basic model | | Model identifying female children | |
|---|---|---|---|---|
| | Odds ratio | 95% confidence interval | Odds ratio | 95% confidence interval |
| Child often attends cooking | 2.6 | 1.5–4.7 | 2.6 | 1.5–4.6 |
| Many flies in kitchen | 2.4 | 1.3–4.6 | 2.4 | 1.2–4.5 |
| Sleeping room < 4m²/person | 2.3 | 1.0–5.2 | 2.3 | 1.0–5.2 |
| Water interruptions are common | 2.2 | 1.0–4.5 | 2.2 | 1.0–4.5 |
| Use mosquito coils | 1.8 | 1.0–3.3 | 1.8 | 1.0–3.4 |
| Always cook indoors | 1.8 | 1.0–3.3 | 1.8 | 1.0–3.0 |
| Roof leaks during rains | 1.7 | 0.9–3.0 | 1.7 | 1.0–3.0 |
| The child (or one of the children) under six years old is a girl | | | 0.8 | 0.4–1.3 |

Number of observations = 527

## CONCLUSIONS

Environmental problems in and around the home are a particularly serious health burden for the women and children of the GAMA.[6] Poverty greatly exacerbates this burden among children: childhood illness is closely linked to the environmental correlates of poverty. For adult women, the key environmental risk factors examined in this report are not so closely tied to poverty. However, the tasks that many women face in managing the home environment are far more onerous in conditions of poverty, even as the need to devote time to income-earning activities is greater. Household environmental management not only involves more difficult and hazardous work in poor neighbourhoods, but also is more likely to require cooperation among households. Moreover, when men are unable to meet their traditional economic obligations, they resent it when women become the principal income earners and are not inclined to take on traditionally female obligations.

Household and neighbourhood-level environmental problems do not receive the attention they deserve in environmental debates, and this probably reflects, at least in part, a form of gender discrimination: once the water has left the tap, the fuels have been purchased, and more generally the environmental problems have entered the home, they are considered less important 'private' problems. But since

---

6 The elderly also spend much of their time at home, and while the survey did not examine the health or priorities of the elderly, one can assume that they would also benefit disproportionately

'private' environmental problems tend also to be 'women's' problems, the seemingly rational emphasis on 'public' problems can easily mask a lack of concern for women's problems.

From the perspective of the women, and particularly the low-income women, improvements in environmental services almost certainly deserve more support. However, simply increasing the level of government intervention is unlikely to be the most effective means of assisting these women.

The future of environmental management in the homes and neighbourhoods of the GAMA will be determined in part by external developments:

1    Changes in formal government policies on environmental services and regulation (eg pricing policy and infrastructure expansion).
2    Economic changes that affect the circumstances of the poor majority.
3    Changes in relations between men and women.

All these processes have global as well as local dimensions and are closely inter-related. Many of the recent shifts in government policy affecting local environmental management reflect adherence to a structural adjustment programme (SAP) that is promoted internationally in support of global capitalism. The economic prospects for the poor majority also depend critically on the global political economy.

The principal focus of this chapter has been on the role of women in environmental management in and around the home. Despite the local focus, the importance of large-scale, and even global processes is evident here. The economic setbacks that have affected large parts of Africa in recent decades have had reper-cussions on household relations in the GAMA, as have the structural adjustment policies that Ghana has had to adopt. Indirectly, international economic processes and economic ideologies have played an important role in shaping the development of gender relations locally. More directly, the international women's movement has changed the meaning of women's daily struggles to improve their position.

While many men are feeling threatened by women's empowerment, the actual gains that women have made have been minimal. There still exists a critical disjuncture between those who manage the household environment and those who take strategic decisions that can help to make environmental improvements possible. The key decision-makers in terms of the allocation of resources to support environmental improvement are principally male household heads and male policy-makers within the state bureaucracy and *not* women. Those who bear the burden of environmental management within the home are almost exclusively women. Compounding the difficulties that may arise due to the dominance of men and male perspectives within government is the related problem that formal state regulations are ill-suited to many of the local environmental management problems that women face.

Like many problems that women have in relation to men, the environmental problems of the home are complicated by the 'intimacy' of the social relations involved. If a factory pollutes the air and damages the health and well-being of local residents, governments around the world recognize this as a public nuisance and accept the need for regulating the factory owners. If workers are adversely affected, most governments also accept the need to regulate their employers. But within the household, the legitimacy of government intervention is more problematic, and it is easy to end up blaming the principal victims.

Is a male household head responsible for the smoke that his spouse is exposed to while cooking if he is the one who purchases the stove? Or is a female homemaker responsible for the poor sanitary conditions that put all household members, and even neighbours, at risk? Historically, the latter view has been more evident than the former. During Accra's colonial period, for example, there were times when the work of the lower courts was dominated by cases of women accused of sanitary offences (Robertson, 1984). Hopefully, such an approach would no longer be considered acceptable. However, alternative strategies, through which the government could actively support women to improve their environmental position, are not evident. Moreover, it is all too easy to imagine, for example, an anti-smoke campaign, warning women not to expose themselves to smoke from cooking fires and smokers not to smoke cigarettes, as if the two problems are comparable: as if women were actively choosing to cook with smoky fuels in the same manner that people choose to smoke cigarettes.

The women in the GAMA did not seem to think that the government had a major role to play in dealing with, for example, indoor air pollution. Only 15 per cent of the almost 1000 women respondents felt that the government needed to take the lead in improving indoor air, as compared to 78 per cent for water, 61 per cent for solid waste, 56 per cent for outdoor air, 44 per cent for insects and 42 per cent for sanitation. The areas where government action was popular were precisely those areas where the government can act without becoming involved in household affairs. Yet at the same time, more than half of these same women felt that improvements in indoor air quality did need to be initiated at the household level.

Serious attempts to improve conditions for these women, and indirectly for the majority of Accra's citizens, will have to work with them. It is not simply a question of providing advice on how to improve home environments and the opportunity to purchase household-level environmental services at cost. Improvements should come with better economic conditions and improved services, but also through changes in gender relations to the advantage of women. In some cases this may involve increasing the status or easing the burden of traditional women's roles, while in others it may involve challenging existing roles. But in all cases it will involve significant changes in relations of power.

While this chapter focuses on Accra, similar concerns undoubtedly arise in many other cities. Indeed, the following fictional account of a change of gender roles in Lagos, Nigeria, captures many of the same issues:

*The cleaning day had a story of its own. It began when the women revolted against having to do all the dirty jobs in the compound, sweeping the corridor and the backyard, unblocking the bathroom drainholes, cleaning out the toilets. They had a meeting and decided to ask the men either to contribute to the work or to pay them for their labours. But the men laughed at the idea. It was simply inconceivable. The next Saturday, however, the women refused to do any cleaning. The bathroom began to stink. The water that couldn't flow from the bathroom into the gutter soon flowed through the compound and gave off an infernal smell. The toilet became unusable. The men were furious. They too held a meeting and came up with the decision to prove that they could do the jobs without grumbling or asking to be paid. They did, and it became a compound tradition. It also became a social event. Every second Saturday, while they cleaned up, they told one another outrageous jokes and improbable stories, they made a lot of noise, they chattered and laughed and sorted out the little quarrels of the week. And after the cleaning was over one of the men would invite the others to his room for an evening's session of drinking and mantalk.* (*Dangerous Love*, Ben Okri, p90)

# 8

# Urban Environmental Justice in a Changing World

Environmental challenges are constantly changing. Many of the emerging regional and global risks that have helped to motivate the green agenda, such as global climate change, ozone 'holes', acid rain, loss of biodiversity and global resource depletion, have less respect for national boundaries than the financial capital that reportedly flows ever more freely around the globe. Simultaneously, the basis for addressing local environmental problems is shifting, partly as a result of changes in global politics and economics, and partly as a result of changing ideas about how they ought to be addressed.

Urban environmental management must adapt to all of these global shifts, relevant to varying degrees in virtually all cities of the world. This implies looking both beyond and within the citywide environmental burdens conventionally associated with urban development: up to the larger-scale problems that may affect the entire globe; and down to the smaller-scale problems that are confined to individual households, workplaces and neighbourhoods. Different cities may have different priorities, but conceptual frameworks that claim international relevance (and most implicitly do) need to be able to accommodate every level.

The transition described in the early chapters of this book clearly has a bearing on the priorities for local urban environmental management. There are systematic wealth-related differences that call for special caution when ideas emerging in affluent parts of the world are represented in less affluent settings as new knowledge. Even if the rhetoric, strategies and priorities of the environmental movement are grounded in globally relevant scientific understandings, they are embedded in a critique of the excesses of affluence rather than the insufficiencies of poverty. To put it crudely, much environmental thinking has lost touch with the environmental dimensions of poverty, which are themselves changing rapidly.

However, the stylized transition also indicates some of the dangers inherent in dividing the world into the haves and the have-nots, and suggesting that while one common agenda is inappropriate, two separate agendas might be sufficient. Even with the three curves displayed in Figure 2.1 (p17), every level of affluence is associated with a somewhat different combination of environmental burdens. Differences are compounded by the wide range of other relevant environmental problems and the substantial variation between cities of comparable affluence. Clearly no crude dichotomy can provide the basis for setting environmental priorities in individual cities.

Similarly, considerable differences were evident within and between the three cities presented in Chapter 4, despite their all being located in 'developing' countries. Ambient air pollution is a widely recognized threat to health in São Paulo, a serious but not widely acknowledged threat in Jakarta, and a comparatively localized threat in Accra. Alternatively, extending household water and sewerage connections to all households in São Paulo is a realistic goal, while in Accra an emphasis on household connections is likely to divert attention from the more immediate health challenge: improving conditions for those who are not going to have household connections in the near future. Moreover, even if these three cities did face comparable environmental challenges, their contrasting political, economic and social circumstances would make any common solutions untenable.

From an equity perspective, it is notable that while the environmental burdens of poverty tend to fall on the poor themselves, the environmental burdens of affluence fall on an increasingly international 'public'. Moreover, affluent lifestyles have already used up the world's environmental 'space', making it virtually inconceivable that the currently deprived follow the development trajectory of the currently affluent. This has added a whole new dimension to the development debate.

While new structures of governance are being constructed at an international level to address the emerging global environmental threats, the governmental structures long assumed to be needed to provide localities with environmental services are being dismantled. In effect, the challenge of finding new means to address old problems, such as providing all households with adequate water and sanitation, has re-emerged.

As described in Chapter 5, the very notion that there is an appropriate organizational solution to local environmental management is doubtful. Public utilities, once assumed to be the best means of extending water supply and sanitation, are no longer favoured. Private provisioning is not in itself a solution, and the voluntary sector does not provide any easy answers. It is easy to say that private, public and voluntary sectors all have important roles to play in local environmental management, and that the appropriate roles depend on both the local configuration of environmental problems, and the local political and institutional context. But while improving living environments is comparatively straightforward when the goal is adequate service provision and public utilities provide the accepted means, once a wide range of goals and institutional forms are involved, the challenge is compounded.

As indicated in Chapter 6, even the techniques of urban environmental assessment tend to remain divided along orthodox lines, with some tools associated with central planning, others with getting markets to work, and still others with supporting community action. If new approaches are to be developed to help manage the local environment, it becomes especially important that good information is available. And just as synergies need to be found in combining different organizational approaches to inform local environmental improvement, so synergies will have to be found in the approaches to environmental assessment.

Urban environmental justice extends beyond issues of the rich and the poor, or present and future generations. Racial, gender and ethnic injustices, for example, also have environmental manifestations. Chapter 7 examined several of the gender dimensions of environmental burdens in Accra. Not only was gender found to be of critical importance to both environmental management and the incidence of environmental burdens, but the roles of women and men were being contested in a debate drawing not only on local experiences but also on international discourse. Moreover, traditional gender roles are themselves related to the scale of environmental problems, and hence to the urban environmental transitions.

A tension has been evident throughout this book: between the 'green' challenge of not depriving future generations of their environmental heritage, and the 'brown' challenge of improving living environments in currently deprived settlements. The 'brown' challenge sits uneasily on the 'green' agenda that now dominates environmental thinking (though not, it should be noted, environmental practice). As noted above, individual cities combine complex configurations that are relevant to both agendas. Moreover, these two challenges have too many physical, political and even conceptual interconnections to allow them to be separated conveniently and pursued independently. They involve a similar range of environmental resources and media, including air, water and land. Both are concerned with the problems that arise when urban activities abuse the environment, and the institutional and behavioural roots to these problems (Atkinson and Davila, 1999). But perhaps most important, both are concerned with environmental equity, and there is at least the potential to merge them in the pursuit of environmental justice.[1]

The first section of this conclusion re-examines the concepts of sustainability and sustainable development as these are the terms that best represent the greening of development discourse. While sustainability is often interpreted very loosely, as a goal it emphasizes clearly the need to avoid damaging future prospects, and hence favours 'green' over 'brown' priorities. Sustainable development encompasses a concern for present inadequacies as well as future prospects, but has still tended to focus environmental attention on 'green' issues rather than on the local and health-threatening environmental problems that predominate in poor cities and

---

1 The discussion of environmental justice in this chapter owes much to Graham Haughton's presentation of equity principles (Haughton, 1999), adapted by David Satterthwaite to the 'brown' and 'green' agendas (McGranahan and Satterthwaite, 2000), and elaborated further by Shalini Bhargava (Bhargava, 1999)

neighbourhoods. More serious, the task of achieving harmony between sustainability and poverty goals is often confounded by politically convenient claims that they are mutually interdependent: that sustainability cannot be achieved without eliminating poverty and vice versa.

The second section re-examines the 'green' and 'brown' agendas, and argues that while they do reflect very different environmental priorities, they both display an underlying concern for equity. The 'brown' agenda focuses on environmental problems involving intragenerational inequities, while the 'green' agenda focuses on those involving intergenerational (or in more radical versions interspecies) inequities. Their common concern for equity helps to provide a conceptual basis for reconciling 'green' and 'brown' priorities. And as demonstrated in the previous chapters, this has implications for how both the current and future urban environmental issues are conceptualized.

## ELIMINATING POVERTY AND ACHIEVING SUSTAINABILITY: THE END OF A HONEYMOON

Two of the most commonly voiced goals in the international development arena, often married in the concept of sustainable development (World Commission on Environment and Development, 1987), are:

1    To provide a secure future for the coming generations.
2    To eliminate poverty.

Urban environmental improvements can serve both of these goals. More sustainable cities can protect the environment for coming generations, while healthier living environments in low-income settlements can reduce poverty. Thus, it might seem that tackling the problems discussed in the previous chapters is fully supported by contemporary development thinking.

Unfortunately, not only have these goals been less influential than many hoped, but also their marriage has been problematic. Rather than providing a clear direction for urban environmental initiatives, their combination has created questionable alliances and unnecessary divisions.

It is not surprising that international measures designed to meet these goals have been scarcer than the rhetoric. After all, neither the impoverished nor the coming generations (and still less other species) are well represented in the international policy arena. While there is widespread acceptance that the interests of these groups ought to be taken into account, there is little concerted political power to effect this. Indeed, it is perfectly understandable that many pragmatists of all political persuasions view high-level pronouncements on the pursuit of sustainable development as empty rhetoric.

Such goals and their interpretation are nevertheless important. The rhetoric influences the scarce measures that are taken in the name of the unborn and the unheard, and is not always empty. Moreover, misguided measures can easily undermine the support that does exist. Failures are quickly seized upon to justify inaction: what better reason to withdraw support for unselfish initiatives than that they do not really help the deserving. Under such circumstances, ill-conceived attempts to draw attention to worthy concerns, or to merge a range of important concerns into a more powerful integrated framework, can easily become counterproductive.

The concepts of 'sustainability' and 'sustainable development' have helped to highlight the environmental pressures that accompany economic growth, but they have also caused considerable mischief. In some circles, sustainability has come to be treated as the pre-eminent goal, with poverty reduction serving this goal inasmuch as it contributes to sustainability. Sustainable development is a more balanced term, but the process that has forged agreement on sustainable development has fostered some potentially serious misconceptions.

## Poverty Reduction as Contributing to Sustainability: An Unequal Alliance

For poverty reduction to achieve prominence in an agenda framed in terms of sustainability, poverty must be held to be either socially or environmentally unsustainable.[2] Scientifically, it is difficult to justify such claims. One could just as well argue that eliminating poverty would be a threat to sustainability, since it could allow billions more people to adopt more resource-intensive lifestyles and increase national capacities to wage globally destructive wars. Politically, justifying poverty reduction with arguments that exaggerate the negative impacts that poor people inflict on others is prone to backfire. Only those with the power to work behind the scenes and influence how political rhetoric is translated into policy practice, can safely manipulate public information efficiently to serve their ends. Those whose influence lies primarily in the public sphere are apt to find that their misrepresentations return to haunt them.[3]

---

2  This requirement not only applies to the use of sustainability as a stand-alone goal, but also to many cases when 'sustainable' is used to describe desirable states (eg sustainable cities). It does not generally apply when 'sustainable' is used to qualify processes, improvements or conditions that are themselves meant reduce poverty (eg sustainable development, sustainable upgrading projects or sustainable livelihoods)

3  The 'fuelwood crisis' of the late 1970s and 1980s is an instructive example of a well-intentioned misrepresentation that backfired. In the wake of the world oil crisis, it became common in development circles to draw attention to the plight of the rural poor by presenting an image of fuelwood-led deforestation and attendant shortages of cooking fuel. However, rather than increase the level of assistance to the rural poor, this largely imagined crisis diverted attention from their real needs and led to numerous ill-conceived stove and tree-planting projects (Leach and Mearns, 1988; McGranahan, 1986)

## Wedding poverty and sustainability concerns by blaming social instability on the poor

The notion that poverty is a threat to social stability, and hence to sustainability, is often implicit and sometimes explicit in attempts to justify treating poverty as a sustainability issue. Munasinghe is among the most explicit:

> *The socio-cultural concept of sustainability seeks to maintain the stability of social and cultural systems, including the reduction of destructive conflicts. Both intragenerational equity (especially the elimination of poverty) and intergenerational equity (involving the rights of future generations) are important aspects of this approach* (Munasinghe, 1993, p3).

In this argument, while intergenerational equity is inherent to sustainability, intragenerational equity sneaks in the back door on the basis of a contingent connection. Poverty, however, does not always lead to social instability, and a fear of instability is not a sound basis for combating poverty.

Poverty does not figure prominently in serious accounts of social conflict or revolution. Social activists have often found the truly impoverished to be conservative and not at all inclined to be disruptive, let alone revolutionary. The more obvious conflicts that have threatened the world in the 20th century have not been those between wealthy and poor, but between great powers. Increasing poverty has been seriously destabilizing in many instances, but not continuing poverty. Moreover, looking at the longer sweep of history, 'When judged by the length of time for which they sustained, some of the most "successful" societies were also among the most exploitative, where the abuse of human rights was greatest' (Hardoy et al, 1992, p178).

Even in cases where poverty is causing unsustainable social disruption, poverty reduction is not the only possible response. Indeed, repression is one of the many conceivable alternatives. The justification for poverty reduction should not have to rely, even implicitly, on the claim that it is an efficient means of curbing social dissent and conflict.

Moreover, advocating poverty reduction as a means of achieving social sustainability may play on the fears of an anxious elite, but it does not represent the aspirations of the impoverished. The impoverished have an immediate interest in eliminating intragenerational inequities, but an ambiguous interest in preventing the social disruptions that result from such inequities. In some circumstances, agitation may be a means of exacting greater equity. From the perspective of a social activist, the view that greater equality is desirable because it prevents conflict is almost perverse.

Finally, even if eliminating poverty were necessary for social sustainability, this would not justify treating sustainability as an overarching goal. Rather, it would argue for giving the goal of poverty elimination more prominence as an end in itself.

## Wedding poverty and sustainability concerns by blaming environmental degradation on the poor

In attempting to reconcile the goal of sustainability with a concern for poverty, it is often claimed that poor people harm regional and global environments. The Brundtland Commission report, for example, first mentions poverty as a 'major cause and effect' of global environmental problems, and follows this up with the claim that it is futile to try to deal with environmental problems without also addressing poverty and international inequality (World Commission on Environment and Development, 1987). The claim that poverty is an effect of global environmental problems is itself very misleading. Of more immediate concern here, however, is the often repeated view that poverty drives people to destroy the environment, thereby undermining sustainability (Holmberg, 1992).

It is reasonable to assume that the struggle for short-term survival can lead people to neglect long-term degradation. Numerous case studies indicate, however, that subsistence cultivators are often very protective of natural resources. Moreover, for the most part, poor people are not in the position to cause much environmental damage, except on a small scale. This was clearly shown in relation to poor urban dwellers in previous chapters, and also applies to a large share of the rural poor. The notion that poverty threatens global sustainability because poor people are especially damaging to the environment is simply wrong.

A more serious but still unconvincing claim is that poor families tend to have more children and that poverty threatens sustainability because of the resulting population growth. The relationship between population, consumption and the environmental impacts that threaten sustainability is often expressed in a very simplified form by the Commoner–Ehrlich equation: $I = PCT$ (where $I$ is the environmental impact, $P$ is population, $C$ is consumption per capita and $T$ an environmental impact coefficient). Since poverty entails a lower $C$, other things being equal it reduces the threat to sustainability. But other things are rarely equal, and if poverty results in a higher $P$, in the long run it can also undermine sustainability. Moreover, if $T$ declines as $C$ increases (as suggested by the environmental Kuznets curve), the environmental disbenefits of poverty reduction will be low and possibly even negative. Baldwin has elaborated the conditions under which economic growth (increasing $C$) not only reduces poverty, but also results in a lower environmental impact in the long run due to the reduction in poverty-induced population growth and the declining marginal impact of consumption (Baldwin, 1995, referenced in Ekins, 2000).

These conditions are likely to be the exception rather than the rule, however (Ekins, 2000). Much clearly depends on the particular environmental threats of concern, and how and where the growth takes place. There are cases where increased population in low-income rural settings actually lead to better environmental management. There are threats to sustainability that do not show declining marginal impacts. Empirically, there is no reason to think that poverty reduction is an effective means of achieving sustainability.

The poverty–population argument is far more convincing if the children of the poor are expected to have higher consumption levels, and especially if they are expected to emulate the consumption patterns of the currently affluent. From this perspective, however, it is not poverty itself that is unsustainable, but a particular sequence of poverty, population growth and poverty reduction. It is an important sequence so long as poverty reduction is viewed as a goal in its own right. But if sustainability is the only concern, then the affluent might be tempted to accept Garret Hardin's arguments and adopt what he termed 'lifeboat ethics', taking measures to ensure that the impoverished are never given a chance to climb on board, and risk upsetting the boat (Hardin, 1974).

More generally, as with social instability, environmental destruction provides a dubious platform for garnering political support for poverty reduction. There are numerous measures that can be used to prevent the poor from causing long-term environmental degradation other than reducing poverty. Many such measures actually increase poverty. Exaggerating the long-term environmental impacts of poverty is more likely to undermine than to serve the interests of the poor (although it may well divert development assistance to programmes led by those who engage in such exaggeration). Moreover, it unfairly portrays the poor as irresponsible, reinforcing the notion that their freedom of choice and political participation should be curtailed.

### Sustainable Development's Honeymoon: Poverty Alleviation and Sustainability as Interdependent Goals

Sustainable development, defined as meeting the needs of the present without compromising those of future generations, clearly voices support for both inter- and intragenerational equity (World Commission on Environment and Development, 1987). When the term first came into common use, 'sustainable' was taken to address environmental concerns, with 'development' addressing poverty and other more conventional social and economic concerns. In effect, the relevant needs of future generations were assumed to be environmental, while the relevant needs of the present were assumed to be social and economic. This distinction is less apparent in many recent discussions of sustainable development, and with good reason.

Clearly, our legacy to future generations does not just include the natural environment, but extends to manufactured capital, and the knowledge and institutions of the societies that people are borne into (sometimes referred to as human and social capital). In recognition of this, considerable efforts have been devoted to refining the definition and measurement of sustainable development to take non-environmental contributions to sustainability into account (as, for example, in the World Bank's efforts to expand the measure of wealth (World Bank Environment Department, 1997)).[4]

It is equally obvious that many unmet needs in the present are environmental, and that this is especially true in poor areas. Less effort has been devoted to taking explicit account of this in the definition or measurement of sustainable development. The definition of poverty itself has broadened (Baulch, 1996). The Human Poverty Index developed for the 1997 Human Development Reports includes access to safe water as one of its five components (United Nations Development Programme, 1997b). In the context of sustainable development, however, environmental concerns are still usually assumed to be issues of sustainability. This is reinforced by contemporary environmental terminology which would apply the label 'environmentalist' to anyone prioritizing biodiversity, climate issues, ecosystem disruptions or other sustainability concerns, but question the credentials of anyone prioritizing the expanded provision of safe water and sewerage. In effect, at least in the environmental arena, sustainable development still favours issues of intergenerational equity over those of intragenerational equity.

Of greater concern, the marriage of development and sustainability has lent support to the claim that poverty reduction and sustainability are interdependent goals: that achieving better harmony with nature entails helping poor people and vice versa (Jackson, 1990). Corroborating this view, the relationship between poverty and environmental degradation has often been portrayed as a vicious spiral, with poverty causing environmental degradation, which in turn leads to more poverty, and so on (Holmberg, 1992). In effect, not only is poverty proclaimed to be unsustainable (as in the attempts to subsume poverty into a sustainability agenda, described above), but unsustainable practices are identified as important causes of poverty.

The origins of this claim are easier to explain in terms of political convenience than in those of empirical evidence. As a concept, 'sustainable development' emerged from policy discussions whose principal aim was not to understand the world but to forge international agreement on how to change it (or to stop from changing it). Arguing that poverty alleviation and sustainability are mutually dependent on one another at least superficially strengthens the case for sustainable development as a unifying concept. It counters both conservationists who are inclined to neglect poverty and advocates of economic growth who are inclined

---

4 In this book, sustainability is often used as a shorthand to refer to what might better be termed environmental sustainability. But we have tried to avoid drawing any conclusions that might suggest that other dimensions of sustainability are unimportant

to neglect long-term environmental degradation. Moreover, once sustainable development was widely endorsed, those wishing to elicit support for poverty alleviation programmes could use the argument to claim that their programmes also served sustainability, and those wishing to elicit support for measures to achieve sustainability could claim the poor as important beneficiaries. At least at the level of international policy rhetoric and fundraising where intellectual rigour is at best a secondary concern, it is very convenient to proclaim that helping future generations also helps the currently deprived, and vice versa. Indeed, within the international policy arena, questioning this relationship could be interpreted as doubting the importance of sustainable development.

Problems arise, however, when one leaves the world of international policy discussions. As noted in the previous section, there is little reason to believe that poverty, in itself, is a major threat to sustainability. The notion that unsustainable practices are a major cause of poverty is equally dubious. Moreover, the policy implications are very misleading, and the ideological content interferes with serious attempts to understand and address the poverty–environment nexus.

Drawing on a wide range of predominantly rural research on poverty and the environment, a recent overview report by researchers at the Institute of Development Studies at the University of Sussex explicitly challenged the view that poverty and environmental degradation go hand-in-hand:

> *The key argument of the report is to challenge the existing orthodox view that poverty and environmental degradation occur in a 'downward spiral'. . . Instead, the report argues that many poor people are able to adopt protective mechanisms through collective action which reduce the impacts of demographic, economic and environmental change. . . The report presents evidence from a variety of case studies in which expected patterns of poverty and environmental degradation occurring in a downward spiral were actually found to be misplaced. In addition, it is also shown that the continued belief in a downward spiral may also lead to land use and resettlement policies that may contribute to poverty and environmental degradation, and also avoid many environmental problems experienced by poor people* (Leach et al, 1998, pp3–4).

It is doubtful whether this 'downward spiral' qualifies as a policy orthodoxy (this point was made by several people commenting on this report in a web-based conference: http://www.sdnp.undp.org/lstarch/povenv/). It is revealing nevertheless that the notion continues to be taken seriously, if only as a crude simplification.

A 'spiral' suggests such high feedback that once the process is initiated, both environmental quality and poverty go into a steady or even accelerating decline. This requires second-order effects to be as large as the first-order effects: if poverty increases by x, causing environmental quality to decline by y, causing poverty to increase by z, then z should be of the same magnitude as x. It also implies that a significant share of poverty can be explained by environmental degradation that can itself be explained by poverty, and so on. This very strong claim that goes well beyond asserting that poverty often causes environmental degradation, and environmental degradation often causes poverty (rocking boats cause waves, and waves cause boats to rock, but the ocean does not rise up as a result).

Moreover, the existence of downward spirals in some extreme circumstances in no way implies that these circumstances are themselves the result of poverty–environment interactions. If, for example, the land that is available to shifting cultivators is curtailed by expanding commercial agriculture, and this eventually leads to a spiral of increasing poverty and land degradation in the remaining area under shifting cultivation, it would be very misleading to ascribe the problem to poverty–environment interactions. Similarly, while an appreciable number of deprived urban households may suffer from a 'spiral' of poverty and ill-health, mediated or at least initiated by unhealthy living environments, this cannot be taken as an explanation of urban poverty or environmental health problems generally.[5]

What emerges from more careful studies is not a clear interdependence between sustainability and poverty reduction, but a complex relationship that is heavily dependent on the particular context. Moreover, it is not even clear that exaggerating the complementarity of poverty reduction and sustainability has really served to garner support for sustainable development as a new goal in the international policy arena. Indeed, very much the same exaggerated claims have been deployed to argue that maintaining the traditional focus on economic growth can address both poverty and sustainability goals, implying that sustainable development is a redundant goal (Beckerman, 1995).

## Sustainable Development after the Honeymoon: Working for Harmony between Poverty and Sustainability Goals

Contrary to images of innate complementarity, one of the major challenges of sustainable development is to prevent conflicts between sustainability and poverty reduction goals from emerging. Hard work is required to make these goals compatible and mutually supportive. Both goals must be given their due respect. Pragmatic compromises as well as idealistic visions are needed. Sustainable development is never going to have the motivational force of such slogans as 'liberty, fraternity, equality'. But like that revolutionary trilogy did in its time, sustainable development brings together some of the major equity issues of the day.

---

5 Dasgupta illustrates how a similar interaction between malnutrition and productivity can convert poverty into destitution, but quite rightly refrains from explaining poverty in such terms (Dasgupta, 1993)

This section briefly reviews some of the obstacles to achieving harmony between poverty and sustainability goals. It should be evident from the previous sections that the pursuit of poverty reduction does not inevitably serve the goal of sustainability. Similarly, as described below, the pursuit of environmental sustainability does not inevitably serve the goal of poverty reduction; indeed, care must be taken not to increase poverty in the name of sustainability. Moreover, while poverty reduction and sustainability both need to be grounded in an underlying concern for equity, they are situated very differently politically. To put it crudely, there is at least the potential for the poor to have more political power and for greater intragenerational equity to be achieved through that route. For future generations and other species, this political route is not an option. Thus, bringing together the pursuit of sustainability and poverty reduction not only requires avoiding substantive conflict, but also merging politically diverse processes.

Those living in poverty tend to be more vulnerable to global environmental disturbances than the more affluent, and not all such disturbances will take place in the distant future. Indeed, earlier phases of human globalization also brought global hazards, and these hazards fell most heavily on the already disadvantaged. The devastating infectious disease pandemics of several centuries ago provide obvious examples. They emerged as a result of both local environmental conditions and the increasing contacts between peoples around the world. These pandemics included the plagues in Europe, but extended well beyond, decimating many populations, traumatizing whole societies and causing untold misery (McNeill, 1989). Within Europe, death rates were particularly high among poor groups. Evidence from colonial encounters is equally revealing of the inequities of such burdens: in cases where the colonizers were the principal victims of disease (as in Africa) colonization was inhibited, whereas in cases where the colonized were the principal victims (as in the Americas) colonization was accelerated.[6]

However, the poor are also especially vulnerable to crude measures designed to reduce global burdens, particularly if those measures are designed according to Northern models or in international forums dominated by the affluent. It is the already impoverished who are likely to suffer most, for example, if forests are protected by excluding local users, pollution emissions are reduced by prescribing high technological standards, population growth is reduced by punishing large families, or water conservation is achieved by discouraging new connections. They

---

6 These pandemics were the among the first large-scale side-effects of globalization and the expansion of the market economy. While considerable progress has been made to help prevent such outbreaks, evidence on newly emergent viruses and the AIDS pandemic indicate that the risks have not been entirely contained (Krause, 1992; Morse, 1993; Wills, 1996). Some scientists believe, however, that pandemics among animals and plants (our life-support systems) are emerging as a more serious long-term threat (Wills, 1996), which conforms at least roughly to the transition described in Chapter 2

are likely to suffer not only because they are vulnerable to an impartial application of such measures, but also because the application is unlikely to be impartial.

International agreements almost inevitably reflect the political advantage of more affluent countries. International agreements on global environmental burdens may seem to favour poorer countries by accepting low income as justification for delaying compliance (as when the Kyoto protocol recognizes 'common but differentiated responsibilities', and the separate social and economic capabilities of developing and industrialized countries (Agarwal et al, 1999)). The context, however, is typically a framework within which existing burdens are used as the benchmark against which improvements are required. In effect, future rights are conferred in proportion with current excess. This not only denies any responsibility for historical contributions, which are generally much higher for affluent countries, but goes very much against the 'polluter pays principle' or a population-based allocation of 'rights' to pollute. Indeed, as Lipietz has pointed out (Lipietz, 1994), it bears more resemblance to the 'enclosures' that left so many peasants landless in late feudal Europe. In effect, population-based rights are too equitable to be easily accepted in the international arena where the politically powerful would rather translate their current overuse into what amounts to a form of ownership to a disproportionate share of the global commons.

Allocating rights (tradable or otherwise) to engage in environmentally degrading activities in proportion to existing activity levels is also, of course, far less favourable to low-income countries than allocating rights in proportion to population.[7] For example, according to the Human Development Report 1999 (United Nations Development Programme, 1999), per capita carbon emissions in 'industrialized countries' were 12.5 metric tons, as compared to 0.2 in the 'least developed countries', 2.1 in 'all developing countries' and 4.1 for the 'world'. Per capita emissions in 'all developing countries' could grow by 3 per cent a year for 20 years and still remain below the current average. Per capita emissions from industrialized countries would have to decline by about 6 per cent a year to reach a similar level. Under most reasonable assumptions, it would require a very long grace period to compensate low-income countries for using current emissions rather than population to allocate emission rights. And yet, the fact that low-income countries are not already held accountable for restraining carbon emissions is one of the sticking points for some Northern negotiators.

---

7 Allocating pollution rights on a per capita basis is more favourable to low-income countries than applying the 'polluter pays principle', assuming that the payments (per capita) required to compensate for the damage of global climate change are less in poorer countries. In theory, a country-based application of the 'polluter pays principle' with equal per capita repayments would result in the same outcome as tradable pollution rights set on a per capita basis, so long as total emission rights were set such that marginal costs equalled marginal benefits

Poor groups are probably at just as serious a disadvantage when it comes to the details of policies adopted in the name of sustainability and how they are implemented – internationally, nationally and locally. Basically, they rarely have the power to influence policy development and implementation. Indeed, this lack of power can be seen as a constituent as well as a cause of poverty (Sen, 1999). In most circumstances, more democracy, enhanced participation and other changes that give the currently disadvantaged more power can be expected to reduce both poverty and the potential conflict between poverty reduction and the pursuit of sustainability. Policies and projects undertaken in the name of the poor are often developed and implemented without even consulting poor groups. This is perhaps better interpreted, however, as an explanation of their frequent failure than as evidence that such consultations, and indeed more fundamental political changes, are not needed.

Future generations and other species are, of course, even more fundamentally disadvantaged politically. They do not even have the possibility of taking more control over the policies and projects initiated in their name. This may make things more comfortable for researchers and policy-makers who cannot be brought to account for failing to give more control to the intended beneficiaries, but it also removes one of the most important procedural mechanisms for achieving greater equity. This makes it all the more important that formal agreements are reached and that the rhetoric in support of sustainability is translated into clearly defined policies. Stakeholder participation is still relevant, but such participation is needed principally to ensure intragenerational equity in the pursuit of sustainability, and to ensure that the measures taken are efficient and have local support.

This book has been concerned principally with intragenerational equity and urban environmental issues. This is in part a reflection of the experiences of the authors and the research agendas they have pursued. It also reflects a concern that the environmental agenda, even in low-income cities, is becoming too narrowly associated with sustainability. These same concerns are evident in the following sections which focus again on urban issues and emphasize the risks faced by low-income dwellers. However, this emphasis should not be interpreted as claiming that sustainability is already being addressed. Rather, as the following subheading suggests, the purpose is to find the means to reconcile the 'brown' and 'green' agendas, and to create the sort of mutual reinforcement that wishful thinking all too often suggests already exists.

## REVISITING THE 'BROWN' AND THE 'GREEN' URBAN AGENDAS AND STRIVING FOR ENVIRONMENTAL JUSTICE

A stereotypical comparison of the two environmental agendas described at the start of this book is provided in Table 8.1. While there is no clear dividing line between the two agendas, they can be distinguished along a number of different dimensions: spatial, temporal and political. The 'brown' agenda addresses issues that are more local, immediate and affect the poor.[8] The 'green' agenda addresses issues that are more dispersed, delayed and affect future generations. In terms of the preceding discussion, the 'brown' agenda addresses the environmental dimension of poverty, while the 'green' agenda addresses the environmental dimension of sustainability.

Superficially at least, these two agendas are in opposition to each other. As described in Chapter 2, 'green' burdens have grown in part because 'brown' burdens have been displaced. Local water shortages have been addressed by drawing on more distant sources. Local air pollution has been reduced by introducing higher stacks or more distant energy conversion facilities. Local solid-waste problems have been addressed by removing the waste from the vicinity of people. Land shortages have been eased by transport systems that encourage urban sprawl. And sanitary problems have been removed by using water to carry away human excreta.

From a 'green' perspective such displacement is inequitable and economically unsound. It shifts the burdens from those responsible on to distant people and ecosystems and even on to future generations. This raises issues of transboundary, interspecies and intergenerational equity:[9] surely people should not have the right to transfer their burdens in this fashion. It also raises economic concerns: if those responsible do not bear the costs and those affected are too distant or dispersed to represent their interests, the resulting environmental damage is likely to be economically excessive.

From a 'brown' perspective, the fundamental inequities and economic inefficiencies lie in the inadequate local water supplies, local air pollution, lack of waste collection, poor sanitation and inadequate land available to the poor. In terms of equity, these people have the right to have their basic needs met – if necessary by the same means that others have historically met theirs. Their poverty is itself a reflection of historic inequities which ought not to be compounded by environmental insults. Economically, local environmental hazards also create collective burdens that do not translate into appropriate individual economic incentives, especially if local organizing is repressed for political purposes.

---

8 This account of the 'brown' agenda is more poverty-oriented than most. In practice, emphasis is often placed on local environmental burdens that fall relatively evenly within a city, such as ambient air pollution, rather than water and sanitation, which is more selectively burdensome for the poor

9 Graham Haughton identified five environmental equity principles applicable in urban settings: social, procedural, transboundary, intergenerational and interspecies (Haughton, 1999). David Satterthwaite noted that the first two are more central to the 'brown' agenda and the last three to the 'green' agenda (McGranahan and Satterthwaite, 2000)

**Table 8.1** *Stereotyping the 'brown' and the 'green' agendas for urban environmental improvement*

|  | The 'brown' environmental health agenda | The 'green' sustainability agenda |
|---|---|---|
| *Characteristic features of problems high on the agenda:* |  |  |
| First order impact | Human health | Ecosystem health |
| Timing | Immediate | Delayed |
| Scale | Local | Regional and global |
| Worst affected | Lower income groups | Future generations |
| *Characteristic attitude to:* |  |  |
| Nature | Manipulate to serve human needs | Protect and work with |
| People | Work with | Educate |
| Environmental Services | Provide more | Use less |
| *Aspects emphasized in relation to:* |  |  |
| Water | Inadequate access and poor quality | Overuse; need to protect water sources |
| Air | High human exposure to hazardous pollutants | Acid precipitation and greenhouse gas emissions |
| Solid waste | Inadequate provision for collection and removal | Excessive generation |
| Land | Inadequate access for low income groups for housing | Loss of natural habitats and agricultural land to urban development |
| Human wastes | Inadequate provision for safely removing faecal material (and waste water) from living environment | Loss of nutrients in sewage and damage to water bodies from its release of sewage into waterways |
| Typical proponent | Urbanist | Environmentalist |

*Source:* McGranahan, G and Satterthwaite, D (2000) 'Environmental health or ecological sustainability: Reconciling the brown and green agendas in urban development' in Pugh, C (ed) *Sustainable Cities in Developing Countries*, Earthscan, London.

This stereotyped version of the 'brown'/'green' debate is not only somewhat simplistic; it is also far more high-minded than the actual push and shove of urban environmental politics. As with global sustainability and poverty reduction, both the 'green' and the 'brown' agendas have distinctly selfless goals (inasmuch as future generations cannot engage in high-level politics and the poor can ill afford to). Self-interest inevitably permeates the politics that surround them, however, both internationally and locally.

One of the politically attractive elements of the environmental agenda is that it promises public benefits that extend to all segments of society. In the urban context, this applies especially to citywide improvements. Even the affluent suffer from outdoor air pollution, polluted waterways, and the like. Neither the 'brown' nor the 'green' agendas, as described here, prioritize the environmental burdens imposed on the currently affluent, but both can make at least some claims to benefit them. Sanitary improvement, for example, can be advocated as a means of avoiding society-wide epidemics, even though the main health burdens arising from poor sanitation are now endemic diseases (and the measures most effective in preventing epidemics, such as controlling the quality of piped water supplies, are not always the most effective in reducing endemic diseases which are more likely to target access to water than water quality (Cairncross and Feachem, 1993)). Similarly, controlling the emissions of ozone-depleting substances can be advocated as a means of protecting health in the present, even if the more obvious dangers still lie in the future.

On the other hand, 'green' arguments can be used as an excuse for ignoring the environmental needs of the poor, 'brown' arguments can be used to justify ignoring more distant environmental burdens, and policy debates can be so confused that it becomes difficult to promote either agenda. It is now often argued, for example, that environmental measures traditionally undertaken in the name of the 'brown' agenda not only fail to reach the poor, but undermine sustainability. Unfortunately, it is also perfectly possible for measures undertaken in the name of sustainability to fail to protect the resources base and still leave the poor unserved.

Public utilities and low water prices, for example, have often been justified as a means of providing water that is affordable to the poor, but have actually left the poor unserved and subsidized the more affluent (see Chapter 3). The new orthodoxy in the water sector is that commercially oriented provision with higher prices can both protect water resources for the future and result in better services to the poor. To support this new orthodoxy, much evidence has been gathered purporting to show that low-income urban households are willing to pay the full cost of better water provision. But, as noted in Chapter 5, many of the institutional weaknesses that led to inadequate public water provision in deprived neighbour-hoods are also likely to affect private sector provision. There are likely to be circumstances when private provision and higher prices not only hurt the poor, but lead to more water consumption in affluent areas where the largest suppressed demand is found. Whether such circumstances are the exception or the rule is, unfortunately, unlikely to be clear until the new orthodoxy is replaced by a still newer approach.

Sacrificing future generations to achieve affluence in the present may be unfair, but so is sacrificing currently deprived people in the name of a potentially affluent future. In any case, it is not urban households struggling to get enough water for basic hygiene, enough fuel to cook with, or some way of disposing of their minimal waste generation that are a threat to sustainability. The physical trade-off between improving the environment for the poor and protecting it for the future is itself in large measure socially constructed. Their contrasting relations to economic growth amplify the trade-offs. Pro-growth environmentalists often emphasize the 'brown' agenda and are openly sceptical of the 'green' agenda (Beckerman, 1995). Anti-growth (or steady-state growth) environmentalists emphasize the 'green' agenda and often ignore the 'brown' agenda altogether (Daly, 1996). But part of the problem with focusing exclusively on economic growth is precisely that it accentuates the conflict between these two agendas. Conventional economic growth reduces poverty, and at least indirectly its environmental correlates, but inevitably it also increases affluence at the upper end of the economic spectrum and creates serious sustainability problems.

Moreover, while Table 8.1 emphasizes the contrasts between the two agendas, they also have a number of common features. Both are concerned with complex and unintended side-effects of human activity, even if the 'brown' agenda focuses more on immediate, localized and health-related effects and the 'green' agenda on delayed, dispersed and ecological effects. A major challenge for both is to ensure that actors whose principal motivations lie elsewhere take environmental effects into account. And again, both are concerned with equity, even if the 'brown' agenda focuses more on burdens affecting low-income groups in the present and the 'green' agenda focuses on burdens that are likely to affect future generations.

Conceptually, the common concern for environmental justice offers considerable potential for integrating 'green' and 'brown' agendas. There are, of course, many conceptions and theories of equity, and little hope of arriving at a consensus on what environmental justice means, let alone how it should be pursued. Historically, most theories of equity have focused on intragenerational equity, and cannot easily accommodate the intergenerational or interspecies issues that are central to the 'green' agenda. Alternatively, narrow conceptions of environmental justice that focus on acts of environmental degradation, cannot easily be extended to the forms of environmental deprivation prioritized by the 'brown' agenda, where the presumed inequities lie more in the lack of capacities to secure environmental services than in injustices originating from environmental abuse. However, there is a widespread presumption that inequities can arise both within and between generations, and that the two are at some level comparable.

The potential for reconciling 'brown' and 'green' concerns at the conceptual level can be conveyed by adopting Rawls' 'veil of ignorance' (Rawls, 1971) and considering the question of environmental justice. Behind this 'veil of ignorance' people make their moral deliberations without being aware of the contingent characteristics they will be born into: their race, class, gender, nationality, and so on (Bhargava, 1999). The generation one is born into can also be considered a contingent characteristic. And just as a veil of ignorance applied across a single generation can help to convey the justice in improving the environmental conditions for the currently deprived, applied across two or more generations it can also convey the justice in protecting the environment for the future. (It is less effective in articulating moral concerns for other species whose numerical supremacy renders the exercise counterintuitive.)

The perspective on environmental justice that one adopts can, to some degree, lend favour to either the 'brown' or 'green' priorities. For example, from a consequentialist perspective 'brown' burdens are more verifiable since current burdens can be measured empirically, while future burdens are inherently more uncertain and debatable. From a procedural perspective, on the other hand, 'green' burdens are more verifiable since actions taken now clearly are restricting opportunities for future generations, while the link between the actions of the affluent and the environmental conditions of the deprived are complex, debatable and involve non-environmental relationships.

By and large, however, the failure to raise and seriously address issues of environmental justice is far more of a threat to equitable political decision-making than any genuine disagreements about how just decisions ought to be made. While philosophers may have difficulties coming to a consensus on how 'brown' and 'green' priorities should be balanced, they also have difficulties coming to a consensus on most other moral decisions that people and politicians make on a day-to-day basis. The consequentialist–procedural opposition referred to in the previous paragraph does often emerge in political debates, but moral arguments from both perspectives are widely accepted, with the tacit assumption that inequitable procedures are more serious if they yield inequitable consequences, and inequitable consequences are more serious if they reflect inequitable procedures.

Environmental justice, in short, can become a common goal guiding both the 'brown' and the 'green' agendas. It can help at once to build a common platform and to help reconcile conflicts that may emerge. Other, non-environmental dimensions of sustainable development are also important. But an adherence to environmental justice does not deny this. What it does deny is wishful thinking that inevitably perceives the currently deprived and future generations as having the same environmental interests or fatalistic thinking that inevitably perceives their environmental interests to be in direct opposition to one another.

There are a number of initiatives that seem to suggest that the 'brown' and 'green' agendas can be merged at the local level (McGranahan and Satterthwaite, 2000). This should not be taken to imply that the task is easy. Rather, it suggests that there is hope in the face of one of the most daunting challenges of this new millennium.

# References

Abbott, J (1996) *Sharing the City: Community Participation in Urban Management,* Earthscan Publications, London

Abeyasekere, S (1987) *Jakarta: A History,* Oxford University Press, Singapore

Accra Planning and Development Programme, United Nations Development Programme and United Nations Centre for Human Settlements (1992) *Strategic Plan for the Greater Accra Metropolitan Area,* Ministry of Local Government, Accra

Agarwal, A, Narain, S and Sharma, A (eds) (1999) *Green Politics: Global Environmental Negotiations,* Centre for Science and Environment, New Delhi

Aidoo, A A (1985) 'Women in the history and culture of Ghana', *Institute of African Studies Research Review* (new series), vol 1, no 1, pp14–83

Alberini, A, Eskeland, G S, Krupnick, A and McGranahan, G (1996) 'Determinants of diarrheal disease in Jakarta', *Water Resources Research,* vol 32, no 7, pp2259–2269

*Ambio* (1990) *Special Report on the Current Status of the Baltic Sea,* Royal Swedish Academy of Sciences, Stockholm

Amuzu, A T and Leitmann, J (1994) 'Accra', *Cities,* vol 11, no 1, pp5–9

Anton, D J (1993) *Thirsty Cities: Urban Environments and Water Supply in Latin America,* International Development Research Centre, Ottawa

Armitage, P and Berry, G (1994) *Statistical Methods in Medical Research,* Blackwell Scientific Publications, Oxford

Atkinson, A and Davila, J (1999) 'The challenge of environmental management in urban areas: An introduction' in Atkinson, A, Davila, J D, Fernandes, E and Mattingly, M (eds) *The Challenge of Environmental Management in Urban Areas,* Ashgate, Aldershot, pp1–12

Bahl, R W and Linn, J F (1992) *Urban Public Finance in Developing Countries,* Oxford University Press for the World Bank, Oxford

Bairoch, P (1988) *Cities and Economic Development: From the Dawn of History to the Present,* Mansell Publishing, London

Bapat, M and Crook, N (1984) 'The environment, health, and nutrition: An analysis of interrelationships from a case-study of hutment settlements in the city of Poona', *Habitat International,* vol 8, no 3/4, pp115–126

Bartone, C, Bernstein, J, Leitmann, J and Eigen, J (1994) *Toward Environmental Strategies for Cities: Policy Considerations for Urban Environmental Management in Developing Countries*, World Bank, Washington, DC

Baulch, B (1996) 'The new poverty agenda: A disputed consensus', *IDS Bulletin*, vol 27, no 1, pp1–10

Beck, U (1997) 'Global risk politics' in Jacobs, M (ed) *Greening the Millennium? The New Politics of the Environment*, Blackwell Publications, Oxford, pp18–33

Beck, U, Giddens, A and Lash, S (1994) *Reflexive Modernization: Politics, Tradition and Aesthetics in the Modern Social Order*, Polity Press, Cambridge

Beckerman, W (1995) *Small is Stupid: Blowing the Whistle on the Greens*, Duckworth, London

Bell, D (1993) *Communitarianism and its Critics*, Oxford University Press, New York

Benneh, G, Songsore, J, Nabila, J S, Amuzu, A T, Tutu, K A, Yangyuoru, Y and McGranahan, G (1993) *Environmental Problems and the Urban Household in the Greater Accra Metropolitan Area (GAMA) – Ghana*, Stockholm Environment Institute, Stockholm

Benzeval, M, Judge, K and Whitehead, M (eds) (1995) *Tackling Inequalities in Health: An Agenda for Action*, King's Fund, London

Berkes, F (ed) (1989) *Common Property Resources: Ecology and Community-Based Sustainable Development*, Belhaven Press, London

Bhargava, S (1999) *Environmental Equity and the Brown and Green Agendas*, Internship Report, Stockholm Environment Institute, Stockholm

Bhatia, R and Falkenmark, M (1993) *Water Resource Policies and the Urban Poor: Innovative Approaches and Policy Imperatives*, United Nations Development Programme–World Bank Water and Sanitation Programme, Washington, DC

Blokland, M, Braadbaart, O and Schwartz, K (1999) *Private Business, Public Owners: Government Shareholders in Water Enterprises*, Water Supply and Sanitation Collaborative Council, Nieuwagein

Blore, I (1989) 'Paying for and getting water in Hyderabad City', *Third World Planning Review*, vol 11, no 1, pp109–119

Boot, M T and Cairncross, S (eds) (1993) *Actions Speak: The Study of Hygiene Behaviour in Water and Sanitation Projects*, IRC International Water and Sanitation Centre and the London School of Hygiene and Tropical Medicine, The Hague

Borja, J and Castells, M (1997) *Local and Global: The Management of Cities in the Information Age*, Earthscan, London

Bowles, S and Gintis, H (1998) 'Efficient redistribution: New rules for markets, states and communities' in Wright, E O (ed) *Recasting Egalitarianism: New Rules for Communities, States and Markets*, Verso, London, pp3–71

Bradley, D, Stephens, C, Harpham, T and Cairncross, S (1991) *A Review of Environmental Health Impacts in Developing Country Cities*, Urban Management

Program Discussion Paper no 6, World Bank/United Nations Development Programme/United Nations Center for Habitat Studies, Washington, DC

Bradley, D J (1980) 'Health aspects of water supplies in tropical countries' in Feachem, R, McGarry, M, and Mara, D (eds) *Water, Wastes and Health in Hot Climates*, John Wiley & Sons, Chichester, pp3–17

Briscoe, J (1993) 'When the cup is half full: Improving water and sanitation services in the developing world', *Environment*, vol 35, no 4, pp7–37

Briscoe, J and Garn, H A (1995) 'Financing water supply and sanitation under Agenda 21', *Natural Resources Forum*, vol 19, no 1, pp59–70

Brugmann, J (1994) 'Who can deliver sustainability? Municipal reform and the sustainable development mandate', *Third World Planning Review*, vol 16, no 2, pp129–146

Brugmann, J (1996) 'Planning for sustainability at the local government level', *Environmental Impact Assessment Review: Special Issue: Managing Urban Sustainability*, vol 16, nos 4–6, pp363–379


Cairncross, S (1990) 'Water supply and the urban poor' in Hardoy, J E, Cairncross, S, and Satterthwaite, D (eds) *The Poor Die Young*, Earthscan, London, pp109–126

Cairncross, S, Blumenthal, U, Kolsky, P, Moraes, L and Tayeh, A (1995) 'The public and domestic domains in the transmission of disease', *Tropical Medicine and International Health*, vol 39, pp173–176

Cairncross, S and Feachem, R G (1993) *Environmental Health Engineering in the Tropics: An Introductory Text*, John Wiley & Sons, Chichester

Cairncross, S and Kinnear, J (1991) 'Water vending in urban Sudan', *Water Resources Development*, vol 7, no 4, pp267–273

Cairncross, S and Kochar, V (eds) (1994) *Studying Hygiene Behaviour: Methods, Issues and Experiences*, Sage, New Delhi

Castells, M (1996) *The Rise of the Network Society*, Blackwell, Oxford

CETESB (1995) *Relatório de Qualidade do Ar no Estado de São Paulo – 1994*, CETESB, São Paulo

CETESB (1998) *Annual Report 1998*, CETESB, São Paulo

Chadwick, E (1965) *Report on the Sanitary Condition of the Labouring Population of Gt Britain*, Edinburgh University Press, Edinburgh

Chambers, R (1994) 'The origins and practice of participatory rural appraisal', *World Development*, vol 22, no 7, pp953–969

Chavasse, D C, Blumenthal, U and Kolsky, P (1994) 'Fly control in prevention of diarrhoeal disease' (letter to editor), *Lancet*, vol 344, pp1231

Chen, B H, Hong, C J, Pandey, M R and Smith, K R (1990) 'Indoor air pollution in developing countries', *World Health Statistics Quarterly*, vol 43, pp127–138

Cliff, A, Haggett, P and Smallman-Raynor, M (1998) *Deciphering Global Epidemics*, Cambridge University Press, Cambridge

Cohen, M N (1989) *Health and the Rise of Civilization,* Yale University Press, New Haven

Cohen, M A, Ruble, B A, Tulchin, J S and Garland, A M (eds) (1996) *Preparing for the Urban Future: Global Pressures and Local Forces,* Woodrow Wilson Center Press, Washington, DC

Cointreau, S J (1986) *Environmental Management of Urban Solid Wastes in Developing Countries: A Project Guide,* World Bank, Washington, DC

Collier, U and Löfstedt, R E (1997) 'Think globally, act locally? Local climate change and energy policies in Sweden and the UK', *Global Environmental Change,* vol 7, no 1, pp25–40

Collier, W L and Santoso, K (1992) *Surabaya Water Environment Study (An Application of Rapid Urban Appraisal Techniques),* Pt Intersys Kelola Maju, Jakarta

Corbin, A (1994) *The Foul and the Fragrant: Odour and the French Social Imagination,* Picador, London

Covich, A P (1993) 'Water and ecosystems' in Gleick, P H (ed) *Water in Crisis: A Guide to the World's Fresh Water Resources,* Oxford University Press, New York, pp40–55

Crane, R (1992) *The Impact of Water Supply Deregulation in Jakarta, Indonesia: Results from Household and Water Vendor Surveys in North Jakarta,* Final Report, World Bank, Washington, DC

Crane, R (1994) 'Water markets, market reform and the urban poor: Results from Jakarta, Indonesia', *World Development,* vol 22, no 1, pp71–83

Cronon, W (1992) *Nature's Metropolis: Chicago and the Great West,* W W Norton, New York

Crouch, C and Marquand, D (eds) (1995) *Reinventing Collective Action: From the Global to the Local,* Blackwell, Oxford

Daly, H E (1996) *Beyond Growth: The Economics of Sustainable Development,* Beacon, Boston

Daly, H E and Cobb Jr, J B (1990) *For the Common Good: Redirecting the Economy towards Community, the Environment, and a Sustainable Future,* Green Print, London

Dasgupta, P (1993) *An Inquiry into Well-Being and Destitution,* Oxford University Press, Oxford

Desai, V (1994) 'Aspects of community participation within low-income housing', *Review of Urban and Regional Development Studies,* vol 6, no 2, pp167–191

Dicken, P (1992) *Global Shift: The Internationalization of Economic Activity,* Paul Chapman Publishing, London

Douglas, I (1987) *The Urban Environment,* Edward Arnold, London

Douglass, M (1989) 'The environmental sustainability of development', *Third World Planning Review,* vol 11, no 2, pp211–238

Douglass, M, Lee, Y F and Lowry, K (1994) 'Introduction to the special issue on community-based urban environmental management in Asia', *Asian Journal of Environmental Management,* vol 2, no 1, ppvii–xiv

Douglass, M and Zoghlin, M (1994) 'Sustaining cities at the grassroots: Livelihood, environment and social networks in Suan Phlu, Bangkok', *Third World Planning Review,* vol 16, no 2, pp171–200

Drangert, J-O, Bew, J and Winblad, U (1997) *Ecological Alternatives in Sanitation: Proceedings from Sida Sanitation Workshop Balingsholm, Sweden 6–9 August 1997,* Publications on Water Resources no 9, Swedish International Development Cooperation Agency (Sida), Stockholm

Drangert, J-O, Swiderski, R and Woodhouse, M (1996) *Safe Water Environments,* Linköping University, Linköping

Easter, W K and Feder, G (1996) *Water Institutions and Economic Incentives to Ameliorate Market and Government Failures,* Staff Paper Series, Department of Applied Economics, University of Minnisota, St Paul

Edwards, M and Hulme, D (eds) (1995) *Non-Governmental Organisations – Performance and Accountability: Beyond the Magic Bullet,* Earthscan, London

Ehrlich, P R, Ehrlich, A H and Holdren, J P (1973) *Human Ecology: Problems and Solutions,* W H Freeman, San Francisco

Ekins, P (1995) 'Economic policy for environmental sustainability' in Crouch, C and Marquand, D (eds) *Reinventing Collective Action: From the Global to the Local,* Blackwell, Oxford, pp33–53

Ekins, P (2000) *Economic Growth and Environmental Sustainability,* Routledge, London

EMPLASA (1998) *Banco de Dados e Informações sobre os Municípios da Região Metropolitana de São Paulo* EMPLASA, Governo do Estado de São Paulo, Secretaria dos Transportes Metropolitanos, São Paulo

Escobar, A (1995) *Encountering Development: The Making and Unmaking of the Third World,* Princeton University Press, Princeton, New Jersey

Esrey, S A, Feachem, R G and Hughes, J M (1985) 'Interventions for the control of diarrhoeal diseases among young children: Improving water supplies and excreta disposal facilities', *Bulletin of the World Health Organization,* vol 63, no 4, pp757–772

Esrey, S A and Habicht, J-P (1986) 'Epidemiologic evidence for health benefits from improved water and sanitation in developing countries', *Epidemiologic Reviews,* vol 8, pp117–128

Evans, P (1996a) 'Development strategies across the public-private divide', *World Development,* vol 24, no 6, pp1033–1037

Evans, P (1996b) 'Government action, social capital and development: Reviewing the evidence on synergy', *World Development,* vol 24, no 6, pp1119–1132

Ewald, P W (1993) 'The evolution of virulence', *Scientific American,* vol April, pp56–62

Ewald, P W (1994) *Evolution of Infectious Disease,* Oxford University Press, New York

Faria, V E (1989) 'São Paulo' in Dogan, M, and Kasarda, J D (eds) *The Metropolis Era: Mega-Cities,* California, SAGE, pp294–309

Fayorsey, C K (1992–1993) 'Commoditization of childbirth: Female strategies towards autonomy among the Ga of Southern Ghana', *Cambridge Anthropology,* vol 16, no 3, pp19–45

Fayorsey, C K (1994) *Poverty and the Commoditization of the Life Cycle,* paper presented at the University of Ghana Research and Conferences Committee Seminar on Poverty on 19 September

Feierman, S and Janzen, J M (eds) (1992) *The Social Basis of Health and Healing in Africa,* University of California Press, Berkeley

Fidler, D P (1996) 'Globalization, international law, and emerging infectious diseases', *Emerging Infectious Diseases,* vol 2, no 2, pp77–84

Frank, A G (1969) *Capitalism and Underdevelopment in Latin America,* Monthly Review Press, New York

Giddens, A (1992) *The Transformation of Intimacy: Sexuality, Love and Eroticism in Modern Societies,* Polity Press, Cambridge

Giddens, A (1994) *Beyond Left and Right: The Future of Radical Politics,* Stanford University Press, Stanford

Giddens, A (1998) *The Third Way: The Renewal of Social Democracy,* Polity Press, Cambridge

Gilbert, A (1994) *The Latin American City,* Latin American Bureau, London

Girardet, H (1992) *The Gaia Atlas of Cities: New Directions for Sustainable Urban Living,* Gaia Books, London

Grieg-Gran, M (1998) *The Waste Hierarchy: Recycling and Solid Waste Management in Developing Countries,* Working Paper, International Institute for Environment and Development, London

Grossman, G M and Krueger, A B (1995) 'Economic growth and the environment', *Quarterly Journal of Economics,* vol 110, pp353–378

Hamlin, C (1990) *A Science of Impurity: Water Analysis in Nineteenth Century Britain,* Adam Hilger, Bristol

Hardin, G (1974) 'Living on a lifeboat' in Hardin, G, and Baden, J (eds) *Managing the Commons,* W H Freeman and Company, San Francisco, pp261–279

Hardoy, J E and Satterthwaite, D (1989) *Squatter Citizen: Life in the Urban Third World,* Earthscan, London

Hardoy, J E, Mitlin, D and Satterthwaite, D (1992) *Environmental Problems in Third World Cities,* Earthscan, London

Harvey, D (1996) *Justice, Nature and the Geography of Difference,* Blackwell, Cambridge, MA

Hasan, A (1999) *Understanding Karachi: Planning and Reform for the Future,* City Press, Karachi

Haughton, G (1999) 'Environmental justice and the sustainable city' in Satterthwaite, D (ed) *The Earthscan Reader in Sustainable Cities,* Earthscan, London, pp69–72

Hirst, P and Thompson, G (1996) *Globalization in Question,* Polity Press, Cambridge

Holmberg, J (1992) *Poverty, Environment and Development: Proposals for action,* Swedish International Development Authority, Stockholm

Holtz-Eakin, D and Selden, T M (1995) 'Stoking the fires? $CO_2$ emissions and economic growth', *Journal of Public Economics,* vol 57, pp85–101

Huttly, S R A (1990) 'The impact of inadequate sanitary conditions on health in developing countries', *World Health Statistics Quarterly,* vol 43, no 3, pp118–126

IRC International Water and Sanitation Centre (1988) *Community Participation and Women's Involvement in Water Supply and Sanitation Projects,* A Compendium Paper, IRC International Water and Sanitation Centre, The Hague

Jackson, B (1990) *Poverty and the Planet: A Question of Survival,* Penguin Books, London

Jackson, T (ed) (1993) *Clean Production Strategies,* Lewis Publishers, Boca Raton, Florida

Jackson, T (1996) *Material Concerns: Pollution, Profit and Quality of Life,* Routledge, London

Jacobi, P (1990) 'Habitat and health in the Municipality of São Paulo', *Environment and Urbanization,* vol 2, no 2, pp33–45

Jacobi, P (1995a) *Environmental Problems Facing Urban Households in the City of São Paulo, Brazil,* Stockholm Environment Institute, Stockholm

Jacobi, P (1995b) 'Moradores e meio ambiente na cidade de São Paulo' in Filho, J M, Jorge, J T, Hogan, D J, and Cal Seixas Barbosa, S R (eds) *A Questão Ambiental: Cenários de Pesquisa – A experiência do Ciclo de Seminários do NEPAM,* NEPAM, Campinas, São Paulo, pp133–168

Jacobi, P (1995c) 'Moradores e meio ambiente na cidade de São Paulo', *Revista de Administração Municipal,* vol 42, no 216, pp26–50

Jacobi, P (1999) *Cidade e meio ambiente (The City and the Environment),* Amablume, São Paulo

Jacobi, P, Baena Segura, D and Kjellén, M (1999) 'Governmental responses to air pollution: summary of a study of the implementation of *rodízio* in São Paulo', *Environment and Urbanization,* vol 11, no 1, pp79–88

Jacobi, P and Carvalho Teixeira, M A (1995) 'Questão urbana: A cidade de São Paulo' in Carvalho, I and Scotto, G (eds) *Conflitos Sócio-Ambientais no Brasil: Volume 1*, IBASE, Rio de Janeiro, pp103–137

Jacobi, P, Kjellén, M and Castro, Y (1998) *Household Environmental Problems in São Paulo: Perceptions and Solutions from Centre to Periphery*, Urban Environment Series no 5, Stockholm Environment Institute, Stockholm

Jacobi, P R (1994) 'Households and environment in the city of São Paulo: Problems, perceptions and solutions', *Environment and Urbanization*, vol 6, no 2, pp87–110

Jepma, C J and Munasinghe, M (1998) *Climate Change Policy: Facts, Issues and Analysis*, Cambridge University Press, Cambridge

Johnstone, N, Wood, L and Hearne, R (1999) 'Private sector participation in urban water and sanitation: realising social and environmental objectives in developing countries', *Natural Resources Forum*, vol 23, no 4, pp287–302

Joint Academies Committee on the Mexico City Water Supply (1995) *Mexico City's Water Supply: Improving the Outlook for Sustainability*, National Academy Press, Washington, DC

Kanji, N (1995) 'Gender, poverty and economic adjustment in Harare, Zimbabwe', *Environment and Urbanization*, vol 7, no 1, pp37–55

Kanji, N and Jazdowska, N (1995) 'Gender, structural adjustment and employment in urban Zimbabwe', *Third World Planning Review*, vol 17, no 2, pp133–154

Kasarda, J D and Rondinelli, D A (1990) 'Mega-cities, the environment, and private enterprise: Toward ecologically sustainable urbanization', *Environmental Impact Assessment Review*, vol 10, pp393–404

Kemper, K E and Widstrand, C (1991) *Environmental Sanitation in Developing Countries: A Selected and Annotated Bibliography*, University of Linköping, Linköping

Khaldûn, I (1981) *The Muqaddimah: An Introduction to History*, Bollingen, Princeton, New Jersey

Kjellén, M, Bratt, A and McGranahan, G (1996) *Water Supply and Sanitation in Low and Middle Income Cities: Comparing Accra, Jakarta and São Paulo*, Urban Environment Series no 1, Stockholm Environment Institute, Stockholm

Kjellén, M and McGranahan, G (1997) *Urban Water – Towards Health and Sustainability*, Stockholm Environment Institute, Stockholm

Kolsky, P J (1992) 'Water, Health and Cities – Concepts and Examples', *International Workshop on Planning for Sustainable Urban Development: Cities and Natural Resource Systems in Developing Countries*, University of Wales, Cardiff, 13–17 July

Krause, R M (1992) 'The origin of plagues: Old and new', *Science*, vol 257, pp1073–1078

Kundu, A (1993) *In the Name of the Urban Poor: Access to Basic Amenities*, Sage Publications, New Delhi

Ladd, B (1990) *Urban Planning and Civic Order in Germany, 1860–1914,* Harvard University Press, Cambridge, Massachusetts

Lafferty, W M and Eckerberg, K (eds) (1998) *From the Earth Summit to Local Agenda 21*, Earthscan, London

Lamba, D (1994) *Nairobi's Environment: A Review of Conditions and Issues,* Mazingira Institute, Nairobi

Lambright, H W and Changnon, S A (1996) 'Urban reactions to the global warming issues: Agenda setting in Toronto and Chicago', *Climatic Change,* no 34, pp463–478

Leach, G and Mearns, R (1988) *Beyond the Woodfuel Crisis: People, Land and Trees in Africa,* Earthscan, London

Leach, M, Forsyth, T and Scoones, I (1998) *Poverty and environment: priorities for research and policy,* Institute of Development Studies, Falmer, Sussex

Lee, Y F (1994) 'Myths of environmental management and the urban poor' in Fuchs, R J, Brennan, E, Chamie, J, Lo, F, and Uitto, J (eds) *Mega-City Growth and the Future,* United Nations University Press, Tokyo, pp428

Leitmann, J (1993) *Rapid Urban Environmental Assessment: Lessons from Cities in the Developing World (Volume 2: Tools and Outputs),* Urban Management Programme Tool no 15, World Bank/UNDP/UNCHS, Washington, DC

Lewis, M A and Miller, T R (1987) 'Public-private partnership in water supply and sanitation in Sub-Saharan Africa', *Health Policy and Planning,* vol 2, no 1, pp70–79

Lindskog, P and Lundqvist, J (1989) *Why Poor Children Stay Sick: The Human Ecology of Child Health and Welfare in Rural Malawi,* Scandinavian Institute of African Studies, Uppsala, Sweden

Lipietz, A (1994) 'Enclosing the global commons: Global environmental negotiations in a North–South conflictual approach' in Glynn, A, and Bhaskar, V (eds) *The North, the South and the Environment,* Earthscan, London

Lippmann, M (1999) 'Air pollution and health – Studies in North America and Europe' in McGranahan, G, and Murray, F (eds) *Health and Air Pollution in Rapidly Developing Countries,* Stockholm Environment Institute, Stockholm, pp29–41

Lipton, M (1989) *Why Poor People Stay Poor: Urban Bias in World Development,* Gower House, Aldershot

Lloyd, C B and Gage-Brandon, A J (1993) 'Women's role in maintaining households: Family welfare and sexual inequality in Ghana', *Population Studies,* vol 47, pp115–131

Lovei, L and Whittington, D (1991) *Rent Seeking in Water Supply,* Discussion Paper, World Bank, Washington, DC

Lovei, L and Whittington, D (1993) 'Rent-extracting behavior by multiple agents in the provision of municipal water supply: A study of Jakarta, Indonesia', *Water Resources Research,* vol 29, no 7, pp1965–1974

Luckin, B (1986) *Pollution and Control: A Social History of the Thames in the Nineteenth Century*, Adam Hilger, Bristol

Mara, D (1996) *Low-Cost Urban Sanitation*, Wiley, Chichester

Marcuse, P and van Kempen, R (eds) (2000) *Globalizing Cities: A new spatial order?* Blackwell, Oxford

Mascie-Taylor, C G N (ed) (1993) *The Anthropology of Disease*, Oxford University Press, New York

McGranahan, G (1986) *Searching for the Biofuel Energy Crisis in Rural Java* [PhD], University of Wisconsin, Madison

McGranahan, G (1993) *Household Environments, Space and Wealth: Reflections on Case Studies of Accra and Jakarta*, prepared for Annual Meeting of the American Association of Geographers

McGranahan, G (1998) 'Health, poverty and the environment: Lessons from a three city study' in Chatterji, M, Munasinghe, M, and Ganguly, R (eds) *Environment and Health in Developing Countries*, A.P.H. Publishing Corporation, New Delhi, pp93–101

McGranahan, G and Kaijser, A (1993) *Household Energy: Problems, Policies and Prospects*, Stockholm Environment Institute, Stockholm

McGranahan, G, Leitmann, J and Surjadi, C (1997) *Understanding Environmental Problems in Disadvantaged Neighborhoods: Broad Spectrum Surveys, Participatory Appraisal and Contingent Valuation*, Urban Environment Series no 3, Stockholm Environment Institute, Stockholm

McGranahan, G, Leitman, J and Surjadi, C (1998) 'Green grass and brown roots: understanding environmental problems in disadvantaged neighbourhoods', *Journal of Environmental Planning and Management*, vol 41, no 4, pp505–518

McGranahan, G and Satterthwaite, D (2000) 'Environmental health or ecological sustainability: Reconciling the brown and green agendas in urban development' in Pugh, C (ed), *Sustainable Cities in Developing Countries*, Earthscan, London, pp73–90

McGranahan, G and Songsore, J (1994) 'Wealth, health, and the urban household: Weighing environmental burdens in Accra, Jakarta, and São Paulo', *Environment*, vol 36, no 6, pp4–11, 40–45

McGranahan, G and Songsore, J (1996) 'Wealth, health and the urban household: Weighing environmental burdens in Accra, Jakarta and São Paulo' in Atkinson, S, Songsore, J, and Werna, E (eds) *Urban Health Research in Developing Countries: Implications for Policy*, CAB International, Wallingford, pp135–159

McGranahan, G, Songsore, J and Kjellén, M (1996) 'Sustainability, poverty and urban environmental transitions' in Pugh, C (ed) *Sustainability, the Environment and Urbanization*, Earthscan, London, pp103–133

McMichael, A J, Haines, A, Slooff, R and Kovats, S (eds) (1996) *Climate Change and Human Health*, World Health Organization, Geneva

McNeill, W H (1989) *Plagues and Peoples*, Doubleday, New York

Meadows, D L, Meadows, D H, Randers, J and Behrens, W (1972) *The Limits to Growth: A Report for the Club of Rome's Project on the Predicament of Man*, Universe Books, New York

Mitchell, R C and Carson, R T (1989) *Using Surveys to Value Public Goods: The Contingent Valuation Method*, Resources for the Future, Washington, DC

Mitlin, D and Thompson, J (1995) 'Participatory approaches in urban areas: Strengthening civil society or reinforcing the status quo', *Environment and Urbanization*, vol 7, no 1, pp231–250

Morse, S S (ed) (1993) *Emerging Viruses*, Oxford University Press, New York

Mosley, W H, Bobadilla, J L and Jamison, D T (1993) 'The health transition: Implications for health policy in developing countries' in Jamison, D T, Mosley, W H, Measham, A R, and Bobadilla, J L (eds) *Disease Control Priorities in Developing Countries*, Oxford University Press, Oxford, pp673–699

Munasinghe, M (1992) *Water Supply and Environmental Management: Developing World Applications*, Westview, Boulder

Munasinghe, M (1993) *Environmental Economics and Sustainable Development*, World Bank Environment Paper, World Bank, Washington, DC

Munasinghe, M (1999) 'Introduction to Special Topic I: Structural adjustment policies and the environment', *Environment and Development Economics*, vol 4, no 1, pp9–18

Murray, C J L and Lopez, A D (1996) *The Global Burden of Disease: A Comprehensive Assessment of Mortality and Disability from Diseases, Injuries, and Risk Factors in 1990 and projected to 2020*, Harvard School of Public Health, Cambridge, Massachusetts

Nickson, A (1997) 'The public–private mix in urban water supply', *International Review of Administrative Sciences*, vol 63, pp165–186

Nijkamp, P and Perrels, A (1994) *Sustainable Cities in Europe: A Comparative Analysis of Urban Energy–Environmental Policies*, Earthscan, London

O'Connell, H (1994) *Women and the Family*, Zed Books, London

Oliveira, C N E and Leitmann, J (1994) 'São Paulo', *Cities*, vol 11, no 1, pp10–14

Olson, M (1975) *The Logic of Collective Action: Public Goods and the Theory of Groups*, Harvard University Press, Cambridge

Ostrom, E (1996) 'Crossing the great divide: Coproduction, synergy, and development', *World Development*, vol 24, no 6, pp1073–1087

Otten, L (1996) *Integrated Solid Waste Management*, prepared for strategies for a Sustainable Greater Jabotabek Seminar, 8–10 July, Jakarta

Pickering, H (1985) 'Social and environmental factors associated with diarrhoea and growth in young children: Child health in urban Africa', *Social Science and Medicine*, vol 21, no 2, pp121–127

Potgeiter, F, Venter, D, Thomas, E P, Seager, J R, McGranahan, G and Kjellén, M (1999) *Port Elizabeth 1000 Household Environment and Health Survey,* Urban Environment Series no 6.1, Stockholm Environment Institute, Stockholm

Pretty, J N (1995) 'Participatory learning for sustainable agriculture', *World Development,* vol 23, no 8, pp1247–1263

Pugh, C (1996) 'Sustainability and sustainable cities' in Pugh, C (ed) *Sustainability, the Environment and Urbanization,* Earthscan, London, pp135–177

Ravallion, M and Chen, S (1997) 'What can new survey data tell us about recent changes in distribution and poverty?', *The World Bank Economic Review,* vol 11, no 2, pp357–382

Rawls, J (1971) *A Theory of Justice,* Belknap Press of Harvard University Press, Cambridge, MA

Reed, D (1996) *Structural Adjustment, the Environment, and Sustainable Development,* Earthscan, London

Rees, W E (1992) 'Ecological footprints and appropriated carrying capacity: What urban economics leaves out', *Environment and Urbanization,* vol 4, no 2, pp121–130

Rees, W and Wackernagel, M (1996) 'Urban ecological footprints: Why cities cannot be sustainable – and why they are a key to sustainability', *Environmental Impact Assessment Review: Special Issue: Managing Urban Sustainability,* vol 16, no 4–6, pp223–248

Reid, D (1993) *Paris Sewers and Sewermen: Realities and Representations,* Harvard University Press, Cambridge, Massachusetts

Rismianto, D and Mak, W (1993) *Environmental Aspects of Groundwater Abstraction in Dki Jakarta: Changing Views,* Report, Jakarta

Roberts, J T and Grimes, P E (1997) 'Carbon intensity and economic development 1962–91: A brief exploration of the environmental Kuznets curve', *World Development,* vol 25, no 2, pp191–198

Robertson, C C (1984) *Sharing the Same Bowl: A Socioeconomic History of Women and Class in Accra, Ghana,* University of Michigan Press, Ann Arbor, Michigan

Robinson, M (1994) 'Governance, democracy and conditionality: NGOs and the New Policy Agenda' in Clayton, A (ed) *Governance, Democrary and Conditionality: What Role for NGOs?* INTRAC, London, pp35–51

ROG/UNDP/UNCHS (1989) *Environmental Study of Accra Metropolitan Area,* Final Report, Government of the Republic of Ghana, Accra

Rosen, G (1993) *A History of Public Health,* Johns Hopkins University Press, Baltimore

Rothman, D S (1998) 'Environmental Kuznets curves — real progress or passing the buck? A case for consumption-based approaches', *Ecological Economics,* vol 25, no 2, pp177–194

SABESP (1998) *Annual Report 1998*, Companhia de Saneamento Básico de São Paulo, São Paulo

Saleh, D (1996) *Strategies for a Sustainable Greater Jabotabek: Solid Wastes Management and Sanitation Sectors*, prepared for strategies for a Sustainable Greater Jabotabek Seminar, 8–10 July, Jakarta

Sassen, S (2000) *Cities in a World Economy*, Pine Forge Press, Thousand Oaks, California

Satterthwaite, D (1995) 'The underestimation of urban poverty and of its health consequences', *Third World Planning Review*, vol 17, no 4, ppiii–xii

Satterthwaite, D (1997) 'Environmental transformations in cities as they get larger, wealthier and better managed', *The Geographical Journal*, vol 163, no 2, pp216–224

Savitch, H V (1996) 'Cities in a global era: A new paradigm for the next millennieum' in Cohen, M A, Ruble, B A, Tulchin, J S, and Garland, A M (eds) *Preparing for the Urban Future: Global Pressures and Local Forces*, Woodrow Wilson Center Press in cooperation with the United Nations Centre on Human Settlements (Habitat II), Washington, DC, pp39–65

Schofield, C J, Briceno-Leon, R, Kolstrup, N, Webb, D J T and White, G B (1990) 'The role of house design in limiting vector-borne disease' in Hardoy, J E, Cairncross, S, and Satterthwaite, D (eds) *The Poor Die Young*, Earthscan, London, pp189–212

Scrimshaw, N S and Gleason, G R (eds) (1992) *Rapid Assessment Procedures: Qualitative Methodologies for Planning and Evaluation of Health Related Programmes*, International Nutrition Foundation for Developing Countries, Boston

Sen, A (1999) *Development as Freedom*, Oxford University Press, Oxford

Serageldin, I (1994) *Water Supply, Sanitation, and Environmental Sustainability: The Financing Challenge*, World Bank, Washington, DC

Serageldin, I, Barrett, R and Martin-Brown, J (1995a) *The Business of Sustainable Cities: Public–Private Partnerships for Creative Technical and Institutional Solutions* (proceedings of an associated event of the Second Annual Conference on Environmentally Sustainable Development) World Bank, Washington DC

Serageldin, I, Cohen, M A and Leitmann, J (1995b) *Enabling Sustainable Community Development* (an associated event of the Second Annual Conference on Environmentally Sustainable Development), World Bank, Washington DC

Shafik, N T (1995) 'Economic development and environmental quality: An econometric analysis', *Oxford Economic Papers*, vol 46, pp757–773

Shapiro, A-L (1985) *Housing the Poor of Paris, 1850–1902*, University of Wisconsin Press, Madison

Shiklomanov, I A (1997) *Assessment of Water Resources and Water Availability in the World*, Stockholm Environment Institute, Stockholm

Sklair, L (1991) *Sociology of the Global System*, Harvester Wheatsheaf, Hemel Hemstead

Smith, K R and Lee, Y-S F (1993) 'Urbanization and the environmental risk transition' in Kasarda, J D, and Parnell, A M (eds) *Third World Cities: Problems, Policies, and Prospects*, Sage Publications, London, pp161–179

Smith, K and Akbar, S (1999) 'Health-damaging air pollution: A matter of scale' in McGranahan, G, and Murray, F (eds) *Health and Air Pollution in Rapidly Developing Countries*, Stockholm Environment Institute, Stockholm, pp15–27

Smith, K R (1988) 'Air pollution: Assessing total exposure in the developing countries', *Environment*, vol 30, no 8, pp16–20; 28–35

Smith, K R (1993a) 'Fuel combustion, air pollution exposure, and health: The situation in developing countries', *Annual Review of Energy and the Environment*, vol , no 18, pp529–566

Smith, K R (1993b) 'The health impact of cookstove smoke in Africa', prepared for Oesterdiekhoff, P et al, *African Development Perspectives Yearbook*, vol 3, Universitat Bremen, Bremen

Smith, K R, Apte, M G, Yuqing, M, Wongsekiarttirat, W and Kulkarni, A (1994) 'Air pollution and the energy ladder in Asian cities', *Energy*, vol 19, no 5, pp587–600

Songsore, J (1992) *Review of Household Environmental Problems in the Accra Metropolitan Area, Ghana*, Working Paper, Stockholm Environment Institute, Stockholm

Songsore, J and Goldstein, G (1995) 'Health and environment analysis for decision-making (HEADLAMP): field study in Accra, Ghana', *World Health Statistics Quarterly*, vol 48, no 2, pp108–117

Songsore, J and McGranahan, G (1993) 'Environment, wealth and health: towards an analysis of intra-urban differentials within the Greater Accra Metropolitan Area, Ghana', *Environment and Urbanization*, vol 5, no 2, pp10–34

Songsore, J and McGranahan, G (1996) *Women and Household Environmental Care in the Greater Accra Metropolitan Area (GAMA), Ghana*, Urban Environment Series no 2, Stockholm Environment Institute, Stockholm

Songsore, J and McGranahan, G (1998) 'The political economy of household environmental management: Gender, environment and epidemiology in the Greater Accra Metropolitan Area', *World Development*, vol 26, no 3, pp395–412

Southall, A (1998) *The City in Time and Space*, Cambridge University Press, Cambridge

Sperber, D (1996) *Explaining Culture: A Naturalistic Approach*, Blackwell Publishers, Oxford

Stenström, T A (1996) 'Tracing bacteria from the latrine to groundwater in dug wells' in Drangert, J-O, Swiderski, R M and Woodhouse, M (eds) *Safe Water Environments*, Linköping University, Linköping, Sweden, pp73–78

Stephens, C, Timaeus, I, Akerman, M, Avle, S, Maia, P B, Campanario, P, Doe, B, Lush, L, Tetteh, D and Harpham, T (1994) *Environment and Health in Developing Countries: An Analysis of Intra-Urban Differentials Using Existing Data*, London School of Hygiene and Tropical Medicine, London

Stiglitz, J (1998) *More Instruments and Broader Goals: Moving Toward the Post-Washington Consensus*, The 1998 WIDER Annual Lecture, Helsinki

Stockholm Vatten (1996) *Environmental Report 1995*, Stockholm Vatten, Stockholm

Surjadi, C (1993) 'Respiratory diseases of mothers and children and environmental factors among households in Jakarta', *Environment and Urbanization*, vol 5, no 2, pp78–86

Surjadi, C and Handayani, Y S (1998) *Solid Waste Management in Jakarta*, Atma Jaya Catholic University, Jakarta

Surjadi, C and Handayani, Y S (1999) *The Problem and Management of Solid Waste in Jakarta*, Centre for Health Research – Atma Jaya Catholic University, Jakarta

Surjadi, C, Padhmasutra, L, Wahyuningsih, D, McGranahan, G and Kjellén, M (1994) *Household Environmental Problems in Jakarta*, Stockholm Environment Institute, Stockholm

Surjadi, C, Padmasutra, L, Wahyuningsih, D, McGranahan, G and Kjellén, M (1995) *Masalah Lingkungan Rumah Tangga di Jakarta*, Universitas Katolik Atma Jaya, Jakarta

Swyngedouw, E A (1995) 'The contradictions of urban water provision: a study of Guayaquil, Ecuador', *Third World Planning Review*, vol 17, no 4, pp387–405

Tarr, J A (1996) *The Search for the Ultimate Sink: Urban Pollution in Historical Perspective*, University of Akron Press, Akron, Ohio

Tauxe, R V, Mintz, E D and Quick, R E (1995) 'Epidemic cholera in the New World: translating field epidemiology into new prevention strategies', *Third World Planning Review*, vol 1, no 4, pp141–146

Theis, J and Grady, H M (1991) *Participatory Rapid Appraisal for Community Development: a Training Manual Based on Experiences in the Middle East and North Africa*, International Institute for Environment and Development, London

Thomas, E P, Seager, J R, Viljoen, E, Potgeiter, F, Rossouw, A, Tokota, B, McGranahan, G and Kjellén, M (1999) *Household Environment and Health in Port Elizabeth, South Africa*, Urban Environment Series no 6, Stockholm Environment Institute, Stockholm

Torras, M (1998) 'Income, equality and pollution: A reassessment of the environmental Kuznets curve', *Ecological Economics*, vol 25, no 2, pp147–160

Turner, J F C (1996) 'Tools for building community: an examination of 13 hypotheses', *Habitat International*, vol 20, no 3, pp339–347

UNICEF (1996) *The State of The World's Children 1996*, Oxford University Press for UNICEF, Oxford

United Nations Development Programme (1997a) *Ghana – Human Development Report 1997*, United Nations Development Programme, Accra

United Nations Development Programme (1997b) *Human Development Report 1997*, Oxford University Press, New York

United Nations Development Programme (1998a) 'Human Development Database', Version 1.1 Statistics from Human Development Report 1998, United Nations Development Programme, Human Development Report Office

United Nations Development Programme (1998b) *Human Development Report 1998*, Oxford University Press, New York

United Nations Development Programme (1999) *Human Development Report 1999*, Oxford University Press, Oxford

United Nations Environment Programme (1996) *Action in Ozone*, United Nations Environment Programme, Nairobi

United Nations Environment Programme and World Health Organization (1988) *Assessment of Urban Air Quality*, World Health Organization, Geneva

Uphoff, N (1993) 'Grassroots organizations and NGOs in rural development: opportunities with diminishing states and expanding markets', *World Development*, vol 21, no 4, pp607–622

Vaa, M (1995) 'Gender relations and the environment of urban poverty', in Holmberg, J (ed) *Tropical Diseases, Society and the Environment*, SAREC, Stockholm

Vallack, H W, Bakker, D J, Brandt, I et al (1998) 'Controlling persistent organic pollutants – What next?', *Environmental Toxicology and Pharmacology*, vol 6, pp143–175

VanDerslice, J and Briscoe, J (1993) 'All coliforms are not created equal: a comparison of the effects of water source and in-house water contamination of infantile diarrheal disease', *Water Resources Research*, vol 29, no 7, pp1983–1995

Vargas, M C (1995) 'Paradigmas socio-institucionais de regulacão do saneamento básico no Brasil: Reflexões em torno da evolucão histórica do setor' in Filho, J M, Jorge, J T, Hogan, D J, and Cal Seixas Barbosa, S R (eds) *A Questão Ambiental: Cenários de Pesquisa – A Experiência do Ciclo de Seminários do NEPAM*, NEPAM, Campinas, São Paulo, pp77–93

Varley, A (1994) 'Housing the household, holding the house' in Jones, G, and Ward, P M (eds) *Methodology for Land and Housing Market Analysis*, University College London Press, London, pp120–134

Vickers, J (1991) *Women and the World Economic Crisis*, Zed Books, London

Vigarello, G (1988) *Concepts of Cleanliness: Changing Attitudes in France since the Middle Ages*, Cambridge University Press, Cambridge

Wallerstein, I (1979) *The Capitalist World Economy*, Cambridge University Press, Cambridge

White, G F, Bradley, D J and White, A U (1972) *Drawers of Water: Domestic Water Use in East Africa*, University of Chicago Press, Chicago

White, R R (1994) *Urban Environmental Management: Environmental Change and Urban Design*, John Wiley & Sons, Chichester

Wijk-Sijbesma, C (1979) *Participation and Education in Community Water Supply and Sanitation Programmes: A Selected and Annotated Bibliography*, WHO International Reference Centre for Community Water Supply, The Hague

Williamson, J (1993) 'Democracy and the "Washington Consensus"', *World Development*, vol 21, no 8, pp1329–1336

Wills, C (1996) *Plagues: Their Origin, History and Future*, HarperCollins, London

Wilson, E O (1992) *The Diversity of Life*, Norton, New York

Winblad, U (1997) *Towards an Ecological Approach to Sanitation*, Sida, Stockholm

Wohl, A S (1983) *Endangered Lives: Public Health in Victorian Britain*, Methuen, London

Working Group on Public Health and Fossil-Fuel Combustion (1997) 'Short-term improvements in public health from global-climate policies on fossil-fuel combustion: an interim report', *Lancet*, vol 350, no 9088, pp1341–1349

World Bank (1988) *World Development Report 1988*, Report, World Bank, Oxford

World Bank (1992) *World Development Report 1992: Development and the Environment*, Oxford University Press, New York

World Bank (1993a) *World Development Report 1993: Investing in Health*, Oxford University Press, New York

World Bank (1993b) *Water Resources Management*, A World Bank Policy Paper, World Bank, Washington, DC

World Bank (1998) *World Development Report 1998: Knowledge for Development*, Oxford University Press, New York

World Bank (1999) *Entering the 21st Century: World Development Report 1999/ 2000*, Oxford University Press, New York

World Bank (1999) *1999 World Development Indicators*, World Bank, Washington, DC

World Bank Environment Department (1997) *Expanding the Measure of Wealth: Indicators of Environmentally Sustainable Development*, The World Bank, Washington, DC

World Bank Water Demand Research Team (1993) 'The demand for water in rural areas: Determinants and policy implications', *World Bank Research Observer*, vol 8, no 1, pp47–70

World Commission on Environment and Development (1987) *Our Common Future*, Oxford University Press, Oxford

World Health Organization (1981) *Drinking-Water and Sanitation, 1981–1990: A Way to Health*, World Health Organization, Geneva

World Health Organization (1996) *The World Health Report 1996: Fighting Disease, Fostering Development*, World Health Organization, Geneva

World Health Organization and United Nations Environment Programme (1991) *Insect and Rodent Control through Environmental Management: A Community Action Programme*, World Health Organization, Geneva

World Resources Institute (1996) *World Resources 1996–97,* Oxford University Press, New York
World Resources Institute (1998) *World Resources 1998–99,* Oxford University Press, New York

Yacoob, M, Brantly, E and Whiteford, L (1994) *Public Participation in Urban Environmental Management: A Model for Promoting Community-based Environmental Management in Peri-urban Areas,* WASH Technical Report no 90, Water and Sanitation for Health Project, Arlington, Virginia
Yearley, S (1996) *Sociology, Environmentalism, Globalisation,* Sage Publications, London

# Index

Page numbers in *italics* refer to tables, figures and boxes